Uncle Rudolf

a novel

'Tremendous.'
Beryl Bainbridge

'It moved me terribly.'
Ali Smith

PAUL BAILEY

4th

A division of
HarperCollins*Publishers*

www.4thestate.com

GRANTA

GRANTA 79, AUTUMN 2002
www.granta.com

EDITOR   *Ian Jack*
DEPUTY EDITORS   *Liz Jobey, Sophie Harrison*
EDITORIAL ASSISTANT   *Fatema Ahmed*

CONTRIBUTING EDITORS   *Neil Belton, Pete de Bolla, Ursula Doyle, Will Hobson, Gail Lynch, Blake Morrison, Andrew O'Hagan, Lucretia Stewart*

ASSOCIATE PUBLISHER   *Sally Lewis*
FINANCE   *Geoffrey Gordon*
SALES   *Frances Hollingdale*
PUBLICITY   *Louise Campbell*
SUBSCRIPTIONS   *John Kirkby, Darryl Wilks, Brenda Cameracanna*
PUBLISHING ASSISTANT   *Mark Williams*
ADVERTISING MANAGER   *Kate Rochester*

PUBLISHER   *Rea S. Hederman*

Granta, 2–3 Hanover Yard, Noel Road, London N1 8BE
Tel 020 7704 9776 Fax 020 7704 0474
e-mail for editorial: editorial@granta.com

Granta US, 1755 Broadway, 5th Floor, New York, NY 10019-3780, USA

TO SUBSCRIBE call 020 7704 0470 or e-mail subs@granta.com
A one-year subscription (four issues) costs £26.95 (UK), £34.95 (rest of Europe) and £41.95 (rest of the world).

Granta is printed and bound in Italy by Legoprint. The paper used in this publication meets the minimum requirements of American National Standard for Information Sciences—Permanence of Paper for Printed Library Materials, ANSI Z39.48-1984.

Granta is published by Granta Publications.

Design: Random Design.
Front cover photograph: Polly Borland/Camera Press. One of a number of specially commissioned portraits taken to celebrate the Queen's Golden jubilee.

ISBN 0 903141 54 x

Royal Festival Hall
Queen Elizabeth Hall
Purcell Room

Meena Alexander
Simon Armitage
Bernardo Atxaga
Alison Croggon
Anne Carson
Kwame Dawes
Maura Dooley
Mark Doty
Ian Duhig
Douglas Dunn
Zena Edwards
Anne Fine
Choman Hardi
Anthony Hecht
John Hegley
Frieda Hughes
Svetlana Kekova
Fatima Kelleher
Mimi Khalvati
Yusef Komunyakaa
Khan Singh Kumar
Yang Lian
Robert Minhinnick
Sinéad Morrissey
Amjad Nasser
Ruth Padel
Vera Pavlova
Evgeny Rein
Robin Robertson
Michael Rosen
Jacques Roubaud
Eva Runefelt
Tatiana Shcherbina
Cathal Ó Searcaigh
Wole Soyinka
Aleš Šteger
Tatiana Voltskaya
Saadi Yousef

POETRY
INTERNATIONAL

26 Oct - 2 Nov 2002
The world's leading poets read live
on the South Bank

www.rfh.org.uk/poetryint

'83% of poetry is not worth reading...
but the other 17% I couldn't live without'
Billy Collins, US poet laureate

Hear the essential 17% at Britain's biggest
poetry festival this autumn.

Box Office 020 7960 4242
Free Online Booking www.rfh.org.uk/poetryint

Now Booking: Susan Sontag
Mon 23 Sep 7.30pm, QEH, £8 concs £5.50

Sponsored by

Bloomberg

GRANTA 79

Celebrity

INTRODUCTION

Celebrities are often seen as fictions, the argument being that they are media inventions, with various amplified, distorted or invented parts of their lives assembled for our benefit and made familiar to us through the media. Of course, a lot of skill and care goes into the presentation, but even unwanted disclosures—drugs, alcohol, childhood abuse—can be turned to marketable advantage: the celebrity, it turns out, is only flesh and blood, human like the rest of us, and now made more dramatic by the fact he or she has this 'other side'. But beyond the obvious fact that even celebrities have more than one dimension, their particular humanity is as elusive as before.

In this way, you might say, they are poor and inadequate fictions—not the rich, real thing at all. As characters, they wouldn't make it into the pages of a good novel, where our knowledge, if not interpretation, of character must begin and end with what the writer has described, suggested or implied—no point in hoping to read further shadings and revelations in the newspapers ('ANGSTROM IN REHAB CLINIC').

A novelist, however, can work the other way round. He can take, or be inspired by, the life of a celebrity and, through imaginative fiction, give us a greater idea of its origins, condition and effects. Andrew O'Hagan has taken on this subject for his new novel, *Personality*, which will be published next year; the piece that begins this issue of *Granta* has been edited from that book, which is certain to raise familiar (but I think still interesting) questions about the dimensions and boundaries of fiction and non-fiction—the place of each within or outside the other. Its leading character, a young singer, Maria Tambini, may remind readers in Britain of another young singer, Lena Zavaroni, a celebrity in her day. Like Tambini in the novel, Zavaroni came from Rothesay on the island of Bute, where her Scottish-Italian family owned cafes. Like Tambini, as a teenager in the 1970s she won a then-famous talent show, *Opportunity Knocks* compèred by the then-famous Hughie Green. Like Tambini, she became a star and suffered many years of anorexia. The similarities are plain and undeniable.

Do they matter? Just before the issue went to press, Andrew O'Hagan and I had a long email conversation about this, which, though we are friends, at times became tetchy. Obviously, I like the book and the piece, but I wondered why he'd chosen fiction rather than biography. We went through a lot of literary precedents.

The case of Madame Bovary: Flaubert here inspired by the life and death of Delphine Delamare, who died, probably at her own hand, in the village of Ry, Normandy, in 1848, and whose gravestone since 1990 has carried the words 'MADAME BOVARY' beneath her real name.

Andrew: 'I think the people of Ry are misguided about literature (if not about tourism). Flaubert didn't write a biography of Delphine Delamare. The important fact is not so much what he took from the Delamare story, but what he made of it, and what he made up. Flaubert, when asked who Emma Bovary was, famously said, *"Emma, c'est moi."* '

The case of Robinson Crusoe: Defoe here inspired by the story of the sea captain, Alexander Selkirk, who has a statue (dressed, as I remember it, in Crusoe-like desert-island gear) at his birthplace in the village of Largo, Fife.

Andrew: 'I think the novel and its modern readers have a capacity for allowing real places [the book has no invented or pseudonymous geography] to live on the page imaginatively. So long as no one is being libelled or hurt, I think novelists should write what they can, and if connections are made with real places or real TV programmes or with real people then that might be admirable if the work sustains it. Lena Zavaroni was a part of my childhood, and her tragedy has influenced what I have set out to do, but the character in my novel is not Lena, nor can she be, and nor is she intended to be.'

Fair enough about Flaubert and Defoe, I wrote to Andrew, but hadn't the world changed since their day? In the villages of Ry, Normandy, and Largo, Fife, folk might have gone around tapping their noses knowingly and saying. 'But this book is really all about Delphine Delamere...all about that sea captain Selkirk (but why didn't he tell us about Man Friday?)' Outside those places, very few people would have seen the parallels. Lena Zavaroni, on the other hand, was on British television for years, her story in every British tabloid. Many millions of people think they know about her life— she was that thing called a star. Now his book might have people tapping their noses all over Britain, not just in Rothesay, saying: 'This is a book about Lena.' Was the possibility of that confusion something that worried him?

Andrew: 'I'd be worried about it if I'd written something that dishonoured that person, or something that made her life smaller than it was. Your question is really about ethics, I suppose. Is it right for an author to make use of a person's circumstances in a book? And the answer is complex and simple at the same time: a person does not own the story of his own life. Even when alive, what happens to them and what they do and who they are does not belong to them—it belongs to the world, and possibly to literature as well. In the case of celebrities this seems to me no less true: their lives are part of our own lives, and part of what we imagine.'

I asked about a different kind of damage—the damage (as some people might see it, and maybe especially some long-standing readers of *Granta*) to the increasingly fudged and fuzzy boundary between fiction and non-fiction. Andrew replied that this damage, if damage it was, had been done long before Don DeLillo got to work on Lee Harvey Oswald in *Libra* or Joyce Carol Oates imagined the life of Marilyn Monroe in *Blonde*. He suggested I consult the four accounts of Jesus's life in the New Testament. And finally: 'Of course, there are people (of whom you might be one) who see a Picasso and admire its colours, are affected by its form and its ideas, but at some level quietly wonder to themselves why it is not a photograph.'

Of whom you might be one. This was the killer punch, because my admission is that, in certain circumstances, I would indeed prefer a photograph to a Picasso. For example, if as a modern Crusoe I wanted to tell a modern Friday what the effects of air bombing were like I would choose a photograph from Dresden or Vietnam over *Guernica*, every time.

My father, who these days would be called an autodidact but forty or fifty years ago was known simply as a working man who read books, used to say: 'Stupid people talk about other people, intelligent people talk about things.' Whole stretches of his conversation denied this statement, but the people concerned were usually the men he worked beside, or friends, neighbours and relations. The famous came under review only in terms of their achievement (H. G. Wells) or lack of it (most British politicians). The Royal Family got nothing more than a snort. And yet recently, sorting out some family snaps, I came across a picture of my mother and the Queen. The Queen was unveiling a plaque to open the new road bridge across the Forth (1964), and my mother was prominent in the crowd behind her. We lived nearby. My mother and a few other women had walked across the fields to see the Queen. The picture was always considered worth keeping.

Michael Collins was interested in this juxtaposition of the famous and the unfamous—celebrities doing their duty by their fans, who have given their camera to a friend and asked the celebrity, 'Would you mind...?' On his own and *Granta*'s behalf, he advertised to find a collection of such pictures and some of the results, including the letters that came with them, begin on page 97. What you notice about these pictures, in nearly every case, is the obliging cheerfulness of the celebrity, and the sweet delight of the 'ordinary' person. Newspaper photographs tend to be interested in celebrity glorification or mishap, but these photographs record treasured moments in the lives of real fans—a moment of equality. One letter said:

'Please find enclosed a photograph of me with Red Rum the Grand National Winner. I do have one of me shaking hands with the Queen, but I look more myself in this one.'

Thinking about how universal and pervasive the fashion for celebrity has become, and trying to recall a time when things were different, I remembered an incident on a London Sunday newspaper's magazine section circa 1977. I'd been editing a piece on the closure of a steelworks in South Wales (the kind of story that has since been repeated endlessly in Britain and America). Now the time had come to take it to the design department and lay it out over several pages. The designer had selected a couple of spreads of the steelworks—smoke and fire, the romance of industry—but I thought we should also have a picture of a foreman described in the story, the man charged with the last ladling out of molten steel. The designer said we couldn't have it. I said it could be very small. We could cut the text, which is always music to any designer's ears. No, he said, no picture.

'Why not?'

'It's not how history should be seen. This is a story about a social class, not about individuals.'

He was a Marxist—more accurately (I think) a Trotskyite. There was a small pocket of them on the paper then, usually serving capitalism happily enough and not at all what Mrs Thatcher a few years later called the 'the enemy within' (the enemy within worked downstairs on the rotary presses—overtimeism, not Marxism, was their big cause). Even at the time the designer's position was extreme. Now, looking back at what has happened to this newspaper since, as to almost every other in Britain, it seems almost impossible that such an argument could ever have occurred. What my colleague may have called the cult of the personality has won the day (as I also won it that day in 1977, I think by referring to the excision of Trotsky from Soviet pictures, and what a sadness this had been). Almost everything is rendered through its distorting prism; the world seems intimate and vivid, small people pass through it and become briefly large, it multiplies the famous and makes them somehow more proximate. A lot of this has to do with transmission technology— the speed and quantity of it, the airtime that needs to be filled—but behind that lies the global victory of the market, against which collective opposition has collapsed. The celebrity as a commodity was waiting to pounce.

Describing the creation of early mass culture in the nineteenth century, the historian, the late Professor Raymond Williams, once wrote that 'the masses' were simply the people our Victorian ancestors had been quite suddenly made aware of but didn't know. The celebrity may be a relief from that oppressive idea; all those unknowable people, but look, here comes one of them that we can seem to know, without the duties and responsibility that come with actual knowing. In the century before that of Professor Williams's study—before trains and newspapers and telegraphy—a stranger might get down from a coach and put up for the night at a country inn. Village children would press their faces against the glass and watch him, boots up against the fender of the dining-room fire, sipping punch. A well-dressed stranger in a shadowy room: he would be up and away the next morning, what was his story? Well, we are all pressed up against the glass now, and hearing some of it.   IJ

GRANTA

YOU, THE VIEWERS AT HOME

Andrew O'Hagan

Hughie Green with young contestants on Opportunity Knocks, 1971

1. Maria

Business was slack. The pubs closed early and the ferry came in for the night. The sky was pink above the school on Chapelhill and at eight o'clock the high tide arrived and the promenade was quiet except for a dog barking. From out in the bay you could see bright lights in all the windows of Rothesay. Inside the rooms there were shadows moving and the shadows were blue from the televisions.

Maria Tambini lived at 120 Victoria Street. The family cafe and chip shop was downstairs and the front window was filled with giant boxes of chocolates covered in reproduction Renoirs; here and there, on satin platforms, were piles of rock that said WELCOME TO ROTHESAY all the way through. Rosa spread her daughter's hair on the pillow and combed it one last time before closing the window to keep out the night. Just a minute before, she had been sitting on the edge of the bed, a silver spoon glinting in her hand, as she fed Maria from a tin of Ambrosia Creamed Rice.

'There,' Rosa said, 'Go to sleep now.' She straightened the edge of the continental quilt and wiped the mirror with a yellow duster. 'And try to keep your head out the quilt, it's nicer for your face.'

Maria closed her eyes and in minutes she was asleep. Her mother went from the room and stood for a while at the top of the stairs. Through the open window in the bathroom she could hear Frances Bone, the woman next door, listening to the shipping forecast. Mrs Bone listened to the forecast every night and often in the day too if she managed to catch it. Standing there, Rosa admitted to herself that the sound was not as annoying as she often made out: she actually liked the sound of the words coming from the radio— 'Forties Cromarty south-east veering south or south-west 4 or 5, occasionally 6. Rain then showers, moderate or good.'

People were laughing down in the shop and Rosa wished someone would go and bring that dog inside. Standing on the stairs she caught the look of the Clyde Firth through the glass over the front door. For a second the sea and the distant lights were something for Rosa alone. Passing over the last stairs she thought of an old song belonging to her father. She remembered her father clearest when she thought of those old Italian songs he sang, and, at the same time, without much fuss or grief or anything else, she thought of him coughing for hours in the bed he died in.

Giovanni was slapping fish in a tray of batter and then laying them into the fryer. He caught himself in the silver top and immediately thought about his hair; it had always been the way with Giovanni, several times an hour he would go into the backshop and take a comb through his black hair. When he smiled and showed his good teeth the women at the tables would look up and in that moment some would consider whether they hated or pitied their own husbands. Giovanni rattled a basket of chips in the fryer and went through the back with a sort of swagger.

Rosa was scouring the top of the freezer with cameo pink detergent paste. She looked over her shoulder and tutted as Giovanni came through. 'This place is pure black, so it is,' she said, scrubbing in circles, her head down, the paste going under her fingernails. 'I work my fingers to the bone in here to keep this place clean and nobody else seems to bother their arse. It's bloody manky, so it is. Why people don't clean after theirselves I don't know.'

She paused. Mention of the efforts she made in life always caused tears to come into her eyes.

'All we need now is a visit from the men, that would just suit you all fine to sit there and for the men to come in and see all this. I try my best and I just get it all thrown back at me. There's no a bugger gives a shite. I'd be as well talking to the wall. If the men come and shut down this cafe for dirt then hell slap it into you. I could run a mile, so I could. I could just put on my coat and run a mile.'

Giovanni moved the peelings from the big sink and ran the cold water over his hands. When he'd dried them he went to touch Rosa's shoulder but she pulled away. 'See what I mean,' she said, picking up the dish towel, 'everything's just left lying about for me to pick up.' But when Giovanni turned to go back into the shop she was shaking at the sink and she put her arm behind her and stopped him. She turned and buried her head in his chest and he sighed. 'Come on, Rosa,' he said, 'you're just tired. There's that much on your mind.'

Rosa cried so often and so predictably that no one really noticed she was crying. Her eyes were always red. People seldom asked what was wrong, or if they could help; her tears had been too frequent and the conditions that brought them on were too general and too common. People just said that Rosa was the type who'd cry at the drop of a hat. She was continuously in a state of moderate distress.

She sometimes cried eating her dinner and she cried running a bath. She cried watching television. She cried at her work and even in her sleep. Nobody really noticed any more.

Just in from a meeting of the Scottish Friendly Assurance Society at the Glenburn Hotel, some customers were waiting for suppers at one of the tables. Giovanni went back and began lifting fish and organizing plates; he juggled a tub of salt and a lemonade bottle full of vinegar. Meanwhile Rosa came through and took the duster from her pocket and climbed on a chair to clean the trays that held the cigarettes. After that she got a damp cloth and did the sweetie jars. She didn't simply clean, she made cleaning into one of life's grand and protracted gestures. As she bent to the task she always looked angry. Rosa hated dust—she hated its settling and gathering, as if it could only throw some terrible light on the failure to cope. In no other respect was she more like her mother Lucia. Every day they went about their housework as if it were an act of violence. Rosa liked to drink tea with a cup and a saucer, and sometimes, after doing the house, she would sit herself down on the sofa, exhausted and flushed, the base of the teacup rattling on the saucer's edge.

Maria's best toy sat on the dressing table in front of her window. The Girl's World: a life-size plastic head, with its hair all honey-blonde and tousled and nylon. The special thing was that the hair could grow; you pressed a button on the doll's pink neck, it made a clicking sound, and then you could pull a long extension from Susie's head.

That was its name: Modern Susie. There were several versions of the Girl's World; this one had Mediterranean-blue eyes and raised eyebrows and a tiny nose, a nose you could hardly breathe through. The toy came with special make-up and special brushes. You could give her earrings and spread lipgloss over her smiling mouth, and all the bits and bobs were kept in a drawer at the base of the doll. Maria could spend whole evenings up in her bedroom playing Worlds. With the record player down low and glitter on all the plastic faces, Maria would sometimes put on a show for her old dolls, and she would make it so that Susie was the big star in the room. Maria would sing to her, as if she was a real person, and late at night, when even the seagulls were asleep and the seafront was quiet, the light from outside, the street lamps, would glance off the diamonds in

Susie's special tiara, causing sparkles to travel over the wallpaper before Maria fell asleep herself.

Maria gave Modern Susie a ponytail. As she pulled the hair through her fingers to trap it in bobbles, the static electricity made Maria's hands feel like somebody else's hands, and, as this happened, the skin along her arms began to feel fizzy, as if tiny bubbles of electricity ran up and down inside them.

Rosa stood behind Maria at a creaky ironing board. Doris Day was on the turntable. 'You need to learn to stand on your own two feet,' Rosa said. 'You know there isn't a man in the world who isn't out for what he can get. Mark my words. Before you know it you're washing nappies and watching the door to see if he's coming back or not. Just you watch yourself, Maria. Keep them at arm's length, hen.'

'I'm thirteen,' said Maria, rolling Modern Susie's lipgloss back and forth over her lips and staring in the mirror.

'That's enough of that,' said Rosa. She drove the iron over the dress and then whipped the dress over. 'That's enough gloss. You don't want to make yourself look greasy. I know what age you are, Maria. I remember the day you were born as if it was yesterday. What a day that was, let me tell you. I was lying up in that ward and not a bugger came to see me. Your Uncle Alfredo came right enough, and my daddy came with gritted teeth. You were such a wee thing.'

Maria's mother often talked like the songs. She didn't care that Maria was thirteen or what age anybody was. She put down the iron. 'Don't ever think I regretted you,' she said. 'I can still see your wee face lying there. That was before I was friends with Giovanni. That man's been a good friend to me, Maria. He's not perfect, I grant you that, but I don't know how I'd have coped lifting and laying for everybody. He's been a good help about here. He's just a friend, but it's nice to have a friend. If you've got a lot on your plate, you know. Men will always be men, Maria.' She propped her arm on the ironing board and rested her chin. 'It's true what they say. When it comes down to it, hen, you've only got your mother. You remember that. There's no another bugger to care about you.' Rosa lifted the iron again and went over the creases.

'Do you think Uncle Alfredo would curl my hair at the bottom?' said Maria, looking into the mirror, folding her hair under her small hand.

'Like Lena Martell? Aye, he'll do that no bother. You've got nicer hair than her, right enough. You'll need to remember to lift your chin up though, Maria. You make your chin look that baggy when you do that. Lift it up. You need to be smarter about yourself. Nobody likes to look at a wee pudgy lassie up on the stage.'

Maria continued to stare at her face and hair. Rosa had taught her to sing by constantly putting the needle back to the start of the record and making her try it again. She told her all the stories. Since as early as she could remember it was all Deanna Durbin this and Judy Garland that, Doris Day wore this, and Lulu said that to the newspaper. 'Nobody ever got to where they want to be by sitting on their backside moaning all the time,' said Rosa.

'I'm not moaning,' said Maria.

'No,' said Rosa, 'but you just need to make the effort and smile a lot more. You need to show your nice teeth. You cannae beat a big smile. There you are.' Her mother let the dress float from her hand to come down softly on the bed. It was covered in yellow polka dots and had a big ribbon at the throat. Maria turned around and made herself smile. Maria liked the look of empty clothes. She liked to imagine famous people in them and then see herself in them when she was dressed up.

'You must try to hold yourself in a wee bit when you're singing,' said Rosa, rooting in the drawer for an Alice band, 'like all the great Italian singers. Hold yourself in one place and let all the lovely sounds come out, 'cause you've a lovely singing voice on you, Maria. You're only letting yourself down if you slouch. You're a woman now. I can't be doing with slouchy lassies. You've got to make an impression.'

Maria took a box from the drawer. Inside there were cardboard models with dresses and skirts and blouses you could fasten on to them. She knew the models weren't very modern; the hair on the women looked like the hair on women during the War. They had long thin legs and the skirts were like wool or something. 'Some men have nothing but filth on their minds,' said her mother, turning a T-shirt inside out, 'they're dirty inside themselves, some men, they aren't clean and you wouldn't want them anywhere near you, good God, you can't be careful enough with some men, hen, they want to ruin people that's what they want to do and you're as well keeping

17

yourself to yourself. You're as well holding on to your dignity, Maria.'

Maria was up on her toes looking down into the street.

'Are you listening to me, Maria?'

Maria spent much of her time in the living room dancing with a hairbrush in front of the mirror. She went to Madame Esposito's dance class ('Modern, Tap, and Ballet') every other night after school, and all day Saturday, but she worked out her best routines in front of the mirror at home. Singing, she did that everywhere: her voice shouted out in pubs and cafes, down the seafront and in the neighbours' living rooms. She didn't dwell in rooms as other children did—rather, she placed herself in the middle of them as if every room was a stage, an echo chamber built for projection and confidence.

A scout for *Opportunity Knocks*, the television talent show, had come all the way to Rothesay to see Maria singing at the Pavilion Dance Hall. Soon after his visit a letter arrived inviting Maria to audition for the show in London. The week before she left, her mother had an Avon party in the living room. It wasn't meant as a send-off party but when Maria thought about it afterwards she realized it had felt like one.

Maria's best friend Kalpana, the Indian doctor's daughter, was allowed to stay overnight. Rosa placed bowls of crisps and nuts around the room and she brought some of the chairs down from the back so all the women could sit. The house was filled with laughter and coughing and everyone had a drink. Kalpana and Maria sat on the stairs in their nightdresses. They could watch everything that was happening in the living room and people passed them up crisps and then gave them chocolates too and they were great.

Maria had noticed that something nice happened to Rosa when she was surrounded only by women. The years seemed to fall away from her, she laughed more, and drank more, she was more girlish, and the weight she carried around seemed to drop. She didn't cry so often in front of other women.

All of the Avon perfumes were named after Greeks. One that Kalpana thought smelled of oranges was called Ariadne. One in a round blue bottle was called Pandora. Mrs Bone liked Medea. Rosa, as saleswoman, liked them all, but her favourites were Jocasta and

Leda and Penelope. She went from chair to chair giving out little glass tubes of free samples and spraying wrists. Maria had not seen her mother so happy in a long time. That was the thing about Rosa: underneath the unsettling everyday buzz of her unhappiness and self-pity, she had the most amazing resources, she liked to be among people, until she perceived they had let her down.

When the women had all filled in their order forms Rosa put on a record and brought the girls downstairs. She turned the music up and hung a curtain across the kitchen door. Maria stood behind it and Rosa put on a new record. 'Ladies,' she said, 'a wee bit of hush. For your own pleasure. Sammy Hush for the proud mother. In a special command performance, for one night only, I am delighted to introduce my own daughter—Maria Tambini!'

'Would You Like to Swing on a Star?' started and Maria jumped through the curtain. All the women clapped and Maria, holding a hairbrush, began swaying and popping her eyes. The women cheered and Kalpana clapped. Rosa swigged from her glass and handed out ashtrays; she kept time to the music and didn't seem to care if things got spilled or if anything went on too long. 'What the hell,' she said, 'it's only us having a nice time for a change.' Maria sang her song three times that night and the phone was ringing in the hall, but they ignored it, going on with the song and then more songs and the drinks.

In the morning the records were out of their sleeves and spread over the living room carpet, and the Rosa who put them back in their sleeves was not the same as the person who'd taken them out. The mother Maria adored was the person who came out when Rosa forgot herself. But that didn't happen often. Maria was still lying in bed, smiling and singing, when she heard the Hoover sweeping over the landing and could tell that her mother had become herself again.

On *Opportunity Knocks* a man-and-wife act from Torquay were doing a routine about clowns. Maria sat on the sofa biting her nails. The woman leapfrogged over the man and they knocked each other over and then returned to the microphone for the finale. Then Hughie Green the compère was back. He had grey hair slicked back and his voice was half-American. There were lines across his forehead and he only smiled on one side of his face. 'I mean that most sincerely folks,' he said.

Maria wondered if Hughie Green had been to all the places in America. He talked as if he knew everyone and had seen everything. He always used the word 'talent'. He said this one had talent and that one had talent and what a lot of talent there is packed into the next act. Maria tried to picture the studio in London. She looked at Mr Green on *Opportunity Knocks* and wondered if he would like her. He looked nice with his grey hair, and she felt he looked like someone she had known all her life.

'What talent is, how you find it, is what *Opportunity Knocks* is all about,' said Hughie Green, 'and we like the public to make the decisions for us. Not just the public here in the studio, but the mums and dads sitting in front of their television sets at home.'

Maria watched each of the acts and watched as the Clapometer recorded the studio audience's response. When she was only a baby Alfredo had told her that the Clapometer could hear applause in Rothesay and all over Britain. She knew that wasn't true, but she still clapped for the act she thought was best, and felt glad when the needle went up.

'That will be you soon, Maria,' said Rosa coming in with the Hoover. 'Don't bite your lip.'

'Oh, Mum,' said Maria, 'what will I wear?'

'Mrs Gaskell—the agent,' said Rosa, 'remember she came to see you at that concert the other week?'

'Uh-huh.'

'Well, Thames Television gave her your tape and that's why she came up. We signed a paper. You're going to stay with her and her husband in London for a wee while. She's talking to a stage school. She's got people working out a costume and everything.'

'Oh, Mum,' said Maria.

'I know,' Rosa said, 'soon we won't know you.' The credits were rolling on the television and the rain was driving against the living-room window. 'Mrs Gaskell said the show is just the beginning. She said people who don't win can still make it if they're as good as you.'

Maria bit her lip again and shook her head. She put her arms around Rosa's neck. 'Do you think I will get to be on the programme for real?' she said. 'Will you all watch me?'

'Yes,' Rosa said. 'We hope so.' Maria pressed her cheek against her mother's and giggled.

'Pyjamas,' said Rosa.

Maria jumped up and made for the door. On the way she grabbed the arm of the Hoover. She pressed the release button with her foot and freed the arm, and then, beaming, she sang the first few lines of 'Rockaby'.

Rosa turned and plumped the cushions on the sofa and smirked with pleasure towards the dusky window. 'You're daft,' she said to Maria and then to the empty room. When Maria had gone upstairs her mother stared at the television screen for ages without blinking.

Maria lay on top of her quilt with a record down low on the Dansette. Her bedroom window was open. Mrs Bone was going deaf and was playing the shipping forecast louder and louder over time; you could hear it at all hours through the wall. When Maria had been in bed for ages and she heard those strange words—Dogger, German Bite—she knew it had to be around one o'clock. Lying in her bed, the radio's London voice coming through the wall, and the lights of Ardbeg glowing orange, her imagination would dance on the window ledge, and she clenched her fists as she thought of singers. She said her prayers, and would open her fist, to find sugar lumps she'd stolen from the cafe, and she would eat them.

Maria had thought the same things at night for as long as she could remember. She imagined there was a camera way out there somewhere. The camera had wings. She knew it was looking for her. All the way over the land and over sea it snapped rapidly as it searched for her face. It took photographs as it flew overhead but really what it wanted was her. It came from Glasgow and tore down the River Clyde. It passed shipyards and hotels and the Erskine Bridge and Dumbarton Rock. It came low out of the mouth of the Clyde and then skirted the tops of the churches and the new computer factories at Greenock. It almost skipped over the water of the Firth of Clyde to Dunoon. It rose sharp over the roofs of the houses there and skirted the cinema, and then it plunged sharp into Innellan and past the craft shops and over the Cowal Hills. The camera could see in the dark. It took pictures of Cumbrae in the distance. Then it swept in low over the sea and clicked all the while: a fishing boat out in the Bay trailing foam and seagulls, and now the lights of Rothesay were obvious and the camera raced ahead. It passed over the pebbles on the short beach. It passed over the promenade and the putting green. It crossed Victoria Street above the cars and then the strange camera-bird stopped and hovered at Maria's window. It just hovered there. She created a look on her face and turned her head on the pillow to face the open window.

After a time she got out of bed, stepped carefully over the squeaky boards on the landing and began to descend the stairs. Part of the way down she noticed a strange blue light coming through the window over the front door. It was very blue and it fell on the wall of the stairs; it made her feel alone and bright in the dark. A trace of the blue light was picked up by the gloss-painted banister, yet, looking up at the wall, she saw the light was useless, though it began to illuminate a photograph hanging there, an old one of Granny Lucia and her dead husband Mario. She leaned in closer to look at their faces. They were barely smiling. Lucia was wearing a ruffled blouse. She had a pretty face, with dimples, and Granda Mario had sticky-up hair. The photograph was in a round frame and at the bottom it said LUCCA.

Maria walked to the kitchen at the back of the cafe. A pile of newspapers sat on the table, fish and chip paper; she put her hand on top of the pile and she noticed how small her hand was and how cold the pile of papers. The headline said HEARTBROKEN: MARIA CALLAS DIED YESTERDAY OF A BROKEN HEART. Bending the papers back she found another one for Friday August 19, 1977: THE HEARTBREAK FAREWELL: THOUSANDS TURN OUT TO BURY ELVIS.

Maria stood in her nightie. She felt sleepy. The kitchen was dark but when she felt the top of the fridge with her fingers she could feel the grooves where Giovanni's cigarettes had burned into the plastic rim. He was always balancing cigarettes there when he was peeling potatoes or stirring the broth. She opened the fridge door. Yellow light beamed out. She sat on the linoleum with her knees pulled up and enjoyed the light that flooded from the fridge. Inside it was white and went on forever.

She reached forward with a finger and touched the cold glass of a milk bottle. There was a plate with butter on it; she drew two fingers over the top and brought them to her mouth. She tasted the salt and then she leaned back on her hands, looking at the chicken and lettuces and the tins of peas that were stored in the fridge for no good reason. She took out a cold egg and licked the shell.

The light from the open fridge was fantastic. Maria spoke a few words to the audience under her breath.

2. Mr Green

Every time I drink a glass of claret it goes straight to my face. I'm not kidding. And when I pass a mirror and check out my chops I know I'll be dead in no time. Don't worry, viewers: don't write in. I'm a hundred and one times happier than the version of myself the doctor's been recommending to me all these years. You can bet your life on that. So just sit back, now put your feet up, relax a little, and stay tuned for the old conversation, for what ails us is present in the world before we are.

Show business. Before you call it an illness you want to think what it does for people. I've met everybody, and I'm telling you there ain't a single soul who couldn't use a little more shine on their shoes. Who can't love a person whose purpose in life is to offer a purpose to life? Show business is glory in the afternoon and sunshine after dark. There you go. I'm a man of definitions, you can ask anybody. Show business is tearing life down and putting it all back together again, funnier, larger, shinier, more harmonious, goddamnit—purer, more special. Don't tell me after all this time the world don't want special. I know it does, I'm telling you straight. I've watched it for sixty-odd years and I know.

You just sit there citizen and laugh yourself silly and scratch your beard, I was here before you were, me and the dawn, me and the bigwigs, me and the professors, me and the great British public at large. My show is called *Opportunity Knocks*. You all know it. We sit here and wait for talent to show up and you know why? We're waiting for something to remind us we're all alive out here. Vocation is the heavenly thing on earth, not opportunity, for Chrissakes. We wait here. We have always waited here. Somebody said it: Vocation acts like a law of God from which there is no escape. That's what we believe around here. Listen. Do you want to know what vocation means? It means 'addressed by a voice'. I, Hughie Green, believe talent will save us all. There. I've said it now.

What talent is, how you find it, is what *Opportunity Knocks* is all about. I found the secret, I think, of making sure that we never made a mistake—by asking the public to make the decisions for us.

Andrew O'Hagan

Not just the folks in the studio, but the mums and dads sitting in front of their television sets at home. And believe me when I say the public is always right. They see talent coming: it might be a born star like my old friend Liz Taylor, it might be a cockney with a personality as bouncy as a beach ball. But the public know. They always know. And they won't be fooled any more than they wish to be. Talent is a demonstration of the fact that there are people in the world—special people, mind you, some of them dear, dear friends of mine—who really believe they are what they pretend to be. I used to say that to my old mother, bless her heart. She'd say, 'Stop talking rubbish, Hughie.' But it ain't rubbish. Talent is the heart's bid for freedom, my friends.

There you are. Listening to me. Stay in show business long enough it begins to seem like philosophy. Who came up with that one? You scratch the silver on a little bit of talent and a whole world begins to show through. You take it from me. Growing up in Ottawa back then we wanted to be good, my friends. We wanted to be the best. Nowadays the kids don't want to be good and they don't care about being the best: they want fame. People nowadays don't think they're alive until they're on the television screen. That's true. There it is, ladies and gents: the biggest known intimacy in the modern world, right there in your living room. But you've got to be good, for Chrissakes. You've got to have the gift.

Talent is the fight against quietness. And yet quietness is always waiting for us—the blood moves round, redder than claret, silent as the frozen air—and one day that quiet circulation inside you gives way to the most perfect silence in the world. I'm telling you. You know it. You can weep for applause but silence is your destiny.

'You want to be watched?' I say to some of the acts who come through the auditions, 'Then start by watching yourself.' But I know the true stars are out there, for sure. They know who I am and I want to take their lives and make them personalities people will never forget. I'm telling you I want to take those kids and give them the world. When the sun climbs down at the end of the day, that is what they deserve, that is what the best deserve and what they will get from me and what they will find reasonable, and surely, viewers, surely, my customers, that is what we all must enjoy if life is sincere.

Hughie Green, that's me, hit pay dirt in the spring of 1955. That's when I brought *Opportunity Knocks* to the BBC. It quickly became the most popular radio show in the country and I guess I was what you call famous overnight. Like a lot of comedians and compères who ended up in radio, I never really danced again, though I have sung sometimes, and I found after a while I wasn't looking for acting parts. It was a new life. Suddenly, I was spinning, popular, and was taken everywhere, and in no time it was Command Performances, and the age of television, my God, and in the middle of all that, in the sweetness of England then, you got the feeling people were rushing at you with hopes. The people wanted you to absorb them, to make them successful too, and in no time you see it, you see your public face emerging, you see it recognized everywhere, and there you are, a personality, smiling, waving, passing into the moment when the slickness of your public face dries into a mask.

Deep down, my father reckoned I was a phoney, and, in his last year, a long time ago now, the disdain he nearly always felt for me softened into an admiring sort of pity. 'You carry your own climate wherever you go, Sonny Jim. I'll say that for you.' And then he was gone, the old bastard. He was gone and the very next day it was a new series of *Double Your Money* and who do you think was up and into the studio early, ironing his own tie, making up, rubbing chalk over his teeth and smiling like a skull? Well yes, the oldest clichés in show business are like the oldest clichés in life, not only true, but truer by the day. The show must go on. Harry upstairs said it was the best *Double Your Money* I'd presented in the whole run.

Never mind all that. You pay the price for being good and being on time. I'm past the point now where I worry about being misunderstood, even by myself. Never mind. There are no prizes in this business for knowing yourself. None. I have worked in show business for forty years. That is all I know and that is all I need to know. I love talented people and as I've told you they sure make the world go round.

A girl came in here the other month. I swear she's thirteen years old, and she doesn't even look thirteen. She is tiny. They found her in Scotland, and I said, 'Where from?', and they said, 'Isle of Bute'. And this little girl comes in, she sings like Barbra Streisand. We bring her into the studio and she sings out of that little body like Ethel Merman, Jesus, the beautiful voice on her, and the feeling in her movements. And she's full of fun too. All that fun the good ones always have, the confidence, she reminds me of myself, working hard, keeping time, rolling her blue eyes and giving it a bit of razzmatazz. She's got the nature. She's got the liveliness, God bless her heart, the maturity.

Well, she just might be the best I've ever heard. Talent is a matter of guts and that girl has guts to spare, you should see her rehearse, unfailing, tireless, and God, she goes the whole bundle and we know nothing about her except she's a little Scottish–Italian girl. Well, we don't need to know anything about her. She's a star. Where did this girl really come from? She sings like you were never born. What a talent. She could do anything in the world, anything at all.

It's snowing outside.

Every time I drink a glass of claret it goes straight to my face.

Quiet now. I get tired in the afternoons.

Talent is the fight against quietness. I mean that most sincerely folks.

3. Showtime

Maria sat on a plastic chair for the dress rehearsals. She tapped her foot on the metal edge of a generator when the orchestra began to tune up; the gold shoes she was wearing reminded her of a pair her mother had back in Rothesay. Maria remembered tottering up the back stairs in them when she was little. Over on the stage, Sid the floor manager held on to his earphones and waved a clipboard. Then he asked for quiet. 'Going for a rehearsal,' he shouted. Then he read some words from the clipboard: Maria could tell they were Mr Green's words, but Mr Green rehearsed with the cameras earlier in the day, and this final rehearsal was just for the performers. Sid read the words quickly as if they were dead, though they were in fact quite lively words, describing the next act, Arthur Field, the Musical Muscle Man, who now stood on the stage between two Greek columns, wearing a tiny pair of trunks.

The orchestra played a jerky tune and Arthur Field lifted his arms. Keeping a composed expression on his face, he began to move his muscles, one set at a time, making them dance in time to the music. First one arm up, then the other; the jiggling, oiled flesh seeming to move separately from the rest of him, then his back muscles, then the mounds of flesh on his bottom, they too moved in time to the music. His body parts seemed to have lives of their own, obeying their own rhythm, and then Arthur Field would strike a pose, curving his arms and clenching his fists. His ribs would show, then he would strike another pose, just as the beat of the music changed, and his stomach would be sucked in to show the shape of his insides.

Maria watched from her seat. She had never seen a man with skin so shiny before and she had never seen a man wearing so few clothes. Arthur Field looked down at his stomach as if it were a pet, as if the moving flesh didn't belong to him. Maria noticed the way his chest moved to the music as if the nipples were eyes inspecting the studio. It was horrible the way the muscles in his thick legs moved and his privates were moving around in his trunks. To Maria his body was alive like nothing she'd ever seen, not like a woman's body, the body she had; the colour of the flesh and the shape of it and the movements were strange, and she wondered if all men looked like that under their clothes. She looked at his concave stomach. She looked at his darting eyes and his nipples and the bulge of his penis and she began to smile behind her hand as if she were watching a cartoon.

Walking along one of the back corridors of the studios Maria smiled professionally to the strangers she passed. Whenever she left her room in Mrs Gaskell's house she assumed people were looking at her, and even in her bedroom, alone, she looked at herself, and in her bed at night she felt watched from above. The corridor's strip lights made the tan on her arms look orange, and, as she walked, the skin round her mouth felt tight from lipstick, foundation and powder, and her eyes felt glued open. Barbara in the tea bar gave her a plastic cup of orange squash. 'You look lovely, darling,' she said as she passed it over.

'You don't think it makes me look silly?'

'Not a bit of it, darling. You look like a right lady tonight.'

'I can't win again,' Maria said.

'Course you can, love.'

'They need a new person.'

'Not at all. We'll all be clapping loudest for you, darling. Wouldn't be the same around here without you now, would it?'

Maria smiled her own smile at Barbara and started walking down the long corridor. There was a smell of disinfectant coming up from the floor as her gold shoes clacked along the tiles. At the end of the corridor the swing doors were open and Marion was staring. 'Chop chop,' she said, 'it's showtime, Maria. Come now. We're all waiting for you.'

Maria quickened her pace down the corridor. She felt as if there was a electric heater inside her stomach. Marion winked and disappeared behind the door and Maria stopped just short, feeling warm, feeling distant, the swing door making its rubbery bump and then shushing. The world was quiet for Maria under the strip lights. She put the cup of orange squash to her lips and drew the sweet liquid into her mouth. There was a bin beside the doors. She moved her tongue in the orange squash for a moment and then she spat what was in her mouth into the bin and threw the cup in after. She disappeared through the swing doors. In seconds they had swung together and were peaceful, and only the yellow overhead lights made a tiny buzzing sound in the empty corridor.

4. Nutrition

Pink coconut snowballs lay on a plate next to the teapot, and on the rest of the tray, around the sugar bowl, heaped between the milk jug and the spoons, was a pile of loose Quality Street, a half-packet of Rich Tea, an Empire biscuit, two fairy cakes with jelly tots in the middle, a Blue Riband, two Penguins, a Breakaway, a Turkish Delight, a packet of Toffos, and a raisin Club.

Blue light from the TV flashed on the edges of the cups. As Giovanni lifted one of the teaspoons it had a reflection of the TV in the cradle of itself, and so did Granny Lucia's spectacles on the arm of her chair, facing the TV, the contorted image of the screen almost watchable on her lenses.

'I've sugared and milked them already,' said Rosa from her place in the corner of the sofa.

'Magic,' said Giovanni.

'It's bigger than it seems in real life,' said Alfredo. He'd taken Maria to London.

'You said that last week,' said Mr Sampson, the oldest man on Bute, who was sitting on one of the dining chairs they'd brought over for him. He didn't have a television set and Giovanni was now in the habit of bringing him up to the living room so he could see Maria.

'And the week before,' said Lucia.

'You say it every week,' said Giovanni.

'All right,' said Alfredo, 'I say it every week and every week it's true. The telly makes that place look much bigger than it actually is.'

'Very good, Alfredo,' said his mother.

'I'm just saying.'

The logo for London Weekend Television came together on the TV screen to the sound of trumpets.

'That's the Telecom Tower. You can see that from the top of the hill where she's living,' said Alfredo.

'Shush now,' said Lucia. The living room door opened and Kalpana put her head round. 'Has it started?' she asked.

'No, hen, come on in,' said Rosa. 'Sit yourself down, it's just starting. Sit here.'

'I'm okay on the floor, Mrs Tambini.'

'Alfredo, pass the lassie some of that stuff over.'

'No, Mrs Tambini, honest. I've just had my tea. No thanks. I'm fine.'

'On ye go,' said Giovanni.

'Shhhhh,' said Lucia.

Just to keep the peace Kalpana took a cake from the tray and placed it on the carpet at her side.

The screen suddenly filled with the face of Hughie Green. His grey hair was slicked back and he was winking into the camera. 'Good evening and welcome ladies and gents and all the viewers at home. What a terrific show we have for you tonight...'

'He must be some age now,' said Mr Sampson. 'I can remember him when he was on the radio. He was good on the radio. They say he's a bit of a lady's man.'

'Let us hear him,' said Giovanni.

Hughie Green made a joke about Concorde and another one about Denis Healey's eyebrows. 'He's good at his job,' said Giovanni. 'He knows his stuff.'

'He uses big words,' said Alfredo.

'There's nothing the matter with big words if you've got something to say with them,' said Lucia.

'Would yez be quiet,' said Rosa.

Hughie Green straightened out his smile and nodded at the camera and did a tiny shuffle. 'Over the last six weeks our first contestant has secured a place in the hearts of the entire nation. She came here as a complete unknown, but since then her vivacious, bubbly personality and beautiful singing voice have proved a winner with people of all ages. From the beautiful Scottish island of Bute, this remarkable little girl has proved to be a breath of fresh air with all of you. I mean that most sincerely folks. A winner of the last six shows, and competing tonight for her seventh, ladies and gents, it's my great pleasure to introduce the fantastic, the sensational...Maria Tambini!'

Lucia could feel the heat of the bar-fire coming through her slippers. She blinked and caught her breath as Maria lifted her eyes and looked right down the camera. She looked into the heart of the living room; and then Lucia remembered she was looking into a million rooms, with people in each one taking the girl to themselves.

'Oh, look at her,' said Lucia, spreading her fingers under her throat. 'Is she not beautiful?'

On the TV, Maria reached the chorus and her whole face seemed to blur with feeling. Her body shook. She drew her arms across the front of her face with the fingers spread; it looked as if she were tearing the song in two, or ripping open the screen that contained her now, and she dived into the song's giant chorus with her head thrown back, holding the notes until the breath left her, and then staring at the floor with wide eyes, closing them, opening the verse with something new in her expression, her arms falling open again as the chorus approached, reaching, climbing, throwing her hands to the audience as if to appeal for understanding. There was a storm of music around her and she wrapped herself up in it and she was gone.

She is gone, thought Lucia. Never was she coming back to this place or anywhere like it.

Rosa followed the movement of her arms. So beautiful, the white gloves along her arms. She didn't phone today.

'Go on, ya wee cracker,' said Giovanni. 'Go on.'

Mr Sampson thought it was all so modern to see the lights behind the wee lassie go from blue to pink and back again as she sang the words. 'Mrs Bone always used to say she was the loveliest thing in a pram,' he said out loud.

Alfredo looked at the television and thought of all the things the camera concealed. He thought of the Green Room and the car waiting in the studio car park. He thought of the drive through

London at night and the look of the skyline from Primrose Hill. He thought of Sid the floor manager and the nice dancers and Mr Green coming past and always speaking in headlines.

'They're doing wonders with her hair,' he said.

And at the end of her song everyone in the living room clapped and they clapped on the television as the camera panned across the audience.

The lights went down. Maria Tambini could hear Mr Green at the other side of the studio talking. She could feel that her brow was damp and could hear herself breathing. She knew that no one could see her face now. She stood on the platform hearing her own breathing and she liked the sound of the audience and Mr Green. There was nobody up on the platform but her. Later in the show she returned to the stage to face the applause of the audience and the Clapometer.

In Rothesay, outside the window of her old bedroom, the wind coming off the Firth was rattling the door of the darkened chip shop and its sticks of pink rock. There was no one about; they were all at home in the glow of the television. Down Victoria Street and past the harbour there was quietness and shadows, and they crowded the seafront, those shadows, flickering around the old palaces of entertainment, the Pavilion, the Winter Gardens, and round the palm trees, over the putting green, to lurk in the bus shelters and the doorways of shops on the road to Craigmore.

Inside Harris's Television Shop a bank of four rental televisions had been left on for the night, and there, behind glass, beaming to the sea, they showed the smiling face of Maria Tambini on her final *Opportunity Knocks*.

5. America

On the plane Maria lay back and watched the shapes of the clouds. She was tired. Marion Gaskell sat next to her reading a programme from an opera she'd seen. 'I never quite find the time to read these,' she said. Two men in front were talking in American accents.

'You should never make the mistake of thinking Las Vegas is normal,' said one.

'I know that,' said the other, 'it's a circus. Jesus Jones. It's the biggest friggin' circus in the world. I've never considered it normal even for a second.'

'Do you know what *Newsweek* said about Elvis when he first appeared there?' said the first man. 'They said he was like a jug of corn liquor at a champagne party. I'm serious.'

They both laughed.

Mrs Gaskell was oblivious to the people in front. She read her programme, she ate petits fours, and occasionally glanced at Maria's tray and suggested she try something. 'It'll be quite some time before they offer us anything again,' she said. Maria scraped some cubes of roast potato under her chicken and stared out the window. Much later on, somewhere over Illinois, Maria pretended she was eating a roll and butter. She dropped pieces of bread down the side of her seat; she rubbed the squares of butter up her arms, into the skin, into the creases around her elbows, and eventually, as the smears of butter began to dry, Maria felt very much at one with the pure air she sensed outside the window.

She was in Las Vegas to sing for one night only. The theatre was in the hotel, the MGM Grand; she was part of Dean Martin's Summer Benefit for the Retinitis Pigmentosa Foundation of America, and was staying in the hotel's Emerald Tower. There were framed posters hung along the corridors. The posters advertised past concerts featuring the great heroes of song and dance, and that night they made Maria feel she was truly part of a special tribe. Mr Martin held her hand and told her she was 'a great little Italian kid from Scotland, *Il Piccolina Signorina Lampadina.*'

Mrs Gaskell seemed almost to grind her teeth with pleasure; she blushed full of pride and professional well-being to be standing there with Dean Martin and the others. 'She's not nearly as young as she appears to be,' she said nervously.

Lucille Ball came over to Maria after rehearsals and said, 'God bless you, honey. You've sure got what it takes.'

'And might you be the fairy godmother?' said Liberace, putting his ringed hand out to Mrs Gaskell.

'I'm simply thrilled to meet you,' she said in return.

'Charmed,' he said, 'I love your English accents.' After a pause, during which Liberace stared at Maria and smiled, he told a story about being a young performer on the *Colgate Comedy Hour.* 'Now, that wasn't the day before yesterday,' he said.

'If you're ever in London...' said Mrs Gaskell.

'I'm very often in London.'

'How exciting. You must come and see us. If you give a concert...'

'So darling of you,' he said, and he smiled. 'I can't tell you how much a boy can begin to miss the Savoy.'

'Quite,' said Mrs Gaskell.

Maria noticed how thin the gentleman's wrists were and how narrow his face. She felt jealous: it came and went.

'Are you Catholic?' he asked her.

'Well, I suppose she is,' said Mrs Gaskell. Liberace ignored her and looked at Maria.

'Is that so, dear?' he said.

'Yes,' she said, 'I'm a Catholic.'

'I still say my prayers,' he said, 'I still say my prayers every night.' Maria didn't know what to say. She smiled. He began to turn away and he winked at her. 'We Catholics oughta stick together,' he said, 'all this performance...' He made the word long and swishy like his coat.

'...We invented it, honey-pie.'

He walked off and was joined by the stage manager.

'Well,' said Mrs Gaskell, 'wasn't he just marvellous?'

Later in the day Maria sneaked down to the gaming hall to see the people winning and losing. The slot machines gripped her most. They seemed frightening after a while. All those lights, and the fixed look in the people's eyes, their fat hands cupping the coins, their fat arms pulling the lever, the wheels spinning. When she walked down the lanes of one-armed bandits the sound of crashing coins and bleepers got to her. The noise was too loud and the people were fat and they didn't care about losing the coins, they just put more into the slots and kept staring at the machines.

Down the street was a Walkway of Fame—golden shoe-prints and handprints—made from casts left by many of the great performers who had come to Las Vegas. To get away from the slot machines, Maria walked the length of the strip. It was good exercise, she said to herself. She stopped and tried her own hands in the pavement prints. Sammy Davis Junior had small hands but long fingers: Maria's were so small they looked lost inside the brass crevices. Yet Maria wasn't satisfied to find her hands were smaller; she wanted them to appear smaller again, and not even to seem like hands in the same way, with similar proportions, and after a while she grew to hate the game. It made her angry.

Some of the casts had been taken from the prints at Mann's Chinese Theatre in Hollywood. It said so on a sign. SHIRLEY TEMPLE BROUGHT AMERICA THROUGH THE DEPRESSION WITH A SMILE, it said. Maria grew suddenly excited when she saw Shirley Temple's prints on the ground. When she put her fingers into the brass she felt the cold of the metal and at the same time realized she was touching something that maybe Shirley Temple had touched. She kept her hands there on the pavement and her mind was full of old pictures. Around Shirley Temple's hand and tap-shoe prints, there were other tiny prints, Jackie Coogan, Baby Leroy, Deanna Durbin. Maria wasn't sure about them, but she put her hands in theirs anyway, and after a moment she felt sick. Her hands were too big for the prints. She felt faint.

She walked up and down the strip. On the way up, she saw her shadow moving on the pavement in front of her—she liked the dryness of the day—and after an hour she began to be happy again, passing food places with smells coming out, breathing in the smells of onions and hamburgers and feeling joyful as she passed them. She passed all the places again and again and felt gratified with her shadow on the ground. She grew so happy at herself it was like levitating. She needed nothing. She would eat nothing. She walked down the street and it was as if the whole street and then the whole of Las Vegas had been built for Maria Tambini and the traffic moved in response to her walking down there, and the people could only move as so many atoms squeezed and channelled by Maria's presence on the street, by her own power as she travelled forward, controlling everything, and her own body seemed almost nothing, her body felt cleansed and empty like the shadow on the pavement, taking up no space at all in the street, the warm breeze itself somehow shaped and commandeered by her mood.

The theatre was hot and full of people clapping and laughing. Along with the excitement, electrical feedback squealed out, but the applause covered it, and the stage was quickly a furnace of good cheer. Dean Martin and Maria Tambini stood there together, smiling into their microphones. Mr Martin put his arm around her waist. Maria wore a smile too big for her face and a skirt a few years too young.

'How are you, darling?'

'I'm fine.'

'You oughta take a rest 'cause you really worked hard there. You sing terrific. That's hard work you know.'

'Uh-huh.'

'You belt out a loud sound. That's hard work for a girl. A girl can't do it a lot and you do it enough for eleven girls.'

She giggled.

'You're cute. You're pretty and everything.'

'Thank you.'

'You sing terrific. I couldn't believe it. I thought there was a ventriloquist back there, like a big bear that was going "raaaaa".'

She covered her mouth with her hand.

'Are you thrilled to meet me? You should be.'

The audience laughed.

'Oh.'

'Do you wanna talk about something?'

'Yeh.'

'Like what?'

'Um. Um. Um. "Swinging on a Star".'

'"Swinging on a Star". You wanna do that first?'

'All right.'

'You don't look like you mean it, little sister. You wanna do something else?'

'Rockaby.'

He laughed. 'Don't start causing me trouble, honey. You're super-terrific. Okay boys—hit it.'

The brass section exploded into the song. Dean Martin stood back holding a drink and smiled approval at the audience while Maria gathered up the sound and belted it over the audience. 'Give it hell,' he said.

In her room that night Maria drank glass after glass of water from the bathroom. Crouching by the bed, with the lights more than visible outside, and the hotel television issuing canned laughter from the corner, she sucked a piece of toast and then spat it back on to the plate. She scraped a line of skin from a nectarine and licked the pulp inside. Her head pounded. She threw all the scraps into the bin and went into a bag in the closet where she found a furry pencil case. She counted out twenty laxatives and swallowed them with the water.

They came into Grand Central Station, the daylight glinting through the compartment. When she opened her eyes Maria saw the tracks and the other trains, the precise movements outside, and at the opening of the final tunnel they all seemed to pick up speed, the trains, and so they turned like silverfish into the depths of New York.

Maria loved the way the station made her feel so small. The windows up there just cancelled her with their beams: she walked beside Mrs Gaskell and felt invisible with so many people around her. Yet she felt tugged by Mrs Gaskell's officious nature to be both present and correct, and she was aware of the persistent pressure to give an account of herself in relation to schedules and expectations, and so they marched across the concourse and out of the station, Maria feeling edged into occupation, while wishing only to fade under the buildings and the glass.

'Will you eat something?' said Mrs Gaskell.

'Not hungry,' said Maria.

'This is a jolly good opportunity for you, Maria,' said Mrs Gaskell, 'so let's have none of your nonsense while we're here. I'm not your mother and I refuse to follow you around with a teaspoon.'

'Good,' said Maria. 'Nobody's asking you to.'

Mrs Gaskell stopped short of the line for the taxi. 'You're too bloody thin!' she said.

'I'm not,' said Maria, 'everybody wants me to walk about like a blob. You just want me to be a blob. I ate my breakfast.'

'You put it in a tissue.'

'No, I didn't! I ate it! It's inside my stomach.'

'Stop it, Maria. This is nonsense.'

'There's nothing the matter. Just leave me.'

'Maria.'

'I won't discuss this any more, okay? I am not standing here talking this kind of rubbish with you. I have eaten my breakfast and I feel very good if you must know. I feel well.'

A driver with a black cap and a sign came out of the crowd and helped them with the bags. 'I have such delightful memories of the park,' said Mrs Gaskell. They drove across town and Maria smiled out of the window on her side. Mrs Gaskell reached into her coat pocket and brought out a flapjack. She placed it on the seat between them. 'Please have a piece before the rehearsal,' she whispered. And then: 'I beg you.'

Maria glanced at it and then continued to look at the buildings on 59th Street and the steam coming out of the ground at the corner of 59th and Lexington. 'I don't deserve it,' she whispered.

'Sorry?'

Maria turned and her eyes were wet. She smiled at Mrs Gaskell. 'I'll have it when we get to the hotel,' she said.

6. The Tonight Show with Johnny Carson

'She just set the whole town on its ear. Blows you right out of the theatre. Here she is—Mary Tambini.'

Applause. Whistling.

'You come from Scotland, huh?'

'Yeah. Scotland, USA.'

'Oh, you're a comedian as well. Do you go back there much?'

'No, things have been busy.'

'Your family are there?'

'Yeah. I speak to them on the phone when I can.'

'I bet they're proud of you, huh?'

'I think so, yes.'

'You like haggis?'

'Horrible.'

'You don't like haggis?'

'God, no. It's a sheep or something.'

'I love your accent.'

'Thank you.'

'You're cute.'

'Thank you.'

'D'you have a boyfriend?'

'No.'

'Can I have your phone number?'

'Cheeky.'

'Cheeeeky. You know I love your accent. I'd like to just take you home and sit you on the sideboard.'

'They told me about you.'

'Uh huh. You play the bagpipes?'

'You're daft.'

'Stay tuned, folks. I'm daaaft. Join us again after this word from our sponsors.'

Maria sang for President Reagan at the White House. He pinched her cheek and she didn't know whether to laugh or curtsy. She stood at the reception and drank her seventh Diet Pepsi of the day, and it felt nice to her, like a passing shower of rain inside, and harmless, under control, the taste of zero, the buzz of Diet Pepsi. At the dinner, when no one was looking at her, Maria got rid of the stuff on her plate. She folded a piece of chicken, two new potatoes, and a heap of julienne carrots in a napkin and passed them into her sparkly handbag.

'Gee,' the President had said, 'I know girls just like you on the West Coast.'

'I'm from the west coast too,' she said. 'The west coast of Scotland.'

'You don't have sunshine there,' he said.

'No.'

'Or oranges,' he said. 'Or Disneyland.'

'I've been in California,' she said.

'You sure don't have that in Scotland,' he said.

Mr Reagan moved on and another man in black tie shook her hand. 'But you have the Loch Ness Monster,' he said.

'Yes,' she said.

'Great to meet ya,' said the man, 'I'm Ed Meese. You sure sing lovely.'

'Thank you,' she said.

Mrs Reagan had a very weak handshake. 'My word,' said the First Lady, 'you're so terribly thin, my dear.'

'I've always been wee,' said Maria.

'Well, never mind,' said Mrs Reagan drawing close to her ear then drawing quickly away, 'a girl can never be too thin.'

Maria went down in an elevator and she asked a security man to order her a car. She felt more and more ill as the car progressed down Pennsylvania Avenue.

From her hotel room that night, Maria could see a white steeple-like thing covered in light outside. She felt very cold. She had a headache and only the crackle of the TV news broke up the silence of how cold it was. There was a drumming inside her head as she lay down on the floor and snuggled up to the radiator; she turned it up full, and the metal was very hot, but she still felt the cold, and for an hour she shivered there, red scorch-marks beginning to show on her back.

She had sung well. The people at the party had made out they liked her. The people had all seemed so happy and so thin and so good-looking in that ballroom, every person in their clean shoes, their bow ties, their long dresses, and what bright teeth they had when they laughed. The President used to be a movie star. So did his wife. She was thin. And when Mrs Reagan smiled it was as if cameras were clicking all over the world. Nobody seemed tired or poor. Nobody seemed to belong in any other place. People were warm: only the air conditioning had made the room cold.

Maria lay thinking about the faces she had seen. Her mind was filled with the room, filled with tonight, and was also filled with other rooms, other nights. She lay on the carpet and suddenly the hotel was too big and so was Washington DC. The world was encroaching, enormous, country within country, city within city, so many rooms, and in the middle, Maria.

7. Mr Green again

I once said to that little girl, I said, 'Honey, this business isn't worth a nickel you can spend if you don't have your health. You have a great talent and you can't argue with that, no siree, but you have to take care of yourself I'm telling you or the talent bombs and you're back where you started.' Years ago I was in Reno, Nevada, and they showed me around the set of a John Huston picture—what you call it? *The Misfits*. Marilyn Monroe and Clark Gable, good God, a whole world of talent, and that poor girl, God Almighty, she was so far gone they couldn't even focus her eyes for the shot. She said to me, 'You think I'm cute, huh?' I said, 'Honey, the whole world thinks you're cute, but the question is, what do you think?'

That Tambini girl spent half her childhood hiding in dressing rooms and starving herself. No wonder she breaks down now and again and she's been out of the business these last years. People said, 'You should've left that girl where she was', and I said, 'Where was she?' I'm telling you a girl like that is travelling under her own steam.

We just made it a bit easier for her by bringing her to the attention of the great British public. Believe you me, you don't invent talent. Talent invents you. It changes your mind and brings you up short. Jesus. The girl wanted a life and she got a life. She spent a little too long in costume, I'll say that: a baby has to grow up eventually and face the music as an adult performer. Don't get me wrong, you have to be honest, people like a bit of suffering, Jesus yes, it adds to a performance no doubt about it, but you got to get a grip on it for Chrissakes before you end up in the drink.

The Variety Club of Great Britain had a tribute for me a few months ago—Lordy Lord, a roast they'd say in New York—and I must say they gave me the works, bags of talent onstage, the speeches, handshakes, the bloody gold watch, all the best acts from the shows I've done over the years, and there we were, down at a theatre in Bridlington with the lovely Princess of Wales in the audience, and all in a good cause, all in a cracking good cause indeed, not me I mean but the National Youth Theatre, all those kids and bless them there's talent in there somewhere.

I came to the theatre early. I know I was supposed to turn up in a car like some la-di-da but Jesus I had to come and see what's what, that's my style you see, and turning up later I'd miss the greasepaint and all that palaver, the stuff I like. They weren't too pleased of course, but hell, I've been out of the business myself these last years, and you don't often get a chance to do the rounds and turn a few door handles. I found that nice Tambini girl rootling around in her dressing room. 'What you doing there, stranger-o-mine?' I said.

'I'm counting my dresses.'

'You're what?'

'I'm counting my blessings. Come in here.'

And she welcomed me into her room, the wee thing. Oh my, what a change in a person, I have to say. Thin. Not an inch of gristle on her. The skin was stretched across her face but, Jesus, there's no use denying it, the girl was lovely and her eyes glittered just the same as they did when she was barely as much as a teenager. 'This is your big night, Mr Green,' she said.

'Hughie,' I said, 'call me that.'

'What you doing here?' she said, 'you should be away having a meal or something.'

'So should you,' I said.

'Oh, don't start,' she said. And the smile, I'm not kidding you, would have upset a chandelier. I said, 'Are you looking after yourself, Maria?'

'I am,' she said, 'I am that.'

Well, good enough, and what do you make of her, she goes and gets me a wee dram and I'm saying to myself this girl has all the class now that we spotted in her years ago. 'The older you get, Mr Green, the more Scottish you sound.'

'Hughie, call me Hughie. My father was Scottish. Well, I always had affection—cheers!—I always loved the Isle of Bute, and you've no idea how lovely a place it is from the air. You fly over there and it's like New Zealand or better than that.'

I drank a malt whisky in front of her and I promised myself a few glasses of wine but you want to look after yourself on a night like that so I kept it down. 'Affection demands a hug from you,' I said to her, and she smiled at me, Jesus, the girl is not your run-of-the-mill, and I said to her I really hoped she was enjoying her career despite everything. 'I am,' she said, and there was no two ways about it. She said, 'I am.'

'Because I get worried for you,' I said, 'and people say we brought you into the business too young.'

'That's nonsense,' she said. She said it herself and I'm not worrying to contradict her, I think she's right enough.

I'm old now and you don't sit down to sup tea with all the pains-in-the-ass, good God, we gave it our best shot to make people's lives a bit easier in our own way. I looked into the face of that wee lassie Maria Tambini and I knew we did honour to who she was and who she will be for years to come if she works hard.

Later on, they sat me in a box. Lord Jesus. Her Royal Highness Princess Diana was over from me and there was another girl who knew how to fix a room with her eyes and everything. As long as I live I'll remember the pink dress she wore, believe you me, it seemed to float about her in slow motion. The Tambini girl came on in the first half and I was proud of her. I really was proud: she came from nothing that girl and nobody in her family had ever been outside a chip shop and the way she sang that night it was as if to confirm every notion you could ever have about talent and what it means.

A thing happened, Her Royal Highness leaned over, you know the way she blushes, and she says to me, 'Is that woman unwell?'

'She's a trouper,' I said.

'No, Mr Green. Is she eating?'

I just told her what had been in the magazines and the papers and told her she was on the mend. You have to hand it to that Princess Diana all the same: she takes an interest in people, and I watched her out the corner of my eye, looking down at the stage and her blonde hair was all swept round in that lovely way and she had such a care for that Tambini girl you could really tell and some of the acts were better acts you'd have to admit.

The TV cameras swung from one end of the place to the other and Les Dawson had us in stitches. After Maria's big number—the way she held those notes!—she came out and her and Les did 'Be a Clown', you know the old Garland–Gene Kelly number, and good Lord, the two of them threw in every joke and every ounce of talent they had between them. I'm telling you: and the energy down there, it's hard to believe, and then they did a scene, you know, where he is supposed to be the reprobate and she's the nagging wife. 'Aw wifie,' he says, 'come and sit upon my knee. Here's a wee seat, my bonny dwarf,' and all that stuff. The audience are killing themselves. The Tambini girl climbs on his knee and the audience are loving it but she is supposed to put her arms around her neck and just pretend to cry for a second.

'She's not pretending.' The lady next to me was waving her programme like a fan and she said it again: 'She's not pretending.' I thought the Tambini girl had missed her cue but it turns out she was holding on to Les's neck and I must say that is not at all professional even if you're tired or whatever, you know how it is in this business, you have to just dust yourself off and we certainly didn't train people to lose the place onstage. But good old Les he can always save the day—what a turn—he just lifts her up and makes a joke to the audience about her being in a coma from too much Scottish mince and tatties and he carries her right off the stage to loud applause. □

GRANTA

NEIGHBOURS

Kyle Stone

Top: The Big House; bottom left, Grandfather and Grandmother Stone; bottom right, Tessie the Terror (on the left)

Neighbours

Not long ago I received an aerial photograph of several enormous white houses stuck together. This is one house, actually, my grandmother's, in Westchester County, New York State. During my childhood, driving over to see my grandparents was known as 'visiting the Big House'. The federal penitentiary, Sing Sing, just up the Hudson River from Westchester, is also known as the 'Big House'. When you are tried and sentenced to jail, it's still known, all over the United States, as getting 'sent up the river', in honour of Sing Sing, even though Westchester's white-collar criminals know they will never end up anywhere close.

Hillary Clinton's independent political career began when she and Bill moved to Westchester, to Chappaqua, fifteen minutes away from my grandparents and their Big House, and took out a mortgage on a place of their own large enough to blend inconspicuously in with the neighbourhood. The shame I feel at looking at photographs of the Big House doesn't go away, even when I realize that, with the arrival of the Clintons in my old neighbourhood, nobody calls my grandparents phoneys any more.

'Why are you moving to Westchester, Mrs Clinton?' the *New York Times* and *New York Newsday* and the *New York Daily News* all asked.

Hillary confided that she admired the county's beauty and its 'stately homes'. In the richest parts of Westchester, a house is not a house, it is a Home. In many parts of the county, including Chappaqua, the Homes are invisible from the road, set off at the ends of private driveways, sometimes patrolled by private police.

When Hillary and Bill moved into their new Home, it was big news in Westchester. Kids rode around Chappaqua on their mountain bikes, reporting Clinton-sightings into cellphones, like miniature versions of CNN's Peter Arnett in the Persian Gulf. The local evening news showed Hillary's removal van. We heard her unpack on National Public Radio. There was a voice-over, as in sportscasting. 'I think a lot of her unpopularity has to do with carpetbagging,' the commentator said. 'It's a high-intensity issue for those that don't like her.'

'Carpetbagger', an epithet from the end of the Civil War, was originally a term for white Northerners who went down to the ruined cities of the post-bellum South to make their fortune. The Clintons had given this elderly insult a new life. The word has overtones: of social climbing, of using people and places transparently, of hick vulgarity, of crashing the party.

The Clintons' house quickly became Westchester's answer to Graceland, the object of Sunday morning drives and the target of radio talk shows. People took the train in from the city to see the Clintons' new Home. David Letterman posed in front of it. There hadn't been this much attention paid to Westchester since Herman Tarnower, the Scarsdale Diet Doctor, was murdered in the late Seventies, shot in the head by his mistress, an elementary school principal. The next day Tarnower's house, mailbox and driveway could be seen on *Eyewitness News*: they resurfaced shortly afterwards in *People* magazine. Every one of us who had ever choked down two weeks of Scarsdale Diet grapefruits—in other words, every woman in Westchester over eleven—felt, suddenly, brightly, in the public eye. Even those of us who couldn't forgive Tarnower his hardboiled-egg dinners and spinach lunches forgave him everything. From then on, something was established, something we remembered twenty years later when Hillary moved in. Westchester seemed to finish off its celebrity residents, one way or another.

My grandparents bought the Big House when my father was thirteen, in 1947, before most of Westchester's present residents were born. Hillary's critics like to point to people like my grandparents, born in Manhattan or the Bronx, with accents thick enough to subtitle. Unlike Hillary, they are real New Yorkers. It doesn't make them any less real or less New York to add that they were fakes from the beginning.

When I ask my grandmother what she thinks of Hillary, she is unequivocal: Hillary is not a New Yorker. She is not from New York. She does not understand New York. She is not real. My grandmother adds that she herself is still a supporter of the Democratic Party. Now that Hillary is in the neighbourhood, she quips, she is looking forward to the Democratic...*parties*. Since my grandmother was born on the Lower East Side, it comes out 'pah-tees'. She then tosses back her head in a laugh that shows me her teeth.

My grandmother is eighty-nine. Her teeth are still hers, her eyebrows are not. Every morning, in a cracked marble bathroom, she plucks them out and paints them back in, along with a beauty mark, like the music-hall flappers of her adolescence. Her hair is a sculptured helmet; it has not been allowed to go white and is instead a delicate, greenish grey-yellow. She puts on a girdle, a garter belt, old-fashioned hose which snaps on to garters, and stuffs her feet into two-tone pumps which still arch her ankles and point her toes with a dusty Forties flirtatiousness. Women of my grandmother's generation do not wear pants, and after seventy-five years of garter belts and hose her legs are as white and smooth as the marble tile underfoot. Both my grandparents have a thing for marble. I've used my grandmother's personal bathroom twice in my life (the house has seven) and both times something—the carved bas-relief, the gilt wall sconces, the cupid's head above the sink—gave me the sacrilegious feeling of relieving myself in a mausoleum. Clutching the railing, she descends the sort of grand spiral staircase that Vivien Leigh might have been carried up. My father relates that as a boy he once fell all the way down the staircase to land at the carpetless bottom: the last sound he heard before losing consciousness, he claims, was my grandfather calling, 'Don't chip the stairs!'

Westchester extends downwards from near Sing Sing towards New York City, fizzling out in the fallen resorts of Yonkers, New Rochelle and Mount Vernon in the south. Once smart summer towns, then nesting grounds for commuters, very white, very WASP, now they're no longer bedroom communities so much as the maid's bedroom, the distant highway exits those who take care of the children and mop the floors take to find their way home to sleep at night. The rest of Westchester considers them far too close, in this freeway era, to scary Harlem and the filthy Bronx. The county ends, in the east, with Long Island Sound, not far from Chappaqua. To the west is the Hudson river, where the robber barons used to sail up and down, and later built, as John D. Rockefeller did, their summer homes.

'God gave me my money,' John D. famously declared. God hadn't given my grandfather his money, exactly. In fact my grandfather was a lower-middle-class Russian Jew with a newly anglicized surname and a mother known, even to her children, as 'Tessie the Terror'. In photographs he is a handsome young buck with a sweet smile and a Mephistophelean glitter in his eyes: the sight of him suggests clichés of the Roaring Twenties, the jalopy chugging to the bootlegger's, the swallowing of goldfish. As it turned out, however, he had none of the era's impulsiveness. He'd protected himself from every disaster, even the Depression, by planning ahead.

My grandmother was the oldest daughter of a self-made immigrant German Jewish clothing merchant, or *shmata* salesman. The clothing merchant opened a store on Union Square, and made a small fortune off an emerging New York middle class of Jews, Italians and Irish too timid to venture into the Episcopalian Abercrombie & Fitch, or the more upmarket Macy's and Bloomingdale's. He became famous for his brutal union-busting tactics and his adept use of Pinkerton men. I can only guess that my grandmother was restless. She eloped with my grandfather at sixteen, his first landmark on the road of upward mobility. A bright girl and an ugly one, she knew his proposal was nothing personal.

The Union Square department store, known as 'S. Klein's… On the Square,' although no other Klein's existed anywhere else, wore well into my own adolescence the same enormous sign it had through hers, a kind of pushy vendor's poem,

UPPRICED?… NO, DOWNPRICED

UPTOWN?… NO, DOWNTOWN

Not a lyric couplet by any means, but it ensured my grandparents a life uppriced and very much uptown, until at last it closed in the late 1960s and the surrounding real estate was sold to a developer who eventually built expensive condominiums for a market too young to remember Klein's.

My grandfather listened to French and Italian Berlitz records in the bathtub, not to learn the languages themselves, but to learn how to speak English like an upper-class foreigner. He cultivated a kind of locked-jaw drawl reminiscent of a Hollywood law professor. He couldn't admit he didn't know the answer to a question, any question. When asked for directions, he would invent non-existent roads and highway turn-offs rather than admit he didn't know where something might be. He could not book a table at a restaurant without giving the impression he was planning to review the place for the food section of the *New York Times*. He was never at a loss for a story, even when the story was what is usually called a lie.

My grandfather claimed the Big House was the last one Stanford

White designed. In reality the tasteful, philandering White had nothing to do with the Greek columns and plantation-style porch, or the forty-four rooms full of red wall-to-wall carpet, red curtains, red leather and Harvard chairs. Hanging up throughout the Big House is my grandfather's art collection, a dozen or so paintings in gilded frames with nameplates reading 'Goya', 'Dürer', 'Turner', 'Constable'. As a child, I once asked my grandmother where she'd gotten all these famous paintings. She said only, 'Your grandfather picked each and every one of them out.'

In my parents' house, just down the road from the Big House, John F. Kennedy, marooned in a rowboat, stared handsomely out at nothing in the middle of a stormy sea. The boat was half-hidden by tossing, crested waves; the presidential forehead was half-hidden by a tossing, crested forelock. It was unclear whether the storm was happening at war in the Pacific or off the shore of the family summer home on Cape Cod. It was clear, however, that this was our household shrine, our episcopal version of a Madonna statue. Unlike my grandmother's paintings, there was no famous artist's name fastened to the bottom. As a child I was bothered by the picture: if he was alone in a storm at sea, who painted his portrait? 'Oh,' my father said, in a dreamy insincere voice, 'someone who knew him well. Maybe his younger brother.'

JFK's younger brother was, in fact, Hillary's predecessor in the role of carpetbagger. Like Hillary, John Kennedy's younger brother had moved to New York to campaign for the Senate. But Bobby Kennedy became New York's adopted golden child, his opportunism looked on indulgently, his opaque Massachusetts accent politely overlooked. Hillary could not have presented more of a contrast. Even her defenders had to admit that, for a Democratic candidate new to the state, moving to Westchester was the equivalent of Bobby Kennedy going to California in 1968 and cold-shouldering Cesar Chavez's migrant grape-picking workers in favour of a shopping spree in Beverly Hills.

Nineteen sixty-eight, the Summer of Love. I was seven. We had just moved back to New York from out west, where my mother's side of the family lived. While students were being tear-gassed in Paris and shot at in Mexico City, we spent the summer living at the Big House while my parents tried to find their own place. My mother hid in the coat closet rather than bump into my grandmother on her imperial way down the stairs. The Big House, in spite of its ante-bellum pretensions, did not have a plantation-style staff. It had, instead, buttons reading MAID, BUTLER, PANTRY, buttons which never budged when you pushed them. Still, it took me a while to realize they were painted on. MAID, BUTLER and PANTRY meant, in fact, an Estonian cleaning lady named Salome. She was in her eighties, shaking, skeletal and bent over so badly she seemed to be permanently on the lookout for carpet lint. 'Salome's weakness is candy,' my grandmother would say, shaking her head pityingly like a broker dispensing unheeded good advice. 'My mother probably wants to pay her in candy,' my father would whisper, as the two of us watched Salome trundle an Electrolux vacuum cleaner up and down the vast front stairs, painfully crunching Hershey's Kisses in her toothless mouth.

In 1968 the prince of my second-grade class in Purchase Elementary School was George Stephanopoulos, the one-time Clinton aide who jumped ship just in time. Even in second grade George S., as he was then known, had more gold stars next to his name than anyone else. In class I remember Stephanopoulos as a silent little boy with a hedgehoglike brush cut, flinching as he was singled out for praise by our teacher, Mrs Nachman. He knew how deeply he was hated by the rest of us.

Mrs Nachman used to talk to us about the troops in what she called 'Vee Ette Nam', rhyming with 'Pam'. In the fall she polled us: How many of you have parents voting for President Nixon? Raise your hands! How many voting for Humphrey? How many for Wallace? Hold them high!

There were seven or eight hands raised for Hubert Humphrey, one of which was mine. There were two hands, I remember, for George Wallace, the segregationist Governor of Alabama. Nixon won the rest of our class, hands down or hands up, as it were: bad news for Hillary, even then. Perhaps if she could have looked in on us then, on her husband's seven-year-old future aide-turned-tell-all-commentator, she would have realized: Westchester didn't always share the rest of New York State's liberal affinities.

Through the early Seventies, the Big House's more incriminating decorative details were lost on us: what we noticed was that it had more than one TV. My little brother and I rode the school bus, which was driven by a succession of longhaired, foul-mouthed Vietnam vets. One, I remember, drove with the wheel between the only two fingers on his maimed hand. All of them scared us, but the rides were exciting. Every day the route to school took us past our grandparents' house. One day Two Fingers jammed on the brake.

'Look at this racist shit!' he yelled, gesturing with his deformed hand at the cast-iron black jockey on Grandma's front lawn. 'What kind of racist pigs live here?'

I made the shushing sign at my brother. We weren't going to give ourselves away as the grandchildren of racist pigs. We said nothing.

'What a symbol, huh?' Two Fingers continued, bringing the school bus to a halt outside my grandparents' place as though he were a tour guide conducting a field trip. 'Look at that.'

The other kids in the bus all twisted in their seats. They were neighbourhood kids: I was certain their grandparents didn't live much differently, but they stared obediently out the windows at the Big House.

'Look at that. Look at that mother.' Two Fingers twisted around in the driver's seat to face his captive audience. I panicked: was he talking about my grandmother? Was she wandering around out there on the lawn? But no, it was the jockey, who stood with his cast-iron visor cap like Bazooka Joe in silhouette.

It was a few years after this episode that I began to notice how many of Westchester's lawn jockeys had suddenly had their heads repainted: innocent baby pinks, the purest of virginal whites. They had become a virtual Aryan Nation of statuary. It was too early, by twenty-one years, for the Los Angeles riots; by thirty or so, for the arrival of Bill Clinton's security detail. In my teens and twenties I thought they had gone white with fear, fear of class insurrection or a race war. More likely, it was simply the first sign, the slow beginning, of Westchester's entry into politics.

In July 1999 Hillary announced her candidacy standing next to the frail outgoing senator, Daniel Patrick Moynihan, on the lawn outside his Westchester summer house. Some prudent campaign staffer had arranged for portable toilets to be installed in Moynihan's garden. It looked like a newly built condo development for dwarfs.

Kyle Stone

Outside stood demonstrators with signs reading NOTHING BUT AN EMPTY CARPET BAG.

Hillary's first opponent, Rudolph Giuliani, is now, of course, a national celebrity in the United States and, in Britain, an honorary knight. At the time, Giuliani made sure we knew Hillary wasn't just his opponent, she was his enemy. Hillary posed for photos with teachers and the teachers' union. No one told her that in Westchester everyone sends their children to private schools. She posed for photos with policemen. No one told her that in Westchester the police are often accused of stealing everyone's missing garden tools. 'I may be new to the neighbourhood,' Hillary told us plaintively, 'but I'm not new to your concerns.' She was new to the neighbourhood: that *was* Westchester's concern.

New York has always linked politics to the clubhouse, and something known as the 'smoke-filled room': it cherishes the hard-edged sound of this the way junior-high students do their cigarettes. The clubhouse used to be the city's Democratic machine, Tammany Hall: it has now evolved into something called the Liberal Party, whose premise and platform are vague enough to stand for anything or nothing, but whose blessing is essential for any political candidate's success in New York. Now that Giuliani has been rediscovered as New York City's father figure, it's easy to forget that he once went so far as to ban not just porn theatres and panhandling but ferrets from the city's streets ('Look at yourself, a grown man, obsessed with *weasels*,' he shouted at the president of the New York Ferret Fanciers on a call-in radio talk show). It's easy to forget that this was the man who posted marksmen on the roof of City Hall during a march by Aids patients. Yet even this authoritarian figure was chasing the state Liberal Party nomination. And doing far better than his more obviously liberal opponent at winning them round.

Upscale magazines began to attack Hillary for her vagueness on the issues. Radio presenters and news reporters ignored the issues, asking instead if she were faithful to her husband. Even the *Weekly World News*, a paper known in the past for stories such as HUMAN SOUL WEIGHS 1/70,000 OF AN OUNCE, ran a cover story on HILLARY'S SECRET LOVER, whom it reported to be a thirty-eight-year-old New York restaurant owner. 'Sooner or later this will get out,' the paper exclaimed, 'and when it does, Hillary's run for the Senate will be toast.' Hillary had had the highest negatives of any Democratic candidate in the state, forty-three per cent. Most of us had written her off as croutons already.

Hillary's campaign released a video entitled *Hillary, The Real Story*. The story went like this: Hillary, in pearls and a pink sweater, made time for Chelsea. 'Barely mentioned,' the *Times* observed, 'is President Clinton.' In response, lunches and buttons pinned to designer collars proclaimed a new organization, WOMEN FOR RUDY. A National Public Radio reporter interviewed a group of women voters in Bedford Hills, ten minutes' drive from Chappaqua. Hillary was not real, the women voters declared. There was nothing to her. They were divided as to whether Hillary had been real once, but agreed unanimously that she wasn't real any more. 'She didn't leave the Creep,' one of them told the NPR reporter. 'I'll never forgive her for that.'

Bedford Hills, a town of golf courses so green they look fertilized by dollar bills, is where my doting father used to take me so I could get on horses and fall off. 'Come on, get up. Get up and get back on. That's the girl,' my father used to call out, worried, as I would lie in the cedar shavings and dollops of horse shit, and cry. I wondered if anyone in Westchester was talking to Hillary the same way.

Why are you moving here, Mrs Clinton? During the Clintons' first term in office Hillary wrote a book entitled *It Takes a Village*. Perhaps, we thought, the move had something to do with the fact that Westchester arranges itself into villages. You can see them from the commuter train: a series of little sets, each with their train station, their parking lot full of Porsches and Pathfinders, their post office, supermarket and Blockbuster Video, and, outside, the police squad car parked with a motionless figure down low behind the steering wheel, either napping or a decoy. Village of Scarsdale, of Harrison, of Rye, of Rye Brook; Village of Larchmont, of Mamaroneck, of Tarrytown; Village of Hartsdale and Ardsley and Armonk; Village of Mount Vernon and Mount Kisco; Village of Yonkers and Pelham and Irvington, of Bedford and Purchase and Pleasantville and Pound Ridge and Chappaqua. The very word 'village' suggests folksy little towns rich in the activities— sidewalk-strolling, doorbell-ringing and the handing out of leaflets— basic to any political campaign. In many parts of Westchester, however, there are no sidewalks, and the hired help, in any case, are instructed never to open the door to strangers when they are home alone during the day.

The houses—the Homes—in Chappaqua and the richer parts of the county are big enough to hide you easily from a ringing doorbell: every kid knew someone who had skipped an entire year of school by simply running upstairs and hiding in a bathroom until the school bus had pulled away. The Homes are too far apart, anyway, for campaign workers leafleting on foot.

My brothers and I never walked anywhere when we were growing up. We saw our neighbourhood from the back seat of Cadillacs, cast-offs from my grandparents. Over time there was to be a string of them, part of the uncomfortable arrangement between my grandparents and my father.

My father tried on a long series of different jobs which grew out of New York-area real estate, ending up in the Koch administration in NYC for a while. New York City employees aren't allowed to live in Westchester, or anywhere else outside the city boundary. Along with all the other city employees who did, my father first asked to be officially classified 'indispensable' ('Nothing's indispensable but air and water,' snapped the *Village Voice*) and then registered as his 'official residence' a post office box in Queens. After Koch had been driven from office, my father drove around the Bronx for New York Health and Hospitals scouting sites for methadone clinics, with a golf club beside him on the front seat. He had hoped to be a painter and a pianist, and he despised his work—most of all his second job, the job he had working for my grandmother. One summer afternoon, prowling illegally around my father's desk, I opened one of its forbidden drawers and found inside a legal pad on which was written over and over again in heavy script:

'I hate my mother.

I hate my mother.'

It was understood that the loaned Cadillacs were an employment perk, and that they were non-negotiable. In time each one found its way back, like a migratory bird, to permanent retirement in the Big House's garage.

As I grew older I developed my own relationship with that garage. In Westchester, as in so many American suburbs, coming of age means owning your first car. Buy one, or have one given to you, and you are officially almost an adult.

By my late teens, I had already flunked my driver's test twice. I had also discovered the narcotic escapism and snobbery of great films, but great films, it seemed, were too good for bad drivers. The county had one art-house cinema at the time, in Scarsdale, an especially rich town, otherwise full of preppie clothing stores and overpriced liquor. It was crucial to find a way to get there. It was difficult, however, to see Fellini or Fassbinder or Werner Herzog in the urbane manner such films called for when afterwards you had to accost Mrs Gasparini, your brother's best friend's mother, in the supermarket parking lot for a ride home in a station wagon full of frozen turkey.

After I finally passed my driver's test, at nineteen, my grandmother loaned me a car: a light yellow Cadillac Coupé de Ville from the early Seventies, slow, long, uncrashable, unparkable. It had pointy buds over its tail lights, like the peaks on a meringue pie. 'When you get into an accident,' my father explained, 'it'll protect you the way a smaller car can't. Besides, you can put the top down. It's sporty.' During the summers, I drove around stuck to the hot upholstery feeling as though I were steering a hot, melting, oversize dessert. We called it the Lemon Chiffon Clunker. I spent the summer months trying to drive to summer jobs, laboriously backing in and out of parking lots, emerging to the sound of paint scraped off metal. Early in the first summer I would leave notes, begging forgiveness, on the cars whose paint jobs I had butchered. *'Dear owner of the green sedan: I had a lot of trouble backing my grandparents' big old car out of this lot. Please accept my apologies if you find your paint job blemished or disturbed.'* I didn't have insurance, and something stopped me from leaving any information that might have actually been useful to someone trying to collect more than an apology for damages. By July my correspondence had scaled down to a sheet ripped off a notepad on which I'd scrawled *'Sorry'*; by August I scrapped the notes altogether and just concentrated on making a quick getaway. Pale yellow Cadillacs are not good getaway cars. Embedded in the dent left in the other car was always the scrape of yellow, the very colour of my cowardice. My hands would be wet with sweat, knowing that in a land of black and dark blue BMWs, the Lemon Chiffon Clunker was hard to miss; convinced they would track me down and follow me home, knowing that in Westchester, wrongdoing means not getting away with it, or not getting away fast enough.

The Clintons were in trouble as well, in summer 2000. The Clintons, it seemed, were always in trouble, although this didn't mean they wouldn't fit right in.

The Clintons pardoned various scoundrels; Hillary's brother, a lawyer and lobbyist for hire, took $400,000 (later returned) from a drug dealer and a swindler convicted of mail fraud; Hillary's other brother secured earlier pardons for another convicted swindler and his wife. Bill pardoned a man whose ex-wife had given generously to the Clinton presidential library and a tax cheat who had delivered a unanimous vote for Hillary from every adult member of a close-knit Hasidic shtetl on Long Island. Bill and Hillary moved furniture valued at more than $26,000 from their old digs with them to Chappaqua. The move did not poll well. The consensus was that the Clintons were trying to make off with stuff meant to gather dust in a sanctified way at the White House. Reading about this, I remembered that every one of the towels in the bathrooms at my grandparents' place had a logo on it: the logo of someplace like the Savoy Hotel or the Barcelona Ritz, the Copley Plaza or the Copenhagen Sheraton. My grandfather maintained that, along with the Bible in the bedside drawer, the hotel expected towels to be taken home as souvenirs.

Hillary had been grilled around the state about these helpful efforts on behalf of others. She had told reporters over and over she was 'very disappointed'. On television, the shaking of talking heads: will this hurt her run for the presidency? Westchester was, like Hillary, very disappointed. Westchester wasn't fooled. It knew the difference between the powerful and the merely notorious, between summer homes and exile, between going into retirement and going into hiding.

Westchester sits, like a big car, on twin blocks: theft, and the fear of it. Robber barons were Westchester's colonizers, its real First Families. One robber baron after another paddled up the Hudson river, the county's western border. First there were Cornelius Vanderbilt and Daniel Drew, who built and owned New York's railroad infrastructure. Then Jay Gould, who bought himself the New York Democratic party machine and Ulysses S. Grant's presidency, and who destroyed, in the 1870s, much of New York's public transportation system through speculation and embezzlement (and who, with his friend James Fisk, cornered virtually all of the city's available money supply). Then there was Andrew Carnegie; his sidekick Frick; John D. Rockefeller, who came from Ohio to build Standard Oil's headquarters at the foot of Broadway before building a second mansion in Westchester; Morgan, who financed them; Mellon; Astor; Cassatt. Vanderbilt's fortune rested in part on the Harlem Line, which still brings trainloads of Westchester commuters into Grand Central every morning from Scarsdale and Tarrytown. The robber barons started this line, and it started the robber barons: Vanderbilt's face on the railroad bonds sold during the 1860s reassured New Yorkers that, in the words of an admirer, 'he would never let anyone else steal anything'.

It was Jay Gould who began the Westchester cult of the Big House with what historian Michael Josephson called his 'queer Gothic gingerbread castle' in Irvington-on-Hudson, a few miles down the river from the Rockefellers. His yacht, the *Atlanta*, bobbled up and down in the river below. Westchester's taste for kitsch started with the robber barons: their mansions and castles and schlosses infested Westchester and parts of Long Island; their wives wore diamond tiaras and diamond chokers, which they themselves called 'dog collars'. They hired genealogists to trace their lineages back, always discovering that history had a pleasant surprise for them: descent from England's King John, or at least one of the Mayflower aristocracy, the First Families of Virginia. The robber barons liked costumes. Gould's friend Fisk, for example, styled himself the 'prince of Erie'. He owned the Narragansett shipping line and paraded about in an admiral's uniform, fat, untidy, and, in Josephson's words, 'bursting with vanity'.

My father's older brother was also fat, untidy and bursting with vanity, even if he didn't wear uniforms. My father didn't get on with him, either. We lived a ten-minute walk away from my uncle, but only saw him two or three times a year. He had dropped out of law school and yet, unlike my father, had still managed to make a success of himself. He had opened a gallery in Manhattan with capital from one of his several marriages. He was a poster boy for Westchester excess. In a town of tanned, lean mesomorphs, my uncle belonged to the Henry Kissinger school of short, tubby, self-adoring rich men. Like Kissinger, he had a blonde second wife a foot taller than he was;

he had, as well, a string of leotard-clad artist girlfriends downtown in the Village, and a collection of Bugattis in the garage. His house was stuffed with modern art, some of it for sale, some of it in a chaotic kind of storage.

In a vain effort to create an heir to the family name, he'd produced another collection, his daughters: six of them. They left home for long periods, came back, moved out, moved in with boyfriends in the city, found their absences unremarked, and quietly moved back home again. On the weekends, my uncle would conduct field trips, and convoys of prospective art buyers, tanned couples in tennis whites, would troop through the house, oohing and aahhing. There would always be a cousin skulking in her bedroom until her door was unceremoniously pushed open and her father announced, 'We're coming in your room a moment to see the de Kooning sketches, babe.'

Westchester, like the world, is divided into North and South. It's the north that has the greatest concentration of Hillary Clinton's constituency of liberal Democrats. And, as with the hemispheres, it's the north that has the most money. Northern and Southern Westchester despise one another. But, like the hemispheres again, they're locked together in a death grip of mutual dependence, since the north needs to shop, and the south needs the north's political clout and its reflected social cachet.

Westchester, south, has shopping malls, designer outlets, computer stores, Toys "R" Us, discount liquor stores, Big Man Tall Man, Lynda's Lovelies for Larger Ladies, Nathan's of Coney Island, The Store Formerly Known as Crazy Eddie's, multiplex theatres, Tropical Fish Barn and Monogram World.

Westchester, north, has horses and horsey people. Literary Westchester tends to the north; Italian Westchester, to the south. The writer T. Coraghessan Boyle, with his piercings, tattoos, beard and dreads, may make like a biker and look like a badass. He too, however, lives in Westchester, and every day his motorcycle passes covens of cold-blooded preppie kids wearing knit shirts with small reptiles sewn above their hearts.

My family lived on a kind of equator of their own between Westchester north and south. My uncle, with his long-legged, small-breasted second wife, had made it solidly into Westchester north—

Neighbours

Episcopalian Westchester, the Westchester of the best real estate and biggest swathes of land, the Westchester unabashedly closest to money. My grandfather never really made it over the invisible Rio Grande that separated north from south, in spite of his affectations and his decorating scheme. My grandparents had separate bedrooms. In my grandfather's, horses in hunting prints jumped all over the walls. There was a pair of metal bedside lamps shaped like horse heads and more horses embroidered on the butch red-and-black bedspread. My grandmother's bedroom had a frilly canopied bed, with lacy pillows and ceramic horse-head bedside lamps and needlepoint ponies capering on the quilt. Both of them were, in real life, frightened of horses; neither of them had ever been within a hundred yards of one. Jewish Westchester made my grandfather ashamed, but horsey Westchester, I suspect, made him anxious.

Italian Westchester was more convivial. My grandfather felt at home among Italians—I think it helped that Italians didn't think about horses much—or perhaps he just preferred Italian stereotypes to Jewish ones. Whenever he had anything to discuss with my father, he would take us to dinner at Frank and Joe's Sawpit.

The Sawpit was widely believed to be owned and run by gangsters. The elderly waiters wore white towels draped over their red-jacketed arms; the tables wore white tablecloths as thick as shrouds. The men at these tables didn't wear the usual Westchester preppie uniform when dining out. Instead they had black hair and black shoes and sometimes dark glasses they kept on indoors. The red leather booths, the smell of gorgonzola and cigars, the dark fish tank of stumbling lobsters, all gave the Sawpit a certain 1940s mob romance. My grandfather liked it because the waiters knew him and greeted him by name. Every dinner had the same ritual: my father would touch my grandfather for money; usually my grandfather would refuse, but, as he would remind my father, at least we all got a dinner out of it. My grandfather never looked at my mother, and whenever he decided the serious conversation should get started, or when one of my little brothers began to wail, my mother and all of us children were sent to go look at the lobsters. One of my brothers would run to the bar, clamber up on a bar stool, and pivot around, shrieking; my mother would have to go over and pluck him off, and the bartender would beam sympathetically and try to look down the front of her dress. We would retreat, and I would watch our reflections in the dark shades of the restaurant's other clientele.

One evening we had just reseated ourselves from one of these forced lobster marches when a convoy of particularly grim-looking shades and tans came up, looked us over, and seated themselves at the next table. The man facing me had a long undertaker's face I knew I had seen somewhere else. I announced, loudly enough for everyone in the restaurant to hear, 'That man looks just like Ed Sullivan!' Ed Sullivan looked up; he and his protectors gave us bright, irritated smiles. The men with him laughed mirthlessly, producing a fish tank sort of bubbling sound: heh-heh-uh-uh-uh-heh.

For years afterwards, the epicentre for me of the world's supply of glamour was that soiled one-storey brick building with FRANK AND JOE'S SAWPIT in looping metal script letters above the door. I heard, some years after I had left, that it had closed abruptly, and then when I came home for a visit a few years back, not long after Bill Clinton had been re-elected, the entire building had disappeared, as though it had suddenly left town.

Some of Westchester's residents count themselves among the more famous figures in American literary culture. Of course, some of these, like Alfred Knopf, his wife Blanche, and Bennett Cerf, are dead, and others, like our neighbour Roger Straus Jr—the 'Straus' in 'Farrar, Straus and Giroux'—are getting there. Roger Straus and his wife, Dorothea, lived on the Upper East Side of Manhattan; the house next door to my parents' was their summer home. The word the Strauses used to describe their house, pool and lawn was 'farm'— SAROSCA FARM said the nameplate—perhaps referring to the work of the gardener couple they had hired to grow organic lettuce and tomatoes for Dorothea. During my childhood, Roger, in his sixties, would pull out the door at seven-thirty every morning in his white Mercedes coupé, giving my father the same stiff little wave he'd just given the gardener couple. 'That Straus, that anti-Semitic Jew, driving that German car!' my father would mutter. Then he would wave back, smiling. Once, Straus called me over—to rein in our dog, maybe, or to ask me to move the platoon of dismembered GI Joe dolls we kept strewn all over the driveway. It was the closest I had ever been to him: big eyes, big nose, deep voice, a smell of nice cologne—and a beige layer of something coating his face from the roots of his hair downward. My father was not surprised. 'Oh, I know. Goddamn Straus, driving that Mercedes to work every day, with more make-up on than Suzanne Pleshette.'

One day my father got the idea that the Strauses, in conversation with their city literati guests, had been passing part of our lawn off as their lawn. My brother and I got off Two Fingers's bus that afternoon to see something metal and chain-link bisecting the green grass. 'You guys like our new spite fence?' my father asked us, happily.

In retrospect it's difficult not to see Westchester as made up of live celebrities, like the Clintons; dead celebrities, like the Rockefellers and the Scarsdale Diet Doctor; celebrities in embryo, like the infant Stephanopoulos; and procurers and retailers to celebrities, people like my uncle. Then there are the sports celebrities, which meant the pitcher Tom Seaver when we were growing up and now means many of the New York Knicks.

My grandmother tells me she has read, in the *New York Post*, that Bill Clinton can't get into a country club. 'Quaker Ridge won't have him,' she tells me, enjoying it. 'Arrowwood won't have him. Westchester Country Club won't have him.'

Having been rejected by all the WASP clubs, Clinton was now apparently trying to get into the Jewish ones. 'We wouldn't have him,' my grandmother says of her own club, shrugging matter-of factly. 'Think of the security. The security problems. The security detail.' The security detail is just what the name-droppers of a country club would want, I think: the Famous Man, flanked by a small private army of unsmiling men in dark glasses. Perhaps, however, what she really means by 'security detail', perhaps what everyone there really objects to, is the idea of a small private army of unsmiling black men, the worry that they may be casting stray looks, behind their dark glasses, at the granddaughters spread out on the deck furniture by the swimming pool.

The Knicks practise at SUNY Purchase, the uninviting state university where Hillary announced her official entry into the Senate race. My grandmother encounters individual Knicks in the drive-in post office. She drives, as always, a Cadillac, but this one is nearly twenty years old. She looks covetously at the Knicks's brand-new sport utility vehicles and convertible roadsters. They have beautiful old farmhouses and beautiful slender wives. They are between one and two feet taller than everyone else in the neighbourhood.

When a Knick strides out the door of the post office and covers, in a couple of steps, the distance across the parking lot, it's hard not to stumble out the door, craning your neck upward, feeling like a third-grader hoping for an autograph. But, since all Westchester's Knicks are black, I'm still tempted, during every sighting, to run after the Knick in question and ask him whether he's tried to get into any of the nearby country clubs, and, if so, which ones have used his celebrity status, like Bill Clinton's, as a reason to turn him down.

On election day two radio commentators pondered the situation: 'You look at it and you wonder, if Rudy Giuliani had been in, whether it would've been any different.'

'Obviously it would have been a different race,' said one. 'A lot nastier.'

'And a lot more expensive,' said the other.

But Giuliani suddenly announced he had prostate cancer—a declaration so abrupt, and so out of character, that many of us speculated whether Hillary had had a secret voodoo consultant. His replacement was Rick Lazio, the junior congressman from New York, who appeared boyish and exuberant to Republicans and like an oversized ten-year-old to the rest of the state. Henry Kissinger stepped in to tutor Lazio on foreign policy.

We watched the returns come in on election night. No word from the presidential election—a tussle, as it turned out, which was going to provide international entertainment for weeks ahead. The talking heads discussed Hillary's victory, instead. The New York press was in a tizzy. Hillary had spent the last sixteen months as a carpetbagger, an ambitious, embarrassing parasite from elsewhere, but now that she had won, she was ours, and we wanted to figure out whether she should run for the presidency in 2004 or 2008.

National television told us that New York had picked 'the first sitting First Lady to be elected to public office'. Bill and Chelsea stood uncomfortably against the wall of a high school gymnasium, while the sitting First Lady paced up and down with her microphone like a nervous televangelist. 'Thank you, New York, for opening your minds! Thank you, for opening your hearts!' We watched New York voters interviewed in the street. One confided that she was originally from Chicago, just like Hillary. New York, she warbled, was a city of out-of-towners. I could almost see my grandmother, the Real New Yorker, grit her small, metal-capped teeth.

George Stephanopoulos, now grown up into an ABC News commentator, was discussing Hillary's victory. 'The Clintons are both politically radioactive,' he said. I watched my grandmother shake her sculptured head. I knew she was thinking of Bill, that unstable isotope, and what he might do, alone and untended, in that house in Chappaqua.

It's been two years now since Hillary became the junior senator from New York. Yet cars still drive past with stickers reading NOT HERE, HILLARY and GO BACK TO ARKANSAS, BILLARY. When Hillary first moved to Westchester, a neighbour of theirs told an interviewer, 'Well, if they lived next door, I'd say hello, and everything, like if we were out at our pool, and they were out at their pool. But I don't think I would invite them over.'

In spite of these reservations, now that Hillary and Bill have found their dream house in Westchester, they will indeed, I'm sure, be invited over. But I can't help remembering one hot summer day in my early twenties. Our neighbours, the Strauses, were away on a trip. It was mid afternoon when we noticed thin trails of black fog coming out of their upstairs windows. My father reluctantly called the fire department, a department composed, as in many other parts of Westchester County, of volunteers. By six o'clock the Strauses' house was its own Towering Inferno, a big stone box invisible behind clouds of black and white smoke. The police later said it was an electrical fire: we were afraid that our house would be next, that it was arson. We heard the crash of glass as the windows fell in; finally we saw, behind the empty window cavities, orange flames. The fire was eventually extinguished, but not before half a dozen station wagons full of neighbours had pulled up on the lawn. They had brought their families, kids, and coolers of beer, and they camped out up and down the driveway and on both sides of the road, on the lawn, around the house, just to sit and watch it burn.   □

Sight and Sound: The film monthly

Critical Cinema

GRANTA

JUBILEE GIRL
Fintan O'Toole

The Mall, June 4, 2002

Jubilee Girl

I came across a portrait of Her Majesty Queen Elizabeth II in the National Gallery in London. In the picture, the Queen is long and thin. Except for her crown and the flecks of gold sprinkled on her pink dress, she might be Olive Oyl from the old Popeye cartoons. From her left hand she swings one of the symbols of her persona, a blue handbag. From her right hand, like the tendrils of some man-eating plant in a 1950s B-movie, dangle nine long leads. Attached to each lead is another of her familiar emblems, a corgi dog. If you did not know that corgis and the queen go together, though, you might think she was taking nine rats for a walk, so rodent-like are their gaunt, pointy faces and tiny little legs.

The Queen is smirking with regal self-satisfaction. Behind her, in a traditional maid's uniform with white cap and apron, a scowling blonde woman is bending down to scoop up with a pink shovel a neat pile of three corgi turds. Above the turds are the wavy lines that indicate a bad smell in children's comics and the word 'Poo!'. The colour of the shovel matches the pink of the Queen's dress, making a visual link between the bad smell and the royal personage.

The painter would seem to be a republican satirist. She has picked up on the outward emblems of Elizabeth's public presence—the crown, the handbag, the odd dress sense, the corgis—and given them a hollow, cartoonish look. Her image of the careless monarch sailing blithely on while the poor servant cleans up the mess she leaves in her wake simmers with class resentment. And the stench rising from the dog shit suggests, crudely but wittily, that the whole business of the British monarchy reeks with the stink of corruption.

If I had not seen the caption underneath, I would be astonished that such an image was on display in an official state institution while outside in Trafalgar Square, a huge crowd is celebrating the Golden Jubilee of Queen Elizabeth II's accession to the throne of the United Kingdom of Great Britain and Northern Ireland. On the other side of the wall from which the portrait is hung, the balcony of the National Gallery is already crowded, for it offers a vantage point over the square and down to the Strand.

The Queen will not pass by the far side of the square for an hour yet, and even then the people on the balcony will catch but a brief and distant glimpse of her gilded carriage before it passes out of sight under Admiralty Arch and down the Strand to Saint Paul's Cathedral.

Before they see her waving from the window, moreover, they will experience a build-up that seems to invite a sense of anticlimax.

They will see the blinding flash of the sun on the helmets and breastplates of the Household Cavalry, smell the sharp, pungent alkaline tang of sweating horses, hear the roar of guns from the King's Troop Royal Horse Artillery as they salute the passing monarch and the blazing trumpets and rattling drums of the mounted bands. They will savour the magnificence of the major generals, colonels and lieutenant colonels, whose order of precedence is mysterious but immutable. They will watch the three ordinary carriages with their extraordinary passengers: the Princes William and Harry; the Duke of York and his daughters; the Earl and Countess of Wessex, strangely alone; the husband and children of Princess Anne. They will spot behind the rococo extravagance of the gilded royal coach, a group of confident riders, among them Princess Anne and Prince Charles.

And in the coach itself, seeming very small and dull amid the splendour, the object of all of this ceremony, the Queen herself. If they are lucky, she may be waving and smiling, but, since she cannot wave and smile forever, she may just be talking to her husband with a slightly exasperated expression on her face. They may find her banal presence rather disconcerting amid all the pomp, like Dorothy discovering that the Wizard of Oz is just a little man behind a screen.

For now, though, they are engaged in the activity that, from the public point of view, is ninety-five per cent of a royal occasion: waiting. Most of the people in the square have placed themselves in front of a giant TV screen which will show her progress, preferring a close-up electronic image to a remote glimpse of reality. Yet for those on the National Gallery balcony the sight is impressive enough: thousands of revellers in the June sunshine, the triumphal column commemorating the naval hero Lord Nelson, the huge stern lions that symbolize imperial might, the black school children singing and dancing on a stage erected for the occasion. This image of relaxed grandeur, this combination of imperial hauteur and vibrant street life, seems utterly at odds with the raucous irreverence of the scandalous portrait inside the gallery.

Out there, they are already five deep against the barriers that line Ludgate Hill and Fleet Street, the Strand and the Mall. There is little to see except the soldiers in dress uniform who are also waiting. Yet the little boys are already on their fathers' shoulders.

'Can you see them?'

'What are they, Dad?'

'They're soldiers.'

'What are they doing?'

'They're guarding. They're guarding the Queen.'

'What are they saying?'

'They're not saying anything. They have to be very quiet.'

'Why do they have to be very quiet, Dad?'

'Because it's respectful. They're showing respect.'

'What's respect?'

'It's what you have for the Queen, you know, like when we go to church and you have to be quiet.'

The portrait, then, should be like an obscene shout in a church. Except that the caption attributes the work to Emma Zayour, age eight. It is not an incendiary work of republican incitement, but part of an official Jubilee event. The exhibition is called *My Queen Elizabeth* and it is a collaboration between the National Gallery and a children's television programme. Emma's picture hangs with the other winners of the competition. Some have a stilted, official look, as if Elizabeth's face has been copied from the back of a coin or the front of a five-pound note. Most, though, are cheerful and intimate, infused with the indulgent fondness children feel for their grandmothers. The Queen is a nice old lady with a handbag. The tone is affectionate, cosy, warm, like a handmade birthday card. Emma's stinking corgi turds are the touch of licensed naughtiness you allow a cheeky but adorable child because you know she loves you.

Standing in front of Emma's picture, it strikes me that, twenty-five years ago, when the Queen celebrated a quarter of a century of the throne, it would not have been displayed. I was in London in that summer of 1977, working as a cashier in a cinema. From a young Irishman, raised with a Catholic hostility towards the English Protestantism which the Queen embodies and a republican disdain for the hereditary aristocracy of which she is the fountainhead, the Silver Jubilee could evoke only a sullen resentment. Most young English people I knew seemed to share this disdain. Our anthem was the Sex Pistols' aural equivalent of Emma's painting, the punk classic

'God Save the Queen'. Its mix of sneering rage and poetic lyricism was a perfect counterpoint to the official hymns of praise: 'God save the Queen/She ain't no human being/There is no future in England's dreaming'.

Back then, to avoid the outrage of having this song as the number one single in the British pop charts in the week of the Jubilee, the charts were rigged, placing, rather aptly, Rod Stewart's 'I Don't Want to Talk About It' at the top. It would have been hard to conceive of a gesture more likely to confirm, for most people under thirty, the hollowness of a monarchy whose image of serenity depended on the suppression of dissent.

Those who control the image of the monarchy did not then know the power of indifference. They did not grasp the simple truth that it is impossible to give offence to someone who will not take it. Looking now at Emma's picture in an official collection of royal images, I realize that they have learned this lesson. 'God Save the Queen' had been reissued a week before, in the hope that it would top the charts on the Golden Jubilee weekend, fulfilling the frustrated destiny of 1977. In fact, amid official indifference, it is merely at number fifteen. A week later it will be at number thirty. Even more tellingly, the Sex Pistols' lead singer, Johnny Rotten, had offered to play at the previous night's pop concert in the gardens of Buckingham Palace. There is, after all, a future in England's dreaming.

It is, though, the kind of future that has become familiar in the fashion and entertainment industries, a future which is the revival of past styles. The Buckingham Palace pop concert was part of the overall strategy of rebranding the Queen, not as an awkward anachronistic presence at the beginning of the twenty-first century, but as an element of retro chic. The event was almost completely dominated by what the official publicity called 'living legends': Paul McCartney, Brian Wilson, Eric Clapton, Ray Davies, Joe Cocker, Rod Stewart, even Ozzy Osbourne who, the official programme acknowledged, was 'perhaps a surprising addition to the bill' but one who would assuredly 'be on his best behaviour'. The implicit message was that the Queen too is to be viewed as a living legend, a fading but historic icon of popular culture, who deserves both the indulgence and the reverence due to an ageing star. She is to be judged not on her rather jaded current output but on her glorious back catalogue. You go to see her, not because she is still electrifying, but so that you can tell your children you saw her live.

It helped that the vast majority of the 'live' audience for the concert was not actually sitting in front of the stage in the palace garden, but watching on giant screens outside. There were two huge screens outside the palace, two in Green Park on one side of the Mall, two in St James's Park on the other side, and ten along the Mall itself.

The million or so people gathered in front of the screens were thus reliving a key moment of Elizabeth's own career. Over 20 million British people watched her coronation in 1953 on television, even though few people actually had television sets. Every set became, at that moment, a communal screen, bringing together as many friends and neighbours as could possibly sit in a room. The television pictures were also relayed to cinemas. For the first time in Europe, television ensured that a public event was genuinely public. As the *News Chronicle* put it at the time, thanks to television 'for once, "the people" was no legal fiction'.

And now here were the people again communally watching the Queen on screen, or, at home, watching a million people watching the Queen together. And it worked. The people watching on the screens, living out a retro event, conducted themselves with a discipline that seemed to hark back to a more orderly time. People kept saying things like 'Isn't it marvellous? Everybody having a good time, with no aggravation.' They were, quite literally, watching their manners, marvelling at their own collective behaviour.

What they were seeing on the screens, though, was in fact a dramatic break with the past. The bargain that the Queen had struck with rock and roll royalty involved huge concessions as well as significant gains. In return for the rewards of becoming a part of retro pop culture, with all the immunity from criticism that brings, she had to accept the irreverence that was so essential to the pop culture of the 1960s. You can be the sacred bearer of a nation's destiny, the anointed embodiment of an immemorial fusion of blood and soil, the spiritual head of the official Protestant church. Or you can appear on stage with Ozzy Osbourne, who bites the heads off live bats. You cannot do both. Quietly, perhaps only half consciously, Elizabeth had chosen the second option.

And so what those people were watching on screen was the monarchy embracing and absorbing the end of deference. When the Queen took her seat towards the end of the show, her arrival was greeted, not with a fanfare bidding the assembled multitude to rise, but with a high-pitched squeal of introduction from Dame Edna Everage: 'The Jubilee girl is here, possums!' On the screens outside there was a pre-recorded sequence featuring Barry Humphries's other caricature, Sir Les Patterson, trying to climb the gates of the palace so he could get in to see his friend 'Betty Britain'. And when Sir Paul McCartney came on stage he immediately sang the cheeky coda to the *Abbey Road* album, the 1960s equivalent of the Sex Pistols' 'God Save the Queen', the little song that claims that Her Majesty's a pretty nice girl, but she doesn't have a lot to say...

At the end of the show, when a dazed-looking Elizabeth came on stage, clutching her handbag for comfort, the Queen's sacred person, until recently untouchable, was pressed against the massed ranks of rock stars. Inside the palace and out in front of the screens, the crowds cheered, not for Her Britannic Majesty, but for Betty Britain, a pretty nice Jubilee girl. At the biggest moment of the jubilee, when most of Britain was watching, the monarchy finally broke its magic staff and stepped out into the warm but treacherous currents of popular culture.

And so next day, as we wait in the mid-morning sun for the royal procession in which the Queen will again have to appear in all her majesty, I wonder how the crowds will react to what they have seen. Will they feel somehow betrayed? Will they abandon the mannerly patience that makes them wait with such cheerful dignity? If royalty itself defers to popular culture, how can the people defer to royalty?

It strikes me that my own country, Ireland, has been through this same process a little earlier. Outwardly, the culture of my childhood was republican. The Queen was doubly despicable: as the living symbol of British imperialism and as the head of the Protestant church whose bullying and blandishments had failed to lure our Catholic ancestors away from the true faith. In revenge for English mockery of Irish religious credulity, we learned to mock the gullibility of a people who bowed their heads to a hereditary monarch.

At parties, I sang a song about the last visit of Queen Victoria to Dublin in 1900:

Jubilee Girl

The Queen she came to call on us,
She wanted to see all of us,
Thank God she didn't fall on us,
She's eighteen stone.

Yet we too had our own princelings. What came into my head as I waited for the Queen to appear was the day, in the mid-1960s, when the Archbishop of Dublin, John Charles McQuaid, visited our local church to conduct the funeral Mass for our parish priest. I remembered walking up to the church early that morning. I was astonished to see, on the mundane streets of our council estate, the Archbishop's Bentley, sleek and stately, parked outside the parish priest's house. The passenger door was open and a pair of small feet, encased in neat black shoes, was sticking out. A uniformed chauffeur was kneeling on the cold concrete, giving the Archbishop's shoes a final polish. Even to a child, the image was disconcerting. Yet it didn't stop me kneeling before him when he came back to the sacristy after the ceremony, or feeling utterly blessed by the afterglow of his presence. A certain kind of public politeness can survive even disenchantment.

Watching the cheerful good behaviour of the crowds waiting for the Queen, I wondered what I would do if she were suddenly to alight from her gilded carriage and walk towards me. I had the nagging thought that I had in fact been prepared for just such an encounter. I had been educated by a militantly nationalist and triumphantly Catholic order, the Christian Brothers. Almost all the leaders of the successful nationalist revolt that resulted in Irish independence were Christian Brothers boys. The Brothers practically invented the story of oppression, resistance and eventual triumph for Catholic Ireland that filled our heads. And yet I could not shake off some vague but insistent memory of having been taught how to behave in the presence of British royalty.

Later, I found the old school book that the Brothers used in their attempts to civilize us, *Christian Politeness and Counsels for Youth*, published in Dublin by the Brothers themselves. It really was true. The section on 'Forms of Address' begins with the Royal Family. We, the sons of bus conductors and office cleaners, needed to know that when writing to the Queen we should begin with 'To the Queen's Most Excellent Majesty', and end with 'I remain, with profound veneration,

Fintan O'Toole

Madam, Your Majesty's most faithful Subject and dutiful Servant.'

Addressing Her Majesty in person was somewhat more complicated. If we were members of the aristocracy or gentry, we could call her Ma'am. The gentry is defined helpfully as 'the Clergy, the landed Gentry, officers belonging to the Army and Navy, Members of the Bar, Medical and other professions, the aristocracy of wealth, and leading city Merchants or Bankers.' If we were to remain in our plebeian station, however, we would have to start our conversation with the Queen with 'Your Majesty,' or 'May it please your Majesty.'

All of this seems laughable to me now, and I feel sure that I would genuflect neither to an archbishop nor to a queen. Yet those lessons in Christian politeness linger in ways so intimate that they have become instinctive: how to walk, how to clean up your accent, how to eat, how to temper your behaviour to the presence of others, how to know what is or is not appropriate. In the English-speaking world beyond Britain, the notions of civility which we have inherited are rooted in a hierarchy which has the royal family at the top. Even if the top is lopped off, the rest of the pyramid remains. Even for those of us who have lived all our life in republics, the Queen remains as a kind of presiding goddess of polite behaviour. Is it this, perhaps, which draws people to her presence—the chance to put one's own demeanour to the ultimate test? The dignity belongs, not to the monarch, but to the crowd. She provides the occasion for the crowd to experience its own capacity to feel proud of itself.

After the formal abandonment of deference at the Buckingham Palace concert, there is no other basis for the deal between the sovereign and her subjects. I have seen an endlessly photographed beauty like Naomi Campbell and caught a glimpse of the radiance that is celebrity in the flesh. I once served champagne at a film premiere to Michael York and Barbara Carrera and could sense the glow of even relatively minor movie stars. I have watched the greatest street politician of the age, Bill Clinton, glad-handing crowds and been caught up in his extraordinary ability to make every individual member feel that he has come to meet them. I can understand why a fan or a devotee would think it worthwhile to expend time and patience for such a return.

Elizabeth does not have a model's beauty or a movie star's

glamour. She does not work a crowd with a fraction of Clinton's mastery. Even her husband, the supposedly curmudgeonly Philip, Duke of Edinburgh, works harder in the presence of a crowd. He is animated, briskly cheerful, shaking hands, accepting bouquets, bestowing encouraging words. She walks and smiles.

She does of course walk gracefully, all those childhood deportment classes stiffening her back against the downward pressure of the advancing years. Up close her fixed smile, so often derided as the 'regal rictus', is a thing of beauty. There is a photograph of her taken in 1928, when she was just two years old, barefooted in a flouncy white dress, perched on a small but throne-like wooden armchair. Her back is completely straight, and eerily, she already wears the official smile. It is not the giggle or the guffaw of a toddler but the carefully arranged smile of a queen, the mouth open just wide enough to show off the teeth, the muscles forming perfectly symmetrical channels of flesh from the edge of the nostrils to the tip of the chin.

In the official Golden Jubilee festival programme that many in the crowd are reading as they wait behind the barriers, they can see it repeated tooth for tooth and muscle for muscle: the adolescent girl smiling among the syringa bushes at Windsor Castle in 1941; the young princess smiling on board ship in 1947; the newly crowned queen disembarking from the State Coach after her coronation in 1953, the smile poised perfectly between the imperial state crown on her head and the imperial orb in her hand; the smiling monarch on the balcony of Buckingham Palace in 1985, pretty grandchildren at her elbow, her son and daughter-in-law, Charles and Diana, posing beside her in a game of happy families; the elegant matriarch smiling out from an official portrait in 1997, defying the surge of popular resentment that year when Elizabeth seemed more visibly upset by the decommissioning of the royal yacht *Britannia* than by Diana's death.

Thus, the Queen's smile, however beautiful, is strangely impersonal. It is one of the crown jewels, an unchanging symbolic object, like the sceptre or the orb. For the crowds who are waiting at the barriers, there is the prospect that it will be turned on them in all its elegant luminosity. But it makes no personal connection. It is no more intended for you and me, as we push against the barriers, than are the crown jewels in their glass cases at the Tower of London. Like them, it is impervious to human contact. And seeing the jewels is a far more efficient process than waiting for hours to catch a glimpse of a fleetingly visible royal display.

The people in the crowd are not unaware of their own boredom. A thirty-something man in front of me is sending a text message on his mobile phone: HI. WE ARE STANDING AT THE MALL. V. TIRED. NOTHING HAPPENING. IF ANY NEWS TEXT BACK. C U. A teenage girl is on her mobile: 'Nah, nothing. A lot of horses shitting on the road. I think we'll go somewhere else and watch it on TV and chill out for a bit.' But her friend won't let her go: 'Come on, it can't be long. We've been here hours. It would be a waste.'

For the London crowds, there is admittedly more to wait for than the Queen. The ceremonials are elaborate, with concerts, military parades and carnival processions. I have seen the Queen in other places, though, and know that many people will stand like this for no other reason than to see her. In the ordinary towns that are graced with her presence on her Jubilee travels, the mystery of their patience is all the deeper.

Such places lack the ceremonial geography of London. Much of central London, especially the long, wide sweep of the Mall from Admiralty Arch to Buckingham Palace, is designed as a stage set for royal processions and imperial triumphs. A suburbanized market town like Uxbridge in Middlesex or Kingston in Surrey is not this kind of theatre. In carefully edited news footage, a royal visit can be framed by picturesque buildings. The old market and Tudoresque pubs on Uxbridge's main street, or All Saints' Church in Kingston, where the Queen unveils a memorial to the coronation of Edward the Elder in AD 902, look suitably historic on television. The crowds on the streets can see, however, that the royal progress through Uxbridge is really a short walk between two shopping centres, the Pavilions and the Chimes, and that the best place to watch Her Majesty enter All Saints' Church is from the roof of John Lewis, the department store that dominates the view.

On these occasions, the real enthusiasts arrive three hours before the Queen, and take the best positions at the barriers. They are mostly elderly and mostly female, so the standing is hard. Over the next hour, mothers arrive with their children, the youngest of whom are allowed to push through to the front by the indulgent old ladies.

After a while, the presence of this growing crowd itself attracts a crowd. People want to know what's going on, and when they hear that the Queen is coming, they stay to watch. They are people like Anil, a sixty-year-old British Asian man who tells me that 'I didn't know anything about it until someone said "The Queen is coming." I'm going to be late back for work but it's an opportunity I can't miss. Such a pity I haven't got the camera.'

There is usually some attempt at entertainment, a military band, or a steel band. In Uxbridge, there is what looks like a very tall man in a diving suit carrying in his lap a very small man in seventeenth-century costume with a mandolin, though in fact the little man's legs are inside the diving suit. He entertains us by shaking our hands and saying, 'I'm not the Queen, by the way.' There is also a lean, crop-haired young man on stilts, wearing a long black dress with footballs stuck down the front for breasts. He is moving in time to the steel band's rendition of a Stranglers' song. A small man in a lion suit walks up and down, holding the hand of a skinny girl in a shiny Union Jack vest. A fat man dressed as a town crier blows a horn and roars, 'Oyez, Oyez, Jubilee showtime in the Pavilions at twelve o'clock.' He is advertising the shopping mall. The man in the lion suit starts to hand out little paper flags with the Union Jack on one side and an ad for the same mall on the other.

On the other side of the barriers, little children from Pied Heath primary school are sitting around a classroom table that has been placed in the middle of the road. Each child has a cardboard crown, like the ones you get at Burger King, but trimmed with fake fur around the bottom. They sit around the table with lumps of dark brown plasticine, half-heartedly making smooth oval shapes which they then roll up into a ball so that they can start all over again. Behind them, at another table, there are older children painting pictures. Further along there is another group holding musical instruments, not playing, just sitting. It is only later, when the Queen spends a few moments viewing them, that I understand that their function is to be a living exhibition of Uxbridge's commitment to the arts for young people.

There is not much else to watch: the policemen looking pleased, the lady mayor in her fussy red robes and tricorne hat, the black-robed town clerk shifting from shoulder to shoulder the heavy steel mace that he must carry before the Queen, looking like Christ preparing to ascend Calvary, the military helicopter hanging overhead. At the front of the crowd, the men test their video cameras. At the back, the elderly ladies push their disposable cameras at friends in the front row. 'Take a picture for me when she comes. I shan't be able to see.'

'But what if she wants to talk to me?'

'You can talk and take a picture at the same time. You can have one hand on the camera and shake her hand with the other.' The woman laughs uproariously at the very thought of being so rude to her sovereign. Mothers keep their children occupied by building up the suspense. 'Guess what colour she'll be wearing?' 'Pink? Lilac?'

What most people in the crowd see when the Queen arrives is the effect of her arrival on other people in the crowd, a flurry of flag-waving from those at the corner who spot the sleek Bentley with its royal crest, followed rather incongruously by the white people-carrier that bears the lady-in-waiting, the aide-de-camp, the press secretary and the bodyguards. The Queen emerges in a dusky yellowish-beige jacket with polka dots, a matching skirt without the dots, and a tall hat with looping appliqué patterns.

The photographers, journalists, camera crew and dignitaries are on the right side of the barriers and can see her clearly, but for most of the crowd, the small children on their parents' shoulders act as periscopes and messengers. 'I can only see her hat.' 'She's wearing yellow! Alex, she's wearing a yellow hat!' 'What are they cheering for? I can't see. Where's she gone? I see her. The Queen is here! There she is, behind the balloons.' 'Does she look like a ten-pence piece?' 'Really got a Golden Jubilee outfit, hasn't she? It's golden!' 'I can't even see if she's in a car or on a horse.'

The Queen moves along the tables, looking at the brown plasticine shapes, smiling at the children. She walks slowly up the street, stopping now and then to take a bouquet of flowers from someone in the front row. As soon as she takes one, I learn what a lady-in-waiting is for. A slightly impatient look comes across the Queen's face as she looks around for the lady-in-waiting to offload the flowers. She walks a few yards up the street, unveils a statue and releases a hundred balloons, purple and yellow, the jubilee colours. Prince Philip looks pleased. The Queen smiles. She walks on for a few more yards but suddenly and silently the Bentley glides in front of her. She gets in, is driven to the top of the street waving from the side window, and is gone. In all, the visit has taken about fifteen minutes.

None of this—and it is typical of the royal visitations I have seen—seems to me at all magical. The word that is so frequently attached to the monarchy—enchantment—has no place here. The policemen, it is true, feel very proud. At Uxbridge, a big, middle-aged constable, Mike, responds to my question about how he feels with a hint of truculence: 'What annoys me is all this stuff about following other people's cultures. They forget our own. We're the only people who can do what we've just done.' Some of the older enthusiasts, the people who got up early to secure their places at the front, have this same edge of mildly belligerent defensiveness. They say nice things about the Queen—'lovely lady, makes you proud to be British', 'a great lady, never thinks of herself, always working for other people'. But what they really want to talk about is the nature of the event itself. It is, they say, uniquely British.

Why, I ask politely, is it unique? Don't famous people appear in other towns, in other countries? Are the crowds not kept back by more or less jolly policemen? Do people not wave flags? Almost invariably, what they say is that the crowd, its politeness, its respect, its good behaviour is what makes it unique. What they are really proud of, in other words, is not the Queen. It is themselves. It is the way they bear themselves in the presence of the Queen, their own forbearance and tolerance, their own cheerful stoicism.

This is neither enchantment nor disenchantment. The more casual members of the crowd, the ones who didn't know what was happening until someone told them that the Queen was coming, take a jokey, self-deprecating but utterly tolerant view of their failure to have a close encounter with the royal person. Anil, who at Kingston caught a momentary sideways glimpse of her hat as she entered the church, laughs and says, 'I saw her about fifty years ago, and it was a similar glance. It's a tradition, I suppose.' Margaret, who got a photograph, she thinks, of the top of the Queen's arm as she reached for a bunch of flowers, gives an ironic chuckle and says, 'Well, that'll be one to show the grandchildren.' There is no anger, no disappointment, no deflation. People seem quite satisfied with events that to me seem deeply unfulfilling.

I am trying to figure out their patience as I walk back up the slowly emptying Uxbridge High Street. I had not seen the statue the Queen had unveiled a few minutes earlier. It is in fact a group of figures. A thin woman in high heels, wearing a skimpy, perhaps translucent dress, carries a small child on her right hip. Her left hand is extended towards a toddler in dungarees. A skinny dog eyes the baby on the woman's hip hungrily. The woman, the children and the dog look like they are waiting with mounting excitement for something to happen.

A plaque on the ground says that the sculpture, by Anita Lafford, was unveiled by the Queen in her Golden Jubilee year of 2002 and is called *Anticipation*. What the figures in the sculpture are anticipating, I realize, is the visit of the Queen herself. The Queen has come to unveil a memorial to the people who waited to see her arrive. The permanent memory of the event is to be frozen at the moment just before the royal Bentley purred into view. It is to be a memory, not of the visitor, but of the visited. Strangely self-reflective as it is, the monument actually captures wonderfully well what I have just seen, for it grasps the truth that what the crowd has really come to see is itself behaving in a manner of which it can be proud.

And this pride, too, can be reflected back on royalty. I stop a middle-aged woman and ask her what she thinks of the sculpture. She doesn't look at the plaque or read the title. She ponders the figures quietly for a moment. A look of enlightenment breaks across her face. She nods and smiles.

'Oh, I know,' she says. 'It's Princess Diana, isn't it? It's her before she married Charles, when she worked with the kiddies in the kindergarten. She's wearing that dress, you know the one you could see through when the photographers made her stand against the sun and the poor girl didn't know that everyone could see her legs. Oh, wasn't it nice of the Queen to come out and unveil a statue of Diana? Just shows how sweet she is, after all that happened.'

She walks off to the shopping centre, having glamorized her sovereign and put a little magic back into the predictable life of the nice old woman who is her queen. □

GRANTA

HOTEL OBLIVION
Geoff Dyer

Although Dave was English and lived in Milan, we—Dazed and I—called him Amsterdam Dave because that's where we met him, in Amsterdam. We were there for the fortieth birthday of our friend Matt. Matt doesn't live in Amsterdam either but his wife, Alexandra, had booked them into a suite at the 717 on Prinsengracht for the weekend. She had also invited a dozen of Matt's friends to spend the weekend in Amsterdam. Obviously Alexandra was not going to spring for everyone's accommodation; the deal was that on Friday she and Matt would take us all out to dinner and then, on Saturday, they would receive us in their lavish suite for drinks: a kind of 'at home' away from home. Matt's more successful friends booked themselves rooms at the 717 but Dazed and I checked into a cheap hotel inconveniently located some way from the centre of town. As it happened, Amsterdam Dave was staying there as well but much more important than this administrative coincidence was our shared sense of the obligations imposed on us by a weekend in Amsterdam. Nearly everyone in our party liked the idea of dinner followed by a few joints in a bar but only Amsterdam Dave was committed to making it a truly memorable weekend in the sense that he would remember nothing whatsoever about it. I was in the twilight, the long autumn of my psychedelic years, and this was to be my last hurrah—or one of them, at any rate. I had never met Amsterdam Dave before but I took to him from the moment he explained the philosophical basis of the weekend.

'It's all about moderation,' he said in the Greenhouse on Friday night, after a deliciously inauthentic Thai meal. 'Everything in moderation. Even moderation itself. From this it follows that you must, from time to time, have excess. And this is going to be one of those occasions.'

'I couldn't agree more,' I said, impressed by the rigour of his thinking. 'As I see it we are here to do the Dam. We want to have the Amsterdam experience.'

'Indeed we do,' said Amsterdam Dave. On Saturday morning, accordingly, we made our way to the Magic Mushroom Gallery on Spuistraat. Amsterdam Dave looked slightly the worse for wear; that is to say, he looked in better shape than he would for the rest of the weekend. This was partly because he had stayed on at a club called the Trance Buddha or Buddha Trance or something long after we had turned in, but mainly it was because Amsterdam Dave never looked better than slightly the worse for wear. I have seen him on several occasions since that weekend in Amsterdam and I have never seen him look anything like as good as he did then. His face had some colour in it. That colour was grey, admittedly, but at least it was a colour. Other times, only his eyes and the hair at his temples were grey; the last vestige of colour had been completely drained from the rest of his face. Even his lips were pale. But that October morning in Amsterdam he looked great, relatively speaking. Dazed looked lovely too, unequivocally so. She was wearing a woolly hat that I had bought her as an advance Christmas present and this, combined with her wonky tortoiseshell glasses, gave her the appearance of an eccentric intellectual beauty, a nutty archaeologist, say, as played by a Hollywood actress who was in her thirties and trying not to rely solely on her looks, determined to show that she could do character. And me? Oh, doubtless I looked a complete joke. From the outside you would have thought I was the kind of person whose over-youthful wardrobe—skateboarding T-shirt, trainers, hooded sweatshirt—could not disguise the fact that he was forty-two, an intellectual with nothing but ink to his name, but, for much of that weekend, I felt myself to be at the height of my powers—or thereabouts. I concede that we may have looked an oddly matched trio as we sat down in a cafe to consume our newly purchased mushrooms but I was not expecting to get thrown out quite as soon as we did. Not thrown out exactly, but given a very stern talking-to by the barman. He didn't want us doing mushrooms in here, he said. This took a moment to sink in: we were being ejected from a bar in Amsterdam for taking drugs?

'That's like getting chucked out of a pub for drinking beer,' said Dazed.

I have achieved very little in my life—perhaps this is why I felt a faint glow of adolescent pride at our undesirable status. The barman had one of those old, fanatically grizzled druggy faces and his dull eyes did not regard us at all sympathetically. I couldn't take issue with him because my gullet was clogged with gag-inducing mushrooms which I was trying to swill down with the remaining drops of water from Dazed's bottle of Evian but, evidently, the three of us collectively registered sufficient surprise to generate some kind of explanation from the barman.

'I don't want you puking,' he said.

'Several things,' said Amsterdam Dave who had succeeded in swallowing his mushrooms. 'First, at my age, I do not need lessons in how to behave. I am a very civic-minded person. Second, my friends and I have a combined age of almost 115 years and we have, I think it's fair to say, no intention of throwing up. Third, if we do feel like throwing up, we'll make sure we step either outside or into the toilet. Fourth, if we are going to throw up it's not going to happen for at least half an hour. In the meantime perhaps you would be so good as to bring us three coffees.'

It was an extremely impressive speech and, for a moment, I thought the barman was going to oblige. Then, with no alteration of expression, he clicked his fingers, pointed to the door and uttered two words. The first was 'Asshole!', the second was 'Out!'

'There is a world elsewhere,' I said to him with all the dignity I could muster—almost none—as we headed for the door. It didn't really matter, getting booted out like this. We simply took our custom elsewhere and went somewhere else. That's basically all we did for the rest of the day. We kept going elsewhere. It was rainy outside and each time we went outside we started thinking about getting inside again. At first this wasn't a problem because it wasn't raining. Oh, it *was* raining all right, but compared with the way it rained later this was nothing, this was clement. There was even a glimmer of sunshine. The leaves—the ones left in the trees, I mean; those lying on the ground in heaps were a different kettle of fish altogether— glowed in the brief intervals when the sun was shining but even when the sun was not shining it was relatively pleasant. Conditions deteriorated later on but at this early stage of the day our main concern was the nauseous canker of doubt put into our minds by the surly barman. We kept expecting to feel sick and then, when we no longer kept waiting to feel sick, we kept going somewhere else. First, though, we ordered three coffees in another, almost identical bar where we waited to feel sick. When that didn't happen we went somewhere else. The sky was silvery grey, there was cloud activity, movement, variant shades of grey, the possibility of things improving. The day had not settled into the unanimous grey pall that indicated things were not going to get better until several days after we left, possibly not until next spring by which time we would be long gone and anything that happened here would be long forgotten except by the one or two people—probably only one, possibly only me—whose business it is to make sure that such things are not forgotten, even if that means they have to be reinvented from scratch.

At some point conditions began to deteriorate. The wind picked up. It began raining heavily and then, once it had begun raining heavily, some kind of maritime gale kicked in. We wanted to get out of the wind-whipped rain but in order to get out of the rain it was necessary to continue walking in it, at least for a while. We headed for the relative tranquillity of the Van Gogh Museum where the paintings pitched and reeled in a blaze of yellow. Not that we saw anything of them. Conditions had deteriorated to the extent that everyone in Amsterdam had just one aim in mind: to get out of the rain, to get out of the rain and into the Van Gogh Museum. Everyone was wet and steaming and at any moment a soggy stampede seemed a distinct possibility. Occasionally, in the background, a sun burst over the writhing corn of Arles, a Roman-candle night—starry, starry—swirled into life. Blossom-tormented trees reared into view, pigment-coloured faces beamed brightly, but mainly there were just the drenched backs of museum-goers in their foul-weather gear, jostling for position. The thirsty yellow of Arles emphasized that here, in Amsterdam, it was the kind of autumn day that is all but indistinguishable from the dregs of winter. More and more visitors were crowding into the museum. The paintings were like the last lifeboats on the *Titanic* and only a lucky few were going to get a glimpse of a gawking sunflower or Gauguin's empty chair (which, for all we knew, was not even there). Everyone else had to take their chances with the drawings or any other bit of art that floated their way.

The mushrooms, mercifully, were not as strong as they might have been and before long we were out in the rain again. Incredibly, conditions had deteriorated still further while we had been in the museum; the weather, to cut a long meteorological story short, had gone from bad to worse to even worse.

'It's like being on the deck of a trawler in the North Sea,' I said. 'Were we not on dry land I would give the order to abandon ship.'

'Aye aye sir,' said Dazed. We pressed on, heads bowed, heading for some other kind of shelter.

'Is it the season of mists and mellow fruitfulness?' Dazed asked as we battled through the rain.

'I suppose it is, technically, but I'm beginning to suspect that this is one of those places where they don't even have autumn. Each year they just plunge headlong from spring into the worst winter in living memory.'

'Is it the time of the falling fruit and the long journey to oblivion?' said Dazed.

'It really might be.'

'Do you think this might be a nice cafe?'

It did indeed look like a nice cafe but once we were inside we became entangled in an impenetrable thicket of chairs. We couldn't move for chairs. With the Van Gogh experience still reasonably fresh in our minds, it seemed as if Gauguin's empty chair had cloned itself and taken up permanent residence in this cafe. Amsterdam Dave's analysis of our situation was less art historical, more pragmatic.

'Normally in cafes it's difficult to get a chair,' he said. 'Here there are too many chairs.' He could not have put it more succinctly if he had tried. There was an hilarious surfeit of empty chairs, so many, in fact, that there was no room to sit. We kept moving them but as soon as we had moved one chair another was in the way. Eventually we managed to create a space in which we had only three or four chairs each, not a bad ratio for those who are weary and damp of limb. We stretched out, ordered refreshments from a punky waitress who was either oblivious to or unperturbed by the superabundance of seating.

'Excuse me,' said Amsterdam Dave when she returned with our drinks. 'We were just wondering. Does it seem to you that there are rather a lot of chairs here?' Although Amsterdam Dave had addressed this question to the waitress it was of course intended entirely for our benefit and amusement. And find it amusing we did. Very much so. Weepingly so. Ha ha. We couldn't stop laughing. The more we tried to stop laughing the more we had to laugh. As far as we were concerned it was just about the wittiest question in recorded history, a truly wonderful remark, right up there with anything ever said by anyone. Good old Amsterdam Dave. Having got us kicked out of one cafe he was now in the process of getting us thrown out of a second. I struggled to get a grip on myself. I thought of the horrible conditions outside, I thought of us walking in the freezing, horizontal rain, I avoided making eye contact with the others, concentrated on thanking the waitress and murmuring non-specific apologies on our behalf. Then, when the waitress had gone off (in something of a huff) we subsided into giggles, wiped the tears from our eyes and succeeded in getting a grip on ourselves.

In the wake of our giggling spasm I recalled that in the morning I had made an impulse purchase of a pair of trousers. Remembering this, I assumed that I had lost them in the course of our journey through the storm-ravaged streets of Amsterdam but, miraculously, they were here beside me, in a bag. I decided, there and then, to change out of my wet trousers which were soaking cold and wet and into my new ones which were dry and lovely and warm. In the cramped confines of the toilet I had trouble getting out of my wet trousers which clung to my legs like a drowning man. The new ones were quite complicated too in that they had more legs than a spider; either that or they didn't have enough legs to get mine into. The numbers failed to add up. Always there was one trouser leg too many or one of my legs was left over. From the outside it may have looked like a simple toilet but once you were locked in here the most basic rules of arithmetic no longer held true. Two into two simply would not go. It was insane, it took a terrible toll on my head. I concentrated hard, applied myself with a vengeance to the task in hand. I got one leg in. I got the other in. Hooray! A man who has finally put behind him the spectre of thirty years of unwanted celibacy—I'm in!—cannot have felt a greater surge of triumph and self-vindication than I did at that point. Such exultation was short-lived, however, for these trousers were wet too. Somehow, I had put back on the wet pair that I had just taken off. The dry ones were still dry, waiting to be put on. I was back where I started. After all the effort of the last—how long? I could have been in here for hours—this was a crushing blow and one I was not sure I could recover from. How had it happened? Human error, that was the only possible explanation. Human error. Somehow, evidently, I had taken off my wet trousers and put them on again. There was no other explanation, but what a huge mystery, what a maze of possibilities is contained by that innocuous 'somehow'. Undeterred—or, more accurately, almost entirely deterred—I started again. I extracted my long limbs from the wet pair and carefully eased them into the dry pair. This time, after much effort, I succeeded in putting them on back to front. By now I was so resigned to failure, to disappointment and frustration, that I scarcely even stopped to consider what had gone wrong (human error again, almost certainly). Without pausing I tugged them off and, head reeling from the effort, put them on again—only to find that I had put them on inside out. In other, less trying circumstances this might have seemed a fairly poor show for a forty-two-year-old intellectual but, as things stood, I was happy to regard it as a qualified success, especially as someone was now banging on the door, claiming I'd been in there for ages, wanting to know what the problem was.

'Good question!' I called back, in high spirits again, stuffing my wet trousers into the bag. All things considered it would have been a high risk venture—who knows what new permutation of disarray might have resulted?—to have attempted to get my new trousers off and on. They might have been inside out but they were on, they were on, that was the important thing.

Back in the cafe, surrounded by a sea of chairs, Dazed and Amsterdam Dave were unconcerned by the state of my trousers. Already, just seconds later, it seemed hard to believe that I could have run up such an enormous bill of difficulties back there in the changing room. It was another world, that toilet, practically a different universe, one with its own extraordinary set of problems and obstacles. A piece of sophisticated electronic music came and went on the sound system, subsiding in a long ambient wash that made a peaceful resolution of human difficulties seem a distinct, almost inevitable possibility. What with one thing and another we were all a bit bedraggled but the cafe was quite a cosy place to marshal our resources or whatever. Quite suddenly, Amsterdam Dave said,

'By the way, did you know your trousers are inside out?'

'No, they're not,' I said.

'Yes, they are,' said Dazed.

'Well that's where you're both wrong,' I said. The interlude of sitting quietly in the cafe had enabled me to see my earlier difficulties in the toilet in an entirely new light and to hold my own in any debate, however fiercely contested. 'It might look to you—to outsiders, as it were—as if my trousers are inside out but they are fine. *I* have turned inside out.'

'That's quite a controversial analysis,' said Amsterdam Dave.

'Controversial but, from my point of view, entirely correct. And now, if you don't mind, I would like to discuss something else.'

'Like what?'

'Like what we do next.' I was all for moving on somewhere else, you see. The others were quite content here but I was all for moving on somewhere else. Somewhere new and possibly better. I was restless and who knows the part played in this restlessness by the fact that my trousers *were*—however strenuously I may have denied it—inside out. Was that why I was so anxious to shift us from inside the cafe to outside on the streets before returning inside once more? All things considered this was an excellent place, but I kept wanting to move on, kept wanting to go somewhere else.

'What I want,' I said, 'is a place where we can sit down, where we can just chat for a couple of hours before we go to Matt and Alexandra's lavish suite. A place with nice music, comfortable seats and nice tea and so forth.' I went on and on about this and as I did so I had a dim sense that I was working through something, some neurosis that refused to manifest itself plainly. And then it came to me.

'D'you know?' I said. 'I have just described exactly the place we're in. I'm already in the place I want to go to.'

'Well done, darling,' said Dazed. 'You've escaped from Samsara.'

And so I had. I had unblocked all sorts of cafe chakras and was experiencing a sense of absolute calm. I was happy to be here, confident in the knowledge that we would soon be basking in the comfort of Matt and Alexandra's lavish suite at the 717.

We turned up there exactly on time, on the stroke of six, and were shown up to Matt and Alexandra's suite by a quite charming waiter.

'Would you be so kind as to follow me?' he said, politely ignoring the fact that we looked like some things the cat had dragged in and one of those things had its trousers on inside out. Matt and Alexandra's suite was every bit as lavish as we had hoped. It was a different world in there. That is something I remember distinctly about our weekend in Amsterdam: there really was a world elsewhere. Everywhere we went was like a different world from where we had just come from. Matt and Alexandra's suite was like the world of Henry James where sentences last for several paragraphs and fine glasses of red wine reflect, dimly, the flicker of the fire, the skewed outlines of framed portraits of men in ruffs. It was horrible outside on the streets but from here, from inside, it was a lovely autumn evening. The suite filled up with Matt and Alexandra's other friends but there was plenty of room for everyone of course, it being a suite. Matt opened the presents everyone had given him. Ours was wrapped up nicely in gold paper with a pale lemon ribbon because Dazed has a knack for doing things nicely, for making things special. If it had been left to me I would have given it— a critically acclaimed novel by a woman half my age—to him in the Waterstone's bag it came in at Gatwick. In the bathroom I took off my trousers and put them back on, correctly, inside in, with no difficulties whatsoever. We stretched out on sofas, drank glasses of fine wine, looked out of the windows at the gale-lashed trees. I hoped that conditions would deteriorate still further, that the rain would turn to sleet, because that would make being inside even nicer, even cosier. I had known Matt for almost twenty years and I felt so happy being with him in all this lavish cosiness that I could quite easily have wept. I think I did weep, actually. I felt happy, content; there was nothing I wanted. It didn't matter at all what one did with one's life, I decided. As long as you had evenings like this the fact that one (I kept switching between 'one', 'you' and 'I') had accomplished next to nothing—none of that made any difference. It was better being forty than twenty when one was full of fire and ambition and hope. It was even better than being thirty when those hopes that had once animated you became a goading source of torment.

'Once you turn forty,' I said to Matt, 'the whole world is water off a duck's back. Once you turn forty you realize that life is *there* to be wasted.' I was so taken by what I had said—by its maturity, insight and wisdom—that I rambled on like this for quite a while, either to Matt or to myself, as I lay on one of several sofas, gazing at my old and new friends and other people in the group I had only smiled at and said hello to. Oh, it was a lovely evening and then, quite suddenly, it was over, or this phase of it was anyway. Somehow we were all out on the streets again, walking through the UV haze of the hookers' windows in the red-light district that might better be termed the black-light district. A guy in an Arctic parka said something to me I did not quite catch, then I realized he was offering me drugs, specifically Viagra. I said I didn't want any.

'You look like you need it,' he said. It was an unkind remark but I pushed it to one side of my mind. Some of our party, including Matt and Alexandra, had already said goodnight and headed off to bed. Those of us who were left went into a bar and smoked some feverish skunk and then there were just the three of us again, Dazed, Amsterdam Dave and I, and we were no longer in the bar but out on the streets, back, in a sense, where we started. Under the influence of this hydro-whatever-it-was grass, the mushrooms, which had not worked very powerfully during the afternoon, made an unexpected comeback and all the accumulated confusion of the day burst in upon us and left us stranded in an alien city that bore only an occasional resemblance to the Amsterdam of maps and guidebooks. We were completely deranged, unsure of our bearings, utterly unsuited to the task of finding our hotel. One moment we were walking up a narrow, canal-bordered street, heading towards a church, say, and the next the church was nowhere to be seen and we were looking in the window of an antiques shop. And then— improbably—we were *in* an antiques shop, looking out at the three bedraggled figures peering in at renovated chairs, old maps and dark desks on which yellow lamps encouraged a life of contemplation and study. The situation was complicated by the way that many of the homes we saw—uncurtained, softly lit, full of furniture, unpeopled, there for all to see—looked like antiques shops and vice versa. The distinction between residence and retail outlet was nothing like as clear as one might have imagined. Other distinctions proved equally hard to sustain. We crossed a bridge only to find that we had crossed back over the bridge which turned out to be a completely different bridge to the one we had been on seconds earlier. At various points I completely lost track of where in the world we had fetched up. It seemed to me that I was in six or seven cities at once. I was in Sydney, in the area known as King's Cross, which meant I was also in the area of London of that name and, at the same time, I was unable to get my bearings because what I saw persuaded me that I was in Paris and Copenhagen. I was everywhere at once.

'There is some place I have not yet been to,' I said in a blur of absolute lucidity, 'some place of which every other place has been no more than a premonition. But how will I know I'm there? If I can't answer that question then, for all I know, I could be there already.'

How easy it was to become confused in Amsterdam, on that autumn night in Amsterdam particularly.

'What we must do,' said Amsterdam Dave, 'is concentrate on finding our hotel.'

'Of course we should,' I said. 'Of course we should. But the phrase "easier said than done" comes to mind.'

'Here's a canal,' said Dazed, as though that solved everything, as though we had not seen hundreds of canals—or this very same canal hundreds of times—in the course of what was starting to seem a long and ill-advised excursion. Nevertheless, we gazed at this canal with baffled wonder and, for a moment, it seemed as if all our problems were over. But then we saw that it was indeed the same canal—dank with fallen leaves but glowing in spite of everything—that we had walked past either ten minutes or several lifetimes ago. Even more demoralizing—I am tempted to say soul-destroying—was the fact that if it had been a different canal this would not have improved our situation in the slightest.

'Same canal, different canal,' I said forlornly. 'Same difference.'

'Well, I gave it my best shot,' said Amsterdam Dave as we looked up at the inscrutable calligraphy of a Japanese restaurant. 'Personally I'd be more than willing to cut my losses and settle for a plate of sushi.'

'You need a sharp knife for sushi,' said Dazed.

'That's not all you need,' I said.

'What else do you need?'

'Ah, you've got me there.'

'Fish,' said Dazed. 'You need fish.'

'Yes, of course. Fish,' said Amsterdam Dave. 'Fish—and a very sharp knife.' All the time we were talking nonsense like this we were also on the trudge, of course, walking and walking.

'For a moment back there I thought I was in Copenhagen,' I said. 'But now I realize that I feel like a Danish businessman, someone in telecommunications, who finds himself more than a little drunk in...in... Oh, I almost had it then. I almost knew exactly where we were. To the centimetre, practically. How maddening it all is, this infernal not knowing. I feel I could just sit down and lament my entire life, every single moment of it.'

Was it still raining? Yes, in the sense that the air was full of moisture, no, in the sense that this moisture could not be said to be falling with any real conviction. It would be more accurate to speak in terms of a very light drizzle, so light that it was a species of mist.

'It makes places look welcoming but it does not make them any easier to find,' said Amsterdam Dave who, I realized, had hacked into my private thoughts. Without really deciding to we had sat down on a bench, not sat down on it as such (it was damp) but gathered in its vicinity.

'Would you say conditions had deteriorated?' Dazed asked sweetly.

'No,' said Amsterdam Dave. 'But I would say that our ability to cope with conditions has undergone a near-catastrophic deterioration.'

'Is there any point in looking at the map?'

'Actually that needs to be rephrased. The question is, "Is there any point in looking for the map?"'

'Don't tell me we've lost the map. Without that map we're totally sunk.'

'I didn't say we'd lost it but I think we may have trouble finding it.'

'Let's put it like this. If we had the map would there be any point in looking at it?'

Dazed said, 'It might help us clarify a few things,' but Amsterdam Dave was adamant.

'Definitely not,' he said. 'We're much better off relying on instinct.' With that we were up and off, on the trudge again.

'Is it still the season of mists and mellow fruitfulness?' said Dazed.

'Yes it is,' I said. 'And, equally, no it's not.'

'Is it still the time of falling fruit and the long journey to oblivion?' asked Dazed.

'I can't say,' I said. 'I really can't say.'

'Do you crave oblivion, darling?'

I confessed that at this moment I did, yes; that at this juncture I hoped the journey might not be so long after all. As soon as I said this, however, I became confused as to where we were heading.

'Is our hotel really called Oblivion?' I said. 'That's a strange and slightly ominous name don't you think, the Hotel Oblivion? Is it really the kind of place we should be staying? I mean, if that's what it's really called, fine. But I think we need to be sure.'

'You know,' said Amsterdam Dave, 'I don't think we're ever going to find it, whatever it's called.'

'Oh, don't be such a pessimist,' said Dazed.

'I'm not sure it even exists any more,' said Amsterdam Dave.

'Oblivion?' I said. 'Are you saying that there is no such thing as oblivion?' It was a terrible prospect—it meant we were doomed to the glare of perpetual consciousness with no possibility of relief—but it was also a ridiculous one.

'If we assume that the hotel doesn't exist,' Amsterdam Dave continued, 'then that puts our situation in a totally different perspective. If that's the case then we can just check in somewhere else.' I heard what he was saying but I was not really listening. The consequences of our hotel not existing were beginning to make themselves felt and I felt all sad. I started thinking about the things that I had left in our room. I couldn't remember what they were but if the hotel no longer existed then probably they didn't either and I was far from ready to kiss them goodbye, whatever they were. And if the hotel had stopped existing before we had officially checked out, where did *that* leave us? Were we a species of the undead, doomed for a certain time to wander Amsterdam in search of lodgings we were unable to enter? In this light, since the consequences of the hotel not existing were identical to there being no such thing as oblivion, it was logical to conclude that we were indeed looking for the Hotel Oblivion. I looked at Amsterdam Dave and Dazed but, from their faces, was unable to discern whether I had said all this or simply thought it. Then, without warning or—as far as I could tell—justification, Amsterdam Dave said,

'Contrary to my previous announcement I now think we're going to be home in less than twenty seconds.'

'Why do you say that?'

'Because there, about ten yards ahead, is our hotel.' I looked up and there, in pale blue letters, was the name of our hotel, just visible through the mist.

It was a moment of heart-stopping happiness. I was so relieved. All our troubles were over. Imagine, then, our confusion when we got to the door and realized that we had made a mistake, that it was not our hotel but a different hotel with the same name. It was incredible but, in the context of our experiences, all too possible, inevitable even. It was also, for me personally, the last straw. I couldn't bear any more of this nonsense, couldn't bear any of this confusion any more. I didn't know what to do. I was at the end of my tether, emotionally and physically. At my age I shouldn't even have been getting fucked up like this; I should have been at home in one of the many interiors we had glimpsed in the course of our walk, toiling away at some lamp-lit desk. I was about to start blaming Dazed and Amsterdam Dave for everything that had happened or not happened in the course of this wretched and stupid weekend. Then Amsterdam Dave tried his key in the door and the door opened and we realized that it may have been a mistake to have concluded that we had made a mistake, that although it did not look like our hotel perhaps it was our hotel after all, and even if it wasn't, it was a good sign, surely, that the key worked. □

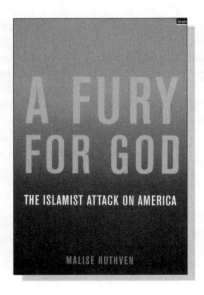

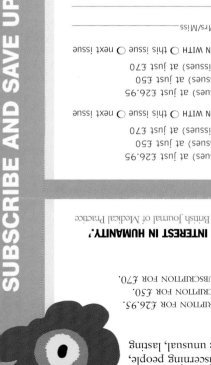

Our subscribers get *Granta* delivered to their homes, at considerable savings on the bookshop price. Why not join them? Or, if you're already one of our select group of nearly 70,000 discerning people, give a subscription to a friend? (It makes a great gift: unusual, lasting and good value for money.)

▶ **YOU SAVE 25%** WITH A ONE-YEAR (FOUR ISSUE) SUBSCRIPTION FOR £26.95.
▶ **YOU SAVE 30%** WITH A TWO-YEAR (EIGHT ISSUE) SUBSCRIPTION FOR £50.
▶ **YOU SAVE 35%** WITH A THREE-YEAR (TWELVE ISSUE) SUBSCRIPTION FOR £70.

'ESSENTIAL READING.' Observer

'RECOMMENDED FOR ANYONE WITH EVEN A PASSING INTEREST IN HUMANITY.'
British Journal of Medical Practice

ORDER FORM

I'D LIKE TO SUBSCRIBE FOR MYSELF FOR:
○ 1 year (4 issues) at just £26.95
○ 2 years (8 issues) at just £50
○ 3 years (12 issues) at just £70
START SUBSCRIPTION WITH ○ this issue ○ next issue

I'D LIKE TO GIVE A SUBSCRIPTION FOR:
○ 1 year (4 issues) at just £26.95
○ 2 years (8 issues) at just £50
○ 3 years (12 issues) at just £70
START SUBSCRIPTION WITH ○ this issue ○ next issue

MY DETAILS (please supply even if ordering a gift): Mr/Ms/Mrs/Miss ——————

Country _____ Postcode _____

GIFT RECIPIENT'S DETAILS (if applicable): Mr/Ms/Mrs/Miss ——————

Country _____ Postcode _____

Gift message (optional): _____

TOTAL * £_____ paid by ○ £ cheque enclosed (to 'Granta') ○ Visa/Mastercard/AmEx:

card no: __ __ __ __   02J8679

expires: __ / __   signature: _____

* POSTAGE. The prices stated include UK postage. For the rest of Europe, please add £8 (per year). For the rest of the world, please add £15 (per year). DATA PROTECTION. Please tick here if you don't wish to receive occasional mailings from compatible publishers. ○

Return details:
POST ('Freepost' in the UK) to: Granta, 'Freepost', 2/3 Hanover Yard, Noel Road, London N1 8BR. **PHONE/FAX:** In the UK: FreeCall 0500 004 033 (phone & fax); outside the UK: tel 44 (0)20 7704 9776, fax 44 (0)20 7704 0474 **EMAIL:** subs@granta.com

Celebrity (as opposed to fame) implies several human conditions: ambition, success and its attendant pitfalls, failure, rehabilitation, redemption. *Granta* offers a guide with these specially selected back issues, all as vital and pertinent now as when they were first published. They are available from Granta at £9.99. Subscribers get the following discounts:

► **30% OFF** WHEN YOU BUY 1-3 ISSUES (£7.00 EACH).
► **35% OFF** WHEN YOU BUY 4-7 ISSUES (£6.50 EACH).
► **40% OFF** WHEN YOU BUY ALL 8 ISSUES (£6.00 EACH).

To order: Please add £1 per issue p&p if you're in the UK; £1.50 per issue if you're in the rest of Europe; £2.00 per issue if you're in the rest of the world. Payment and return contact details are as per the subscriptions form overleaf. We need your name and address and, if you'd like us to send the issues to someone as a gift, their name and address. Our website has details of the complete collection of back issues (lists of contributors, descriptions and extracts). The address is **www.granta.com**.

Granta 71: Autumn 2000 — Shrinks

Granta 37: Autumn 91 — The Family

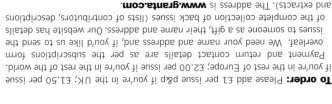

Save up to 40%

Granta 72: Winter 2000 — OVERREACHERS

Granta 74: Summer 01 — Boy

Granta 47: Spring 94 — LOSERS

Granta 58: Summer 96 — AMBITION

Granta 49: Winter 94 — MONEY

Granta 51: Autumn 95 — Big Men

GRANTA

I'VE ALWAYS BEEN A FAN

Have you ever been photographed with a celebrity? Publisher seeks
these snaps. Please send photos, with accompanying letter, to PO Box
no 2110. All letters answered, all photographs returned.

DEVISED AND EDITED BY MICHAEL COLLINS

Elton John

I am enclosing a photograph of myself taken with Elton John at one of his very generous parties given to the employees at Watford Football club in the 1980s. I think this was about 1985. My husband worked at the club from 1984–1987. These parties were fabulous and he used to invite other showbiz people like Michael Parkinson and his wife; Kiki Dee, who was great fun; Nanette Newman, who was a really charming person and many others. These are wonderful memories.

Yours,

Kate Ray (Mrs)

Sir Elton John (b. 1947) is a singer and songwriter of many pop hits (with Bernie Taupin). He was knighted in 1997 and founded and chairs the Elton John Aids Foundation.

Steve McQueen

I enclose a photograph of myself with Steve McQueen, American filmstar, now deceased.

This was taken at the Savoy Hotel on 5th June 1969.

I cannot remember the colour of his suit but I think the shirt was dark moss green and the tie pink. McQueen was smaller than the 'hunk' he appeared to be on the screen and had the rigid features of one who has had plastic surgery. His 'blond' hair was, I am sure, dyed. Although it was said that McQueen was thirty-nine at the time, I am sure he was older; his hands were those of an old man with liver coloured patches associated with old age.

It is interesting to note the cigarette, now considered anti-social.

I worked for the Publicity Dept of Cinema Center Films (a division of CBS) at the time and it was my job to organize press trips, receptions etc., write publicity material.

I wore a green silk dress with green and gold earrings, a green bead bracelet and carried a black bag.

Yours faithfully,

L. Barwell

Steve McQueen (1930–80) appeared in many films including The Magnificent Seven, The Great Escape *and* The Thomas Crown Affair.

Morecambe and Wise

As promised here are the photos of me with Eric and Ernie at the opening of the Co-op supermarket in Morecambe in 1972. It was a very special day and Eric was on top form. His speech at the luncheon was hilarious—Ernie took a back seat that day.

We finally heard the end of the story he so often tried to tell on their TV shows... 'There were two old men sitting in deck chairs...' before Ernie would stop him and say, 'You can't tell that!!' No one stopped him that day, and the ending is: 'One said, "It's nice out isn't it?" The other man said, "Oh is it? I'll get mine out."'!!

Please take very good care of the photos—they are very very special.

Sincerely,

Eileen Davey

Eric Bartholomew (1926–84) and Ernest Wiseman (1926–99) began their vaudeville act in 1941. The Morecambe and Wise Show was one of the most popular programmes on British television during the 1970s and 1980s.

Angela Lansbury

The enclosed photo may be of curio value. Taken in a Montreal night club, August 1942. The attractive young lady is Angela Lansbury in, surely, one of her earliest professional roles as an entertainer. I am sitting on her right. On her left was Dennis Mitchener (unfortunately killed in action a little over a year later). The civilian was a Montreal businessman who generously subsidised an expensive night out.

Yours faithfully,

B. S. Downs

Angela Lansbury (b. 1925) is a British actress currently best known for her television series, Murder, She Wrote. *Her films include* National Velvet, The Manchurian Candidate *and* Bedknobs and Broomsticks.

Reg Varney

Thank you for your letter. You caught me unprepared, but I managed to dig out the old photograph of myself and Reg Varney without much difficulty, which is enclosed herewith.

I hope you will find it useful. As a touch of background, it must have been taken in 1985/86 in my office in Hobart. I was then the Harbour Master and Chief Pilot of Hobart, Reg had been sent round to see me by the Commissioner of Police, as Reg thought one of his forebears had worked for the Marine Board of Hobart. I don't think we were able to confirm this. As you can imagine we were having a bit of a laugh, hence Reg sitting at my desk, and wearing my 'Brass Hat'. Reg was appearing at the Wrest Point Casino theatre. Unfortunately I was leaving for Sydney that afternoon, so was unable to take up his invitation to see his show.

Yours sincerely,

Jim Lucas

Reg Varney (b. 1916) is a British actor, best known for his leading role in the television comedy series On the Buses, *1969–73.*

Eric Sykes

Please find the photo of Eric Sykes as requested. It was taken at a celebrity charity golf tournament at Windlesham Golf Club, in Surrey. Eric was almost blind and his manager guided him around the course. I asked Eric if I could have a picture taken with him and his manager kindly shot this for me on the first green.
Good luck with the feature.

Yours sincerely,

Yvonne Peet

Eric Sykes (b. 1923) is a British comedy actor. His films include Those Magnificent Men in Their Flying Machines *and* The Plank.

Brian Lara

Thank you for your letter. My son, now twenty-two, wonders whether Brian Lara still rates as a celebrity? Anyway, I hope it's of use to you.

Yours sincerely,

Barbara Marsh

Brian Lara (b. 1969) is a West Indies cricketer. He has played for Trinidad and Tobago, and, at club level, Warwickshire and Northern Transvaal. He holds the records for the highest innings score in Test cricket (375 runs) and in First Class cricket (501). Both records were set in 1994.

George Best

As promised, my photos with celebrities. I have had to enclose part of my scrapbook, because unfortunately the newspaper cuttings have 'stuck' to the v. old pages, but I thought the reading will help you to get the 'gist' of the time the photos were taken [1971].

My friends in those days understood and shared my interest in Matt Monroe, because of his incredible voice (still music to my ears). But, with George Best, it was different, as I 'hated' football, that was till I (by chance) saw him play in a Manchester United match on television, and was spellbound by the way he played! Just to watch him running through all the other players, guiding the ball as he went, his lovely black hair flowing in the wind, he was magical, and so talented, he actually taught me to 'like' football, and see it in a different light! Naturally I watched him since then, and whenever I could.

Kind regards to you,

Ebbie Beattie

George Best (b. 1946) was one of Britain's greatest footballers. He played for Manchester United and Northern Ireland. He was voted European Player of the Year in 1968.

Enoch Powell

This was taken at a talk given by Enoch Powell to the Monday Club at Bristol Zoo in May 1988. We had tea together and someone there had a camera and took our picture together. The finest Prime Minister we never had.

Philip Winter

Enoch Powell (1913–83) was a controversial Tory politician. In April 1968 he made a speech predicting that black immigration into Britain would result in 'rivers of blood' and was dismissed from the Shadow Cabinet.

Princess Anne, Anthony Valentine

The enclosed two photographs are the only ones I kept after clearing out piles of 'souvenirs'. There are a lot more of the princess with me but they are in a museum at Landguard Fort here in Folkstone.

Anthony was opening a fête of some sort at Dr Barnardo's children's home. HRH was at Felixstowe College—she was official visitor and came regularly. I was Headmistress.

Yours sincerely,

Elizabeth Manners

Princess Anne, the Princess Royal (b. 1950), is the Queen's only daughter. She has been President of the Save the Children Fund since 1970 and rode as a member of the three-day eventing team at the 1976 Montreal Olympics. Anthony Valentine (b. 1939) is a British film and television actor best known for his leading role as 'Raffles' in the television series of the same name.

Terry-Thomas

I thank you for your letter and enclosed is a photograph of Terry-Thomas and myself at the opening of the fête in aid of the Bohill village hall. It has since been built and is well used.

I hope you are able to make use of the picture.

Yours sincerely,

Thomas Townsley

Terry-Thomas (1911–90) was a classic British character actor. His films include I'm All Right, Jack, It's a Mad, Mad, Mad, Mad World *and* Those Magnificent Men in Their Flying Machines.

Sally Jones

Enclosed photographs as requested. Sorry for delay (been to Holland, to look at the tulips). Not quite sure which you are interested in, have enclosed one of Dad with Sally Jones. If you decide you need to use them and need more details let me know.

Yours sincerely,

Joan Griffiths

If you lose them it's not the end of the world, these things happen.

Sally Jones is a former tennis player. She twice won the British Open singles (1988 and 1990) and became the first woman sports presenter on the BBC's morning news programme, Breakfast Time.

Colin Cowdrey

As promised, the photo of Lord Cowdrey (Colin Cowdrey) & myself [with hat] at Arundel Castle cricket ground in the year 2000, shortly before his death, which was Dec 4 that year. He was a perfect gentleman, a delight to be with, and had time for everyone, young or elderly.

I hope you may be able to use this, if not, I fully understand that you probably have many photos for publication.

I have been associated with cricket for many many years, won my cup and badge for my college in Surrey in 1941, so you can see I am a senior citizen, but take a great interest in the game particularly the County Championship, and number many cricketing personalities as 'friends'.

Very sincerely,

Geoffrey Runacres

Colin Cowdrey (1933–2000) was a distinguished English cricketer. He played for England (1954–74) and captained twenty-three Test matches. At county level he played for Kent, where he was captain 1957–71.

Robbie Williams

The photograph was taken in 1992 at the ticket office of [the Scandinavian airline] SAS at Manchester Airport. Take That were flying to one of the Scandinavian countries and as my father works for SAS he was able to arrange for my friends and I to meet Robbie Williams and Mark Owen while they picked their tickets up. At the time they were just starting to get famous, only the year before they did a gig at our high school, but even so there were plenty of other girls jealously looking through the window as we met them. We were only with them for about five minutes, but that was at least two months' worth of gossip at school!

Yours sincerely,

Katy Farrer

Robbie Williams (b. 1974) is a British pop idol. He joined the boy band Take That at sixteen in 1989 and turned solo in 1995. His records have since earned him over £35 million. A 2002 VH1 poll voted him the Most Important Man in Music, beating John Lennon, Elvis Presley and David Bowie.

Desert Orchid

I enclose some photographs of myself with Desert Orchid and hope they are suitable for your feature.

Whenever I meet Desert Orchid I find myself smiling from ear to ear. He is like a special friend who makes you feel lifted. All right, he is a big show off especially when there are cameras and anyone to stand and admire him. But he has a presence, a charismatic presence which you can feel when you are with him. You remember the races he has won by sheer guts and determination and how, with the same determination, he survived a life threatening illness.

Some of us are besotted with Des and often use him as our inspiration. Some have said, when life doesn't go as planned, 'Des wouldn't give up so neither will I.'

Yours sincerely,

Marguerite Gosney (Miss)

Desert Orchid (b. 1979 by Grey Mirage out of Flower Child) is a champion racehorse. He has won the King George VI Chase four times, the Cheltenham Gold Cup and the Irish Grand National. Now retired, he makes regular appearances to raise money for charity. He leads the annual parade before the King George VI Chase on Boxing Day and has his own fan club.

London's best-selling Eating & Drinking Guide

2002 Guide

Time Out

Eating & Drinking

London's best restaurants, cafés & bars

£9.99

Full colour maps of London's key restaurant areas

In association with

Perrier

SOURCE

MINÉRALE NATURELLE AU SOURCE

NATURAL MINERAL W FORTIFIED W FROM THE

BOTTLED AT SOURCE

VERGÈZE, FRANCE

GRANTA

WHAT SHEBA DID WRONG

Zoë Heller

Zoë Heller

The other night, over dinner, Sheba was talking about the first time that she and the Connolly boy kissed. I've heard about it before, of course—there being few aspects of the Connolly business that Sheba has not described to me several times over. But this time round, something new came up. I happened to ask her if anything about the first embrace had surprised her and she laughed. Yes, she said. The smell of the whole thing had been surprising. She hadn't anticipated his personal odour, and if she had, she would probably have guessed at something teenagey: bubblegum; cola; feet.

When the moment arrived, what I actually inhaled was soap, tumble-dried laundry. He smelled of scrupulous self-maintenance. You know the washing-machine fug that envelopes you sometimes, walking past the basement vents of buildings? Like that. So clean, Barbara. Never any of that cheese and oniony breath that the other kids have...

Every night since we came to Eddie's house, Sheba has been talking to me like this. She sits at the kitchen table looking out on the green darkness of Eddie's garden. I sit across from her, watching her nervous fingers score ice-skating loops in the plastic tablecloth. It's often pretty strong stuff she tells me in that newsreader's voice of hers. But then one of the many things I have always admired about Sheba is her capacity to talk about low things and make them seem perfectly decent. We don't have secrets, Sheba and I.

The first time I saw him undress, you know what I thought of, Barbara? Fresh garden vegetables wrapped in a clean white hanky. Mushrooms, fresh from the soil. No, really. He was edible. He washed his hair every night, Barbara. Imagine! It was limp with cleanness. The vanity of adolescence probably. Or no—perhaps the anxiety of it. His body was a new toy still: he hadn't learned to treat it with the indifferent neglect of adults.

Her account was wending back to familiar terrain, now. I must have heard the hair rhapsody at least fifteen times in recent months. (I've never cared for Connolly's hair, myself. It's always struck me as slightly sinister—like that spun fibreglass snow that they used to sell as Christmas tree decoration.) Still, I kept giving her the cues.

'And were you nervous, when you were kissing him, Sheba?'

Oh no. Well, yes... Not really. [Laughter] Can you be nervous and calm at the same time? I remember being quite relieved that he wasn't using his tongue. You do need to know someone a bit, first, don't you? It's too much otherwise. All the slobber. And that slightly embarrassing sense of the other person trying to be creative in a limited space... Anyway, I relaxed too much or something, because the bike fell—there was this awful clatter—and then, of course, I ran away...

I don't say much on these occasions. The point is to get Sheba to talk. But even in the usual run of things, I tend to be the listener in our relationship. It's not that Sheba is cleverer than me. Any objective comparison would have to rate me the more educated woman, I think. (Sheba knows a bit about art—I'll give her that; but for all her class advantages, she is woefully ill-read.) No, Sheba talks because she is just naturally more loquacious and candid than I am. I am circumspect by nature and she...well, she isn't.

For most people, honesty is such an unusual departure from their standard modus operandi—such an aberration in their workaday mendacity—that they feel obliged to alert you when a moment of sincerity is coming on. 'To be completely honest,' they say, or, 'To tell you the truth,' or, 'Can I be straight?' Often they want to extract vows of discretion from you before going any further. 'This is strictly between us, right?... You must promise not to tell anyone...' Sheba does none of that. She tosses out intimate and unflattering truths about herself all the time, without a second thought. 'I was the most fearsomely obsessive little masturbator when I was a girl,' she told me once when we were first getting to know each other. 'My mother practically had to Sellotape my knickers to me, to stop me having at myself in public places.'

'Oh?' I said, trying to sound as if I were used to broaching such matters over coffee and a Kit Kat.

It's a class characteristic, I think—this insouciant frankness of hers. If I had had more contact with posh people in my life, I would probably be familiar with the style and think nothing of it. But Sheba is the only genuinely upper-class person I've ever known. Her throwaway candour is as exotic to me, in its way, as a plate in an Amazonian tribesman's lip.

She's meant to be taking a nap at the moment. (She's not sleeping well at night.) But I can tell from the creaking of the floorboards overhead that she's pottering about in her niece's room. She often goes in there in the afternoons. It was her bedroom when she was growing up, apparently. She'll spend hours at a time handling the little girl's things—reorganizing the vials of glitter and glue in art-kits, making inventories of the dollies' plastic shoes. Sometimes she falls asleep up there and I'll have to go and wake her for dinner. She always looks rather sad and odd, sprawled out on the pink and white princess bed, with her big, rough feet dangling over the edge. Like a giantess who has blundered into the wrong house.

This place belongs to her brother Eddie now. After Sheba's father died, Sheba's mother decided the house was too big for one person and Eddie bought it from her. Sheba is rather bitter about that. It isn't fair, she says, that just because Eddie is rich, he should have been able to buy their shared past for himself.

Eddie and his family are away in New Delhi. The American bank he works for has posted him there for six months. Sheba rang him in India when her trouble started, and he agreed to let her stay in the house until she found something permanent. We've been here ever since. It's anyone's guess what we will do when Eddie returns in June. I gave up the lease on my little flat some months ago and Sheba's husband, Richard, seems determined not to have her back under any circumstances. Even if we had the money to rent a new place, I'm not sure that any landlords in London would have us. I try not to worry, though. Sufficient unto the day is the evil thereof, as my mother used to say.

This is not a story about me. But, since the task of telling it has fallen into my hands, and since I play a minor role in the events I am going to describe, it is only right that I should offer a brief account of myself and my relationship to the protagonist. My name is Barbara Covett. (From time to time, one of my colleagues will call me 'Barb' or, even less desirably, 'Babs', but I discourage it.) Until I retired earlier this year, I had been living in Archway, north London, and teaching history at St George's, a comprehensive school in the same neighbourhood, for the last nineteen years. It was at St George's, a little over eighteen months ago, that I met Bathsheba Hart. Her name will probably be familiar to most of you by now. She is the forty-two-year-old pottery teacher, who was recently charged with indecent assault on a minor, after being discovered having a sexual affair with one of her fifteen-year-old students.

What Sheba Did Wrong

Since it first came to light, Sheba's case has received nigh on unstinting media coverage. I try to keep up with all of it, although, frankly, it's a pretty depressing task. There was a time when I placed a certain amount of trust in the integrity of this country's news organizations, but now that I have seen at close hand the way in which reporters go about their business, I recognize how sadly misplaced that trust was. Over the last fortnight I must have spotted twenty errors of fact about Sheba's case in the newspapers alone. On Monday of this week, some bright spark at the *Daily Mirror* described Sheba as a 'buxom bombshell'. (Anyone who has ever so much as glanced at her knows that she is as flat as the Fens.) And yesterday, the *Sun* ran an 'exposé' on Sheba's husband, in which it was claimed that Richard, who lectures in Communications Theory at City of London, is 'a trendy prof who gives sexy seminars on how to read dirty magazines'.

It was the papers that finally did Sheba and Richard in, I believe. After she was given bail, the two of them tried to soldier on for a while. But it was too much—too much for any couple—to bear. When you think of the reporters camped outside their house, the awful headlines every day—SEX TEACHER PASSES HER ORALS WITH FLYING COLOURS, TEACHER TAKES KEEN INTEREST IN THE STUDENT BODY, and so on—it's a wonder, really, that they lasted as long as they did. Just before Sheba made her first appearance in the magistrate's court, Richard told her that her presence in the house was making the children's lives a misery. I believe he thought this was a kinder rationale for throwing her out than his own feelings of revulsion.

That was when I stepped in. I put Sheba up for a week or so in my flat and then, when she got Eddie to let her stay, I came with her. How could I not? Sheba was so pitifully alone. It would have taken a very monstrous individual to desert her. There is at least one more pre-trial hearing—possibly two—to be got through before the case goes before the Crown Court and frankly, I don't think Sheba would make it on her own. Her barrister says that she could avoid going to the Crown Court altogether, if she pleaded guilty to the charges. But Sheba won't hear of it. She regards a guilty plea—even one that includes a clear denial of 'coercion, duress or bribery'—as unthinkable. 'There was no assault and I've done nothing indecent,' she likes to say.

In becoming Sheba's caretaker these last few months, I have inevitably drawn some of the media glare to myself. It seems to be

Zoë Heller

a source of some amusement and discomfort to the journalists that a respectable older woman with nearly thirty-five years' experience as an educator should choose to be associated with Sheba. Every single reporter covering this case—every single one—has made a point of describing, with varying degrees of facetiousness, my handbag: a perfectly unexceptional, wooden-handled object, with a needlepoint portrait of two kittens on it. Clearly, it would suit them all much better if I were off somewhere, with the other jowly old biddies, boasting about my grandchildren or playing bingo. Not, at any rate, standing on the doorstep of a rich banker's house in Primrose Hill, defending the character of an alleged child molester.

The only possible explanation that the journalists can find for my having voluntarily associated myself with Sheba's debauchery is that I am, in some, as yet, shadowy way, debauched myself. In the months since Sheba's arrest, I have been required, on several occasions, to speak to reporters on her behalf, and as a result I am now known to readers of the *Sun* as 'the saucy schoolteacher's spin-mistress'. (Those who know me can attest to what an unlikely candidate I am for such a soubriquet.) My rather naive hope, in acting as Sheba's spokeswoman, has been to counter some of the sanctimonious hostility towards my friend, and to shed a little light on the true nature of her rather complex personality. But alas, my contributions have done no such thing. They have either been cruelly and deliberately distorted, or they have simply gone unnoticed in a torrent of lubricious lies propagated by people who have never met Sheba and would, very likely, not have understood her, even if they had.

This is chief among the reasons why I have now decided to risk further calumny by writing my own account of Sheba's downfall. I am presumptuous enough to believe that I am the person best qualified to write this small history. I would go so far as to hazard that I am the only person. Sheba and I have spent countless hours together over the last eighteen months exchanging confidences of every kind. Certainly, there is no other friend or relative of Sheba's who has been so intimately involved in the day-to-day business of her love affair with Connolly. In many cases, the events I describe here were witnessed by me personally. Elsewhere, I rely upon detailed accounts provided by Sheba herself.

I should acknowledge straight away that, from a moral point of view, Sheba's testimony regarding her and the boy's conduct is not always entirely reliable. Even now she is inclined to romanticize the relationship and to underestimate the irresponsibility—the wrongness—of her actions. What remorse she expresses tends to be remorse for having been found out. But, confused and troubled as Sheba still is, her honesty remains utterly dependable. While I may dispute her reading of certain events, I have found no cause to doubt the factual particulars of her account. Indeed, I am confident that everything she has told me regarding the how, when and where of this affair is, to the best of her knowledge, true.

The first time I ever saw Sheba I was standing in the St George's car park, getting books out of the back of my car, when she came through the gates on a bicycle—an old-fashioned, butcher-boy model with a basket on the front. Her hair was arranged in one of those artfully dishevelled up-dos: a lot of stray tendrils framing the jaw, and something like a chopstick piercing a rough bun at the back. It was the sort of hairstyle that film actresses wear when they're playing sexy lady doctors. I can't recall exactly what she had on. Sheba's outfits tend to be very complicated—lots of floaty layers. I know she was wearing purple shoes. And there was definitely a long skirt involved, because I remember thinking that it was in imminent danger of becoming entangled in her pedals. When she dismounted—with a lithe, rather irritating little skip—I saw that the skirt was made of some diaphanous material. Fey, was the word that swam into my mind. *Fey person*, I thought. Then I locked my car and walked away.

Our formal introduction took place later the same day when the deputy head brought her into the staffroom at afternoon break for a 'meet and greet'. I was off in a corner when Sheba was ushered in, so I was able to watch her slow progress around the room for several minutes, before having to mould my face into the appropriate smile.

Her hair had become more chaotic since the morning. The loose tendrils had graduated to hanks, and where it was meant to be smooth and pulled back, tiny, fuzzy sprigs had reared up, creating a sort of corona around her scalp. She was a very thin woman, I saw now. As she bent to shake the hands of seated staff members, her body seemed to fold in half at the waist like a piece of paper. 'Our new pottery teacher!' the deputy head was bellowing with his customary, chilling good spirits. Sheba smiled and patted shyly at her hair. *Pottery*. I repeated the word quietly to myself. It was too perfect: I pictured her, the dreamy maiden poised at her wheel, massaging tastefully mottled milk jugs into being.

Women observing other women tend to be engrossed by the details—the bodily minutiae, the clothing particulars. We get so caught up in the lone dimple, the excessive ears, the missing button, that we often lag behind men in organizing the individual features into an overall impression. It was only now, watching Bill Rumer, the head of chemistry, smile wolfishly at Sheba, that the fact of her beauty occurred to me. *Of course*, I thought. *She's very good-looking.* Sheba made another nervous adjustment to her hair. As she raised her long, thin arms to fuss with the chopstick hair ornament, her torso lengthened and her chest was thrust forward slightly. She had a dancer's bosom. Two firm little patties riding the raft of her ribs.

After a few moments, the deputy head turned and beckoned to me. 'Barbara!' he shouted. 'Do come and meet Sheba Hart.'

I stepped over to join them.

'This is Barbara Covett,' he said. 'She's one of our stalwarts. If Barbara ever left us, I'm afraid St George's would collapse.'

Sheba looked at me carefully. She was about thirty-five, I estimated. (She was actually forty, about to be forty-one.) The hand that she held out to be shaken was large and red and rather coarse to the touch. 'How nice to be so needed,' she said, smiling. It was difficult to distinguish her tone, but it seemed to me that it contained a note of genuine sympathy—as if she understood how maddening it might be to be patronized in this way.

'Sheba—is that as in Queen of?' I asked.

'No, as in Bathsheba.'

'Oh. Were your parents thinking of the Bible or of Hardy?'

She smiled. 'I'm not sure. I think they just liked the name.'

'If there's anything you need to know about anything concerning this place, Sheba,' the deputy head continued, 'you must ask Barbara. She's the St George's expert.'

'Oh, smashing. I'll remember that,' Sheba said.

During her first couple of weeks, Sheba kept very much to herself. At break times, she often stayed in her pottery studio. When she did come into the staffroom, she usually stood alone at one of the windows peeking round the curtains at the playground outside. She was perfectly pleasant to her colleagues—which is to say, she exchanged all the standard, weather-based pleasantries. But the women tended to the opinion that Sheba was 'stuck up', while the men favoured the theory that she was 'cold'. Bill Rumer, widely acknowledged as the staff expert on such matters, observed on more than one occasion that 'there was nothing wrong with her that a good boning wouldn't cure'.

Sheba did not exempt me from her general aloofness. Somewhere in her second week, she greeted me in the corridor. (She used 'Hello', I was pleased to note, as opposed to the awful, mid-Atlantic 'Hiya' that so many of the staff favour.) And another time, walking from the Arts Building after an assembly, we shared some brief, rueful comments about the choral performance that had just taken place. But my feelings of connection to Sheba did not depend upon these minute exchanges. The bond that I sensed, even at that stage, went far beyond anything that might have been expressed in quotidian chit-chat. It was an intuited kinship. An unspoken understanding. Does it sound too dramatic to call it spiritual recognition? Owing to our mutual reserve, I understood that it would take time for us to form a friendship. But when we did, I had no doubt that it would prove to be one of uncommon intimacy and trust—a relationship 'de chaleur' as the French say.

For most of the staff, Sheba's dignified self-containment acted as a sort of force field, repelling the usual impertinent enquiries about home life and political allegiance. But elegance loses its power in the presence of the properly stupid, and there were a few who were not deterred. It was from these eager little fishwives that the rest of the staffroom learned that Sheba was married with two children; that her husband was a lecturer; that her children were educated privately; and that she lived in 'a ginormous house' in Highgate. The other thing that became known in those early weeks was that Sheba was experiencing 'class-control issues'.

In Sheba's third week at the school, a geography teacher called Jerry Samuels was patrolling the school property for truants when he passed the art centre and heard what sounded like a riot going on inside Sheba's hut. When he went in to investigate, he found the studio in uproar. The entire second-year class was having a clay fight. Several of the boys were stripped to the waist. They had evidently been using clay to daub tribal markings on their chests and faces. Two of them were endeavouring to topple the kiln. Samuels discovered Sheba cowering, tearfully, behind her desk. 'In ten years of teaching, I've never seen anything like it,' he later told his colleagues in the staffroom. 'It was *Lord of the Flies* in there.'

Notwithstanding her difficulties with discipline, Sheba, like every other member of staff, was expected to participate in the full range of school duties—playground patrol, canteen shift, and, perhaps most daunting of all for her, Homework Club supervision. 'Haitch Cee' as it is known to the pupils, is held every weekday, between the hours of three-thirty and six p.m., in a Middle Hall classroom. It was set up a few years ago by the Head, with the official purpose of 'providing a calm working environment for those who might have difficulty finding one in their own homes'. It is a deeply unpopular institution among the staff, mainly because it tends to double up as a dumping ground for children who have received detentions. Club supervisors usually find themselves having to deal with the school's worst pupils at a point in the day when those pupils are at their most restive and difficult.

There were ten children in the Homework Club on the afternoon that Sheba was supervising. Almost immediately that she began taking down names of attendees, a violent dispute broke out between two third-year girls, one of whom was accusing the other of putting chewing gum in her hair. For the next three quarters of an hour, Sheba's attention was taken up with keeping the girls physically apart from one another. It was only after she sent one of the girls to the head of the third year that things calmed down and she had leisure to notice the other children in the room. There were now three girls and six boys present, all of whom, according to the teacher's notes that they had brought with them, were attending HC as punishment. They returned Sheba's gaze with the surliness that she had come to expect. Only one boy, at the very back of the room, sat working quietly. Sheba remembers being rather touched by his childlike posture of concentration—the way his tongue was peeping out from his mouth and his left arm was curled protectively around his labours. This was Steven Connolly.

A little while later, when she had issued the usual reminder about assigned tasks having to be completed by five o'clock, she got up and wandered over to where the boy was sitting. He winced slightly when he saw her approaching and drew himself upright. 'What?' he said. 'I'm not doing nothing wrong.' From across the room, Sheba had assumed he was a second- or third-year pupil. But up close, he seemed older, she recalls. His upper body had a solid, triangular look. His hands and forearms were unexpectedly large. She could see the beginnings of bristle on his chin.

Sheba has always maintained that Connolly is a terrifically attractive boy. To be fair to her, several female newspaper columnists have made observations to similar effect. ('Glowering and exotic' one woman in the *Mail* called him a few weeks back.) I don't see it, I must confess. Of course, since I have never been physically drawn to any of the pupils, I may not be the best person to assess the boy's charms. Yet I rather think that if my tastes *had* run in that direction, I would have fixed upon someone a little prettier: a delicate-boned, downy-faced boy in the lower school, perhaps. Connolly is not pretty in the slightest. He is a coarse-looking fellow, with hair the colour of pee and a loose, plump-lipped mouth. His nose, owing to a childhood accident (an ardent game of kiss-chase, an unanticipated pothole), is quite severely squished. His eyes are heavy-hooded and so downturned as to bring to mind a tragedy mask. Sheba insists that he has superb skin and it is true, I suppose, that he has been spared the suppurating carbuncles to which boys of his age are prone. But what she refers to as his 'olive complexion' has always struck me as rather dingy. I can never lay eyes on the boy without wanting to give his face a good going-over with a hot flannel.

On Connolly's desk, Sheba saw a torn-out magazine advertisement for a fur sale at Harrods. It was illustrated with one of those highly stylized pen-and-ink sketches of a woman in a fur stole: all hourglass waist and scornful expression. Connolly was copying the image into the back page of his maths workbook. Sheba assured him she had not come over to tell him off. She had merely wanted to see what he was up to. His sketch was good, she said. The embarrassment, or perhaps the pleasure, caused by this praise made him squirm. (Sheba remembers him twisting his head from side to side, 'like a blind person'.) 'But you know,' she went on, 'you don't have to copy things. Why don't you draw something from life? Or even your imagination?' Connolly's face, which had momentarily softened under flattery, closed up again. He shrugged irritably.

Sheba struggled to correct herself. 'No,' she said. 'Because, I mean, I bet you could do really brilliant things. This is really, really good.' She began asking him a few questions about himself. What was his name? How old was he? She expressed some disappointment that he wasn't in her pottery class. What option was he taking instead?

Connolly looked stricken when she asked this and muttered something that Sheba couldn't make out.

'What's that?' she asked.

'Special Needs, Miss,' he repeated in a croak.

Contrary to some of the reports that have since emerged, Connolly was not 'backward' or 'retarded'. Along with a good twenty-five per cent of St George's students, he had been identified as having 'literacy issues'—difficulties with reading and writing—and was therefore eligible for daily Special Needs sessions in the remedial department. On questioning the boy further, Sheba discovered that Special Needs also prevented him from participating in art classes. She told him that she was surprised about this and suggested that perhaps something might be done to rectify the situation. Connolly was shrugging non-committally when Sheba was suddenly called away. One of her second-year charges was attempting to burn a first year with a disposable lighter.

A few days after meeting Connolly for the first time, Sheba found a picture in her pigeonhole. It was a rudimentary pencil sketch of a woman, executed on lined foolscap, in the romantic style often favoured by pavement artists. The woman had vast, woozy eyes and long, long arms that resolved themselves in odd, fingerless trowels. She was gazing into the distance with an expression of dreamy, slightly cross-eyed eroticism. Ballooning out from her low-cut blouse, there was a good amount of heavily cross-hatched cleavage. In the bottom right-hand corner of the page, the anonymous author of the sketch had written in large, unwieldy italics, the words, 'Foxy Lady'.

Sheba understood, more or less straight away, that she was the Foxy Lady in question, that the picture was intended as a portrait of her, and that it had been drawn by the shy, blond-haired boy from the previous week's HC. She was not alarmed. On the contrary, she was pleased and rather flattered. In the brutal atmosphere of St George's, the gesture struck her as eccentrically innocent. She didn't seek out Connolly to thank him for the drawing. She assumed that, since he had sent it anonymously, any approach on her part would embarrass him. But she expected that he would sooner or later make some approach to her. And sure enough, one day, shortly before the half-term break, she found him dawdling outside her studio as she was leaving for lunch. 'Did you get that picture, then?' he asked.

Sheba remembers Connolly being poorly dressed for the weather. It was late October and he had on only a T-shirt and a flimsy cotton jacket. When he lifted his T-shirt to scratch absent-mindedly at his belly, Sheba saw how his pelvic bone jutted out, creating a wide, shallow cavity just above his groin. She had forgotten that about young men's bodies, she says.

'What,' she said, feigning surprise, 'you mean it was from you?'

Connolly allowed, coyly, that this might be the case.

Sheba told him it was a lovely picture and that if he really had drawn it, he ought to have signed it. 'Wait a minute,' she said. She unlocked the door and went back into the studio where she took the drawing out from the bottom drawer of her desk. 'Why don't you sign it for me now?' she asked.

Connolly, who was still standing in the doorway, looked at her uncertainly.

'Why, Miss?' he asked.

Sheba laughed. 'No reason. I just thought it would be nice. You don't have to. But usually artists like to take credit for their work.'

Connolly came over to the desk and looked at the drawing. It was not as good as some of the other things he had done, he told her. He couldn't really do hands. Sheba agreed that hands were very hard and went on to utter some encouraging words about the value of practice and of studying life models. At a certain point, she noticed him gazing at her own hands. She felt shy, she recalls, because her hands were so rough and unkempt. She put the picture down and folded her arms. She told Connolly that she had spoken to the deputy head about changing his timetable. It was not going to be as easy as she had thought, she said. But she had not given up. She would keep on trying. In the meantime, the most important thing was for him to keep drawing.

There was a short silence. Then Connolly confessed hesitantly that his picture had been intended as a portrait of her. Sheba nodded and told him that she had guessed as much. The boy was flustered by this. He began to stammer. In a clumsy attempt to put him at his ease, Sheba made a joking comment about the generous bosom he had given her in his portrait. 'Wishful thinking,' she said. But this only exacerbated the boy's embarrassment. He turned quite purple, apparently, and did not say anything for a long time.

Sheba was rather tickled by this episode, I believe. It was a novelty, she says, to be so candidly admired. When she first told me this, I remember expressing some incredulity. Certainly, I could believe that Richard's affection might have grown complacent over the years, or perhaps just so reliable as not to count. But she surely wasn't suggesting that she had been in want of admirers before Connolly? Sheba, who made the men in the St George's staffroom gaga with her flimsy blouses? No, she insisted. That was quite different. There had always been men who made furtive google eyes at her, men who made it clear that they found her attractive. But no one, before Connolly, had ever truly pursued her. She used to think it was out of respect for her having a husband. But it couldn't really have been that. If everybody was so reverent of the institution of marriage, how did all the adultery get committed? Probably, she thought now, it was the kind of men she had spent her life around. Most of Richard's friends were academic types, and they were all terrified at the thought of being 'cheesy'. Their ultimate nightmare, she said, was to be called insensitive. If they flirted, it was always an arch, joking sort of thing. Even when they told you that your dress was nice, they put it in quotation marks—just in case you took offence and slapped their faces. Only Connolly, who was either too young, or too obtuse, to appreciate the outrageousness of his ambition, had dared to reach out to her. He hadn't been scared of her, or angry with her, she said. He hadn't tied himself in rhetorical knots trying to be equal to her beauty. When he looked at her, it was as if he were gobbling her up, she said. 'Like a peach.'

Right after half-term, Connolly turned up at Sheba's studio again. She was alone at the end of the school day, collecting up some animal figurines that her last class of first years had made, when he appeared. He had some pictures that he wanted to show her, he said. It had been raining on and off throughout the day. His hair was sticking close to his head and there was a sweet, steamy smell of damp clothes about him. When he came close to her, she caught a whiff of his breath and that smelled sweet, too—candied almost, Sheba thought. They sat down and looked at his sketches—all of which, in deference to her advice, he had drawn from life models. Then they examined some of the first years' pandas and lions, laughing together at the particularly clumsy ones. At a certain point, Sheba started to explain to him the principles of glazing. She was impressed by his attentiveness. He seemed genuinely interested, she thought; genuinely eager to learn. This, she told herself, as she pointed out the various features of the kiln, was what she had hoped teaching would be: drawing children out of themselves; cultivating tender young sensibilities.

Shortly before Connolly left that afternoon, he looked up at a British Museum poster of an ancient Roman urn and remarked on how odd it was to think of an actual person—'a real bloke, thousands of years ago'—making the artefact. Sheba glanced at him warily. No one, until now, had shown the slightest interest in her posters. Connolly's comment was so much the sort of sentiment that she had wanted to inspire that she half-suspected him of mocking her. 'It does your brain in, doesn't it?' he said, flicking shyly at his fringe. His face yielded no trace of satirical intent. 'Yes,' she replied, eagerly. 'Yes. *Exactly.* You're right. It does do your brain in.'

He put his jacket on. Sheba told him to drop by with his sketches whenever he wanted. 'Perhaps the next time you come,' she added, 'we'll have a go at making something with clay.' Connolly nodded, but made no other response and Sheba feared that she had overstepped the mark in some way. When Connolly didn't show up on the following Monday or Tuesday or Wednesday, she took it as confirmation that she had.

The next Friday, though, just as Sheba was loading the kiln, Connolly reappeared. He had been unable to come earlier in the week, he explained, because he had been tied up with detentions. Sheba, determined not to be overbearing, merely shrugged and said she was glad to see him. He had brought more of his sketches with him, and again, they sat for a long time examining his work before going on to chat more generally about school and other matters. He stayed with her for almost two hours. Towards the end of his visit, Sheba recalls that she was discussing the science of kiln temperatures, when he interrupted her abruptly to comment on how nicely she spoke. She didn't need to be a teacher, he told her earnestly. She could get a job 'doing the weather on the telly, or something'. Sheba smiled, charmed by his gaucheness. She would keep the career tip in mind, she told him.

As time went on, and Connolly's visits became routine, he was emboldened to volunteer more of his insights about art and his ideas about the world. Sometimes, when he and Sheba were talking or looking at pictures, he would get up suddenly, she says, and go to the studio window to comment on the shapes of the clouds, or the purplish colour of the early evening sky. Once, in what was surely a rather desperate moment, he even stroked the nubby mustard material of the studio curtains and pronounced it 'an interesting fabric'.

It is pretty clear to me that there was a strong element of calculation in these little bursts of wistfulness and wonderment. By which I do not mean to imply that the boy was cynical, exactly. Merely anxious to please. He had observed that Sheba liked him best when he was saying sensitive things about paintings and so on, and he was beefing up his moony ponderings accordingly. If this was cynical, then we must allow that all courtship is cynical. Connolly was doing as all people do in such situations—tricking out his stall with an eye to what would best please his customer.

For a long time, though, Sheba didn't see any of this. It did not occur to her that Connolly's schoolboy profundities were anything other than heartfelt. And when, at last, it did occur to her, she seems to have been touched rather than disillusioned. To this day she passionately defends Connolly's 'brilliance' and 'imagination'. If he did feign interests that weren't his, she says, the pretence demonstrated 'a very sophisticated social adaptiveness' on his part. The school is embarrassed by the idea that Connolly might be clever, she claims, 'because they've always written him off as dim'.

The school has never written off Connolly as dim. The fact that he has been identified as a Special Needs pupil—that he receives help for his dyslexia—indicates quite the contrary. No one on the staff has ever been quite as excited about his intellectual capacities as Sheba, it is true. But then, the plain fact is that Connolly is not a very exciting boy. He is a perfectly average boy in possession of a perfectly average intelligence.

Why, then, was Sheba first moved to such an extravagant estimation of his virtues? The papers will tell you that Sheba's judgement was clouded by desire: she was attracted to Connolly, and in order to explain that attraction, she convinced herself that he was some kind of a genius. This is reasonable enough. But it is not the whole story, I think. To completely understand Sheba's response to Connolly, you would also have to take into account her very limited knowledge—and low expectations—of people of his social class. Until she met Connolly, Sheba had never really had any intimate contact with a bona fide member of the British proletariat. Her acquaintance with that stratum did not—and still doesn't—extend much beyond what she has gleaned from the grittier soap operas and the various women who have cleaned her house over the years.

She would vehemently deny this, of course. Like so many members of London's haute bourgeoisie, Sheba is deeply attached to a mythology of herself as 'street-smart'. She always howls when I refer to her as 'upper class'. (She's 'middle' she insists, or at the very most, 'upper-middle'). She loves to come shopping with me in the Queenstown street market or the Save-On next to the Chalk Farm council estates. It flatters her image of herself as an inner-city dweller, to exchange drolleries about produce with cockney stallholders—to stand cheek by jowl in checkout queues with teenage mothers buying quick-cook macaroni in the shape of Teletubbies for their children. You can be quite sure, however, that if any of these prematurely craggy-faced girls were to address her directly, she would be frightened out of her wits. Though she cannot say it, or even acknowledge it to herself, she thinks of the working class as a mysterious and homogeneous entity: a tempery, florid-faced people, raddled with food additives and alcohol.

Little wonder that Connolly seemed so fascinatingly anomalous to her. Here she was, a frightened snob, surrounded by hostile north London plebeians and along came a young man who sought out her company, who listened, open-mouthed, when she lectured him on Great Artists. Who proffered dreamy aperçus about the curtains. Poor old Sheba regarded Connolly with much the same amazement and delight as you or I would a monkey who strolled out of the jungle and asked for a gin and tonic.

Connolly understood all this, I think. I don't mean that he would have been able to articulate, or even consciously to formulate the role that class played in his relationship with Sheba. But that he sensed the anthropological dimension of Sheba's interest in him and played up to it, I have no doubt. When describing his family and home to Sheba, he seems to have been at pains to leave her naive notions of prole mores intact. He told her about his family's holiday caravan in Maldon, Essex; about his mother's part-time job as a dinner lady and his father's job as a taxi driver—but he omitted to mention that his mother held a college diploma or that his father was a classical music buff. These facts, now that they have emerged in the papers, are so astounding to Sheba—so at odds with the cartoon thugs she has been encouraged to envisage—that she chooses either to ignore them, or to dismiss them as lies. In a recent newspaper interview, Connolly's mother mentioned that when her children were young, she and her husband often played them recordings of *Swan Lake* and *Peter and the Wolf*. Sheba threw the paper down when she got to this bit. Mrs Connolly was lying, she said—trying to make her son's home life seem more wholesome and happy than it really was. 'Steven's father hits him, you know,' she screeched at me. 'He beats him. She doesn't mention that, does she?'

This rather melodramatic accusation is based on something that Connolly told Sheba once, at the very beginning of their relationship. Sheba has spoken of this conversation often because Connolly's claim about his father's violence—true or not—prompted their first physical intimacy. It was towards the end of Winter term. Connolly had come to see her in the studio and the two of them were looking out of the window at the darkening playground, discussing the possibility that it might snow. Connolly mentioned that snow always put his father in a bad mood. When Mr Connolly 'had the hump', he added, he often hit him. Sheba was not particularly surprised by this admission. She had watched several made-for-television dramas about domestic violence and considered herself well acquainted with council house brutality. She murmured something consoling to Connolly. And then she reached out and rubbed his head. When her fingers came away, strands of his hair rose up with them in an electric spray. Sheba laughed and made a light-hearted comment about the static in the air that day. Connolly closed his eyes and smiled. 'Do that again, Miss,' he said.

Prior to this incident, Sheba had occasionally wondered about the extent of Connolly's sexual experience. She had been inclined to place him at the innocent end of the scale, she says; not technically a virgin, perhaps, but still fundamentally inexperienced. Now, something about his smile—the confident way he commanded her to touch him again—made her revise her original estimation. She had been wrong, she thought. He was worldlier than she had imagined.

She declined to repeat the gesture. It was time for her to go home, she told him. She put on her coat and the funny Peruvian hat that she was wearing that winter. Then she locked up the studio and the two of them walked through the playground to the car park together. Even though she told him not to bother, Connolly hung around while she undid the lock on her bicycle. When they got out on the street, they paused awkwardly, unsure of how to effect their farewells. Sheba resolved the matter by prodding Connolly abruptly in the ribs and jumping on to her bike. 'Bye then!' she cried as she rode away. When she glanced behind her, she saw that he was lingering on the pavement where she had left him. She waved, and after a moment he waved rather mournfully back.

On her way home that evening, Sheba felt troubled. Unsettled. She kept going over what had just happened in her studio and telling herself that there was really nothing to fuss about. She had ruffled the boy's hair, for goodness' sake. Just as an auntie might. But why, then, she wondered, was she feeling so shifty? Why was it necessary to reassure herself? Things that really are innocent don't need to be labelled as such.

Had Sheba pursued this interrogation of herself with any rigour, things might have turned out very differently. But almost as soon as the promising line of enquiry had been opened, she abruptly shut it down. What did it matter what other people might think, as long as she knew that the thing was harmless? People were hyper-vigilant these days, because of child abuse. In the rush to guard against the sickos, the world had gone slightly mad. For heaven's sake, there were people who wouldn't take pictures of their naked children any more, for fear of being shopped by the chemist. Surely she wasn't going to succumb to that sort of craziness and become her own tyrannous Neighbourhood Watch? She had ruffled his hair. His hair. She had wanted to comfort the boy. Perhaps she would have been less inclined to make the gesture with another, less appealing pupil.

But what of that? She couldn't expect herself to be oblivious of what the kids looked like and smelled like and felt like. She spent all day confronting their corporeal reality: inhaling their farts, gazing with pity upon their acne. Some of them were vile-looking and some of them were attractive. What kind of saint wouldn't notice the difference? Whatever pleasure she took in Steven's physical self was no more or less suspect, she told herself, than the pleasure she had once taken in the plump, velvety bodies of her own babies. A sensuous pleasure, certainly, but far from sensual.

A couple of weeks into Spring term, Sheba was wheeling her bike out of the school car park when she found Connolly waiting for her on the street. It was six o'clock and the main road that runs along the west side of the school grounds was busy with rush hour traffic. All the children—even Homework Club attendees—had gone home now. Sweet wrappers and crisp packets—remnants of the afternoon exodus—were skittering about the pavement in the pinkish dusk light. Sheba smiled hello to Connolly and asked him what he was doing there. He shrugged. 'Waiting for you,' he said.

She knew right then what was going to happen, she says. It came to her, as these things sometimes do, in a perfect and fully formed revelation. He had a crush on her, he had been developing this crush for some time. She had encouraged it, or, at the very least, failed to discourage it. Now, he was going to declare himself, and she—because she could think of no other feasible reaction—was going to affect amazement and horror.

'What did you want to see me about?' she asked him. 'You know, Steven, if you need to talk to me about anything, you can do it in school.'

She started walking fast, wheeling her bicycle beside her. Connolly trotted to keep up. No, he said, shaking his head, he couldn't tell her in school.

'Well, then,' Sheba said, 'you have to arrange a...'

'I really like you,' he interrupted.

She was silent.

'I think about you all the time. I was...' He broke off and gazed at her unhappily.

Sheba smiled. 'I'm glad you like me,' she said, maintaining her tone of teacherly brusqueness, 'but I can't talk to you now. I have to get home.'

'It's more than liking,' Connolly objected impatiently.

They had reached an intersection. Sheba hesitated. Her way home was to the left, down a long shopping street called Grafton Lane. She needed to get rid of the boy—she couldn't have him trailing her all the way to her house—yet it seemed callous to abandon him there on the street corner. She made the left turn, and continued to walk with him—past the cheap shoe shop with its wire baskets of cut-price slippers out in front, past Dee-Dar, the tatty little Indian where St George's teachers hold their staff dinners, past the post office and the chip shop and the ancient chemist's with dusty boxes of Radox in the window. Connolly said nothing for a while. Then, as if unable to contain himself, he burst out, 'I'm really into you, Miss.'

Something in his voice made Sheba think that he was about to cry. She stopped and looked at him, but he had his head down, looking at the pavement. 'Steven,' she said 'This isn't...' She broke off. 'This just...it won't do!' She straddled her bike, preparing to mount it.

'I can't help it,' Connolly said, looking up. 'I swear, I can't help myself.' She had been right. There were tears in his eyes. 'Oh, Steven,' she said. She was about to reach out her hand and pat his shoulder when his face suddenly came pressing in at hers.

Sheba says I couldn't possibly understand what it feels like, after twenty years of faithful marriage, to be kissed by someone other than your husband; to feel the pressure of a stranger's mouth on yours. 'Things fall asleep in a marriage,' she told me once. 'They have to, really. You have to lose that mad sexual alertness you had when you were out in the world on your own. All these years with Richard, I don't think I've ever consciously suppressed anything. I've always been so grateful to be married—so relieved that I would never have to be naked in front of a stranger again. But I'd forgotten how exhilarating it is to expose yourself...to be a little scared. As soon as Steven kissed me, it all came back in an instant. The...the...you know, the high of it. I was amazed, really, at how I could have lived without that all those years.'

It must have been a pretty comic sight—the little suitor reaching on tippy-toe for his middle-aged mistress, the bike smashing to the ground. But the farcical element of their first embrace seems never to have occurred to Sheba. Or if it has, she has never mentioned it. She has spoken about the warmth of Connolly, the soap smell of him, the bristle at the back of his neck, the texture of his jumper and any number of other tedious details connected with this first embrace. But never about how immensely silly the whole thing must have looked.

In the immediate aftermath of the bicycle's collapse, there was confusion and speechless embarrassment. Connolly tried to help Sheba up but she waved him away. She remembers looking around to see who might have witnessed their kiss. One elderly woman with a wicker shopping basket on wheels was staring at them as she hobbled by. But that was all.

'Can I see you properly?' Connolly asked, even as she was still righting herself.

'No,' Sheba said. She held her bike in front of her, defensively. 'No. Look... Stop it now, please.' She got on her bike.

'Miss,' Connolly pleaded. But she only shook her head and rode away.

Over the following days she began working out possible compromises on what she called 'the Connolly situation'. She would allow Connolly to visit her, on a strictly platonic basis, once a week. No, once a fortnight. Or perhaps there would be no limit on the number of times he could visit her but she would restrict their conversation to matters relating to art. After a week, Connolly came to her again. She was just leaving her studio when he came running up to her and thrust a note into her gloved hand. Without uttering a word, he rushed away again. Upon unfolding the little square of paper, Sheba found a terse, handwritten plea to meet him on Hampstead Heath the following night at seven p.m.

For the next twenty-four hours, Sheba debated whether or not to comply with his request. On her way home from school the following afternoon she had made up her mind, she says, to ignore the note. Clearly the boy was intent on a romantic relationship with her. The only thing to do was to keep him at a distance. But as soon as Richard arrived home, she heard herself telling him that her old school friend Caitlin was up from Devon for the night, and that she had made plans to see her. She felt that she had to go, she says now. She had to explain to Connolly, in person, why their friendship could not continue and why his advances had to stop.

Sheba rode to the Heath on her bicycle. She chained her bike to the railings and walked up the path to the pond. It was a large place for such an assignation, and she felt sure that she and Connolly would miss each other. She remembers being struck by the depth of her own disappointment. And then, suddenly, Connolly appeared before her. He seemed younger and smaller than usual that evening, she says. As always, he was not wearing enough clothes. He expressed surprise that she had come. He had been sure, he told her, that she would 'chicken out'. Sheba explained gravely that she was there only because she had been worried by the tone of his note. There was no hope of 'anything happening' between the two of them, she said.

Connolly responded with surprising calm. He nodded, understandingly, and suggested that they walk together for a bit. Sheba refused. That wouldn't be a good idea, she said. But when a man with a dog appeared on the path and glanced at the two of them curiously, she changed her mind. Connolly was behaving so sensibly and maturely, it was bound to be all right, she told herself.

As they set off up the path, Connolly promised not to 'try anything on'.

'I should hope not!' Sheba said, amused by his presumption.

But even as she said that, it occurred to her that perhaps he *would* try something on. Perhaps, she thought, he had plans to rape her. She kept walking anyway. She had begun to feel 'detached' from the proceedings, she recalls, 'as if I had become my own rather heartless biographer'.

As they approached an area of the Heath that was more densely wooded, Connolly turned to her, clasped her hands in his, and began walking backwards, into the trees, pulling her along with him. 'Come on. In here,' he said.

'What are you doing?' Sheba asked, but she allowed herself to be pulled. It was much darker here than it had been on the path. She could barely see Connolly's face. A fairy-tale image came to her, she says, of a goblin dragging a princess back to his forest lair.

They continued to walk for another minute or so, and then, just as Sheba was about to protest again, Connolly stopped and released her from his grip. They were standing in a little clearing. Connolly grinned at her. 'We can be private here,' he said. Then he sat down, and took off his jacket, so that she could sit on it. Sheba told him he would freeze to death. But he just sat, looking at her.

'This is ridiculous,' she said. 'I'm not going to sit down. It's just not on.' Connolly was silent for a while. And then, to her surprise, he lay back on the ground and shut his eyes.

'You're going to catch pneumonia like that,' she said. But he didn't reply. She looked down at him, feeling sillier and sillier. Eventually he opened his eyes. 'Fuck, it *is* cold isn't it?' he said. This made her laugh, apparently. Then she said, 'I'm afraid I shouldn't have come. I'm going to go back now.'

Connolly sat up. 'No you're not,' he said.

She remembers smiling at him, knocking her arms against her sides like a little girl. And then she sat down.

They did not have sex on this occasion. It was far too cold, according to Sheba, and she was far too anxious. I know that they kissed. And Connolly must have lain on top of her at some point, because in speaking of this encounter, Sheba has mentioned having been astonished by how 'light and narrow' Connolly was. (She was accustomed, no doubt, to her husband's more substantial girth.) I also know that at a certain point in the proceedings, Sheba asked something woe-struck and rhetorical along the lines of, 'What are we doing?' To which Connolly responded with a terse reassurance in the vein of, 'Don't worry about it.' Sheba thought he sounded terribly grown up and capable. She knew he was neither of these things, of course. But she seems to have taken comfort in the illusion.

Going home that night, Sheba was convinced that she would not be able to face Richard without presenting some physical manifestation of her sin. She pictured herself dissolving in tears. Fainting. Spontaneously combusting. But when she arrived at her house she surprised herself with how expertly she dissembled. Richard had waited up for her. He was lying on the sofa, watching *Arts Tonight*. He held up his hand in greeting when she entered the living room, but continued squinting at the television. I've seen Richard watching television once or twice. He has a particular way of turning his head away from the screen and looking at it sidelong. Sheba says that this has something to do with his bad eyesight. But to me, it's always seemed a fitting manifestation of Richard's generally superior attitude: it is as if he is trying, in his pompous way, not to let the telly know that he's interested.

'God, you won't believe what crap these people are talking,' he said. They were both quiet for a moment, watching the panel discussion. After a while he turned to her and asked her if she'd had a nice time. Sheba looked away, pretending to inspect split ends in the mirror. No, she told him, it had been a rather dull evening. She hadn't planned to say that, she recalls, but somehow, when it came to it, grumpiness seemed easier to pull off than enthusiasm. 'Oh dear,' Richard said. He was only half listening. Sheba told him she was going to bed and he humphed. Then, just as she grasped the door handle, he looked up again. 'So how's Caitlin?' he asked.

'Oh, okay,' Sheba said. 'Actually a bit lumpy and mumsy these days.' She beamed out silent apologies to her innocent friend.

'Well,' Richard said yawning, 'that's what life in the provinces does to a person.'

'Yes,' Sheba said. 'Probably.' She paused a moment and then, when Richard did not reply, she opened the door. 'Okay, I'm off upstairs,' she said. 'I'm knackered.'

The next day, at the end of school, Connolly came to her studio again. Sheba had been telling herself all day that she was going to send him away. There was a brief, awkward struggle when he first walked in. And then she changed her mind and let him kiss her.

'You know, Steven,' she said, after a while, 'it's very, very important—incredibly important—that we keep this secret. You haven't said anything to anybody, have you?'

He assured her, indignantly, that he had not. 'I mean,' he added, 'apart from my mates and that.'

Sheba looked at him, thunderstruck. He looked back at her for a long moment. Then he laughed. 'Fooled ya,' he said.

Sheba was quiet. She put her hands on his shoulders and studied his grinning face. She told him never to joke about this. She told him that it could be very difficult keeping a secret and that one of these days he might feel tempted to confide in someone, but that even if he thought the person trustworthy—even if they swore on their mother's grave not to tell—he was never to say anything.

'I'm not like that,' he protested. 'I wouldn't grass on you.'

'Grass on *us*,' Sheba corrected him. 'You would be in a lot of trouble, too, you know.' She knew this was probably untrue, but she thought it best to give him as much incentive as possible for keeping quiet. Connolly stood before her, twisting his head from side to side just as he had done the first time they met. 'Come on,' he said gruffly, 'let me kiss you.'

Shortly after that they repaired to the far end of the room and there, behind the kiln, they engaged in their first act of sexual intercourse. 'Everyone always wants to know, How could I?' Sheba said to me once. 'You know, What made me do it? But it was easy. Like saying yes to another drink when you know you're going to have a hangover tomorrow, or taking a bite of a doughnut, when you know it's going to give you fat thighs. You keep saying *No, no, no,* until you say, *Oh bugger it. Yes.*'

It's hard, I tell her, to explain such drastically incautious behaviour, other than as a symptom of sexual obsession. But Sheba always objects to that phrase. She says that it places undue emphasis on the carnal aspect of her relations with Connolly. The remorseless vulgarity of the press coverage has made her defensively high-minded. She wants it to be known that she and Connolly were not merely engaged in 'kinky romps' and 'sex sessions': they were *in love*.

Just after the scandal broke, a *Sunday Express* reporter ambushed Connolly outside his house and asked him what had drawn him to his teacher. Connolly, in what is his sole public statement about the affair to date, replied, 'I fancied her, didn't I?' before being whisked by his mother into his father's waiting cab. The line is now famous. I understand it has even become a kind of humorous catchphrase in the media. For Sheba, however, it is a terrible humiliation. When she first heard it, it seemed to her that Connolly was wilfully belittling their romance—disowning his true feelings in order to gratify the coarse expectations of the tabloids. She has since forgiven him. He didn't know how it would sound, she says. But the quotation itself— and the widespread perception that the relationship was the smutty stuff of *Carry On* films—remains a very sore point.

There were a few occasions, she will acknowledge, when the two of them only had time to make love hurriedly before parting again. But such encounters were unsatisfactory to both of them, she insists. They were always looking for opportunities to spend 'real' time with one another. Connolly had a pager and whenever Sheba found herself with an unforeseen spare moment, she would call him. It was difficult to make time for proper outings, without arousing the suspicion of their respective families, but, even so, they managed it on at least three occasions.

Once they went to the National Portrait Gallery. Another time, they went to a West Indian restaurant in Hammersmith. (She made Connolly eat goat for the first time.) Once, for reasons that history does not relate, they visited Hampton Court. On each of these occasions, they took taxicabs, she says, and always laughed with slightly hysterical relief when the cab drivers pulled up, revealing themselves not to be Connolly's father. Inside, they would press themselves into a corner and pretend that the driver could not see them while they groped and panted at each other all the way to their destination.

I sense from what Sheba has told me that these dates, beneath their surface larkiness, were rather tense for her. In the classroom, or on the Heath with Connolly, Sheba could believe that theirs was a beautiful, forbidden love—something sweet and healthy and, if only the circumstances were tweaked, infinitely viable. Out in the world, however, she was forced to recognize their radical oddness as a couple. Once, as they were walking down St Martin's Lane together—this was their National Portrait Gallery trip—she caught a glimpse of their reflection in a shop window. It took a moment before she made the connection that the bony, middle-aged housewife clutching the hand of her teenaged son was *her*.

At the restaurant in Hammersmith, Connolly apparently requested a sickly cocktail to go with his curry. Sheba suggested he have a soft drink instead, or a lager, but he was insistent—he wanted his rum and coke—and she did not press the matter. She could hardly hector the boy about the dangers of strong drink, she felt, when she was about to take him to the park for sex.

Early on in the affair, Sheba started buying underwear for herself— nylon flowery things, intended for girls her daughter's age. She kept them at the back of her underwear drawer and only put them on when she knew she would be seeing Connolly. Once, she says, while she was picking through a bin of thongs in the noisy basement of an Oxford Street boutique, she looked up to see Diana Selwood, the wife of one of Richard's colleagues, approaching her. Diana was with her teenage daughter, Tessa. Sheba stepped back from the bin and folded her arms. She greeted Diana and they chatted for a while about their children and husbands. Then Diana looked down at the bin. 'Golly, Sheba,' she said. 'I take my hat off to you. I stopped bothering with fancy underwear years ago. How the hell do you wear these things?'

'God, no idea,' Sheba said, staring blankly at the floral scraps. 'I thought they were headscarves to tell you the truth.'

Connolly was always cooing over her beauty in those first months—stroking her hair, placing his beefy little arm around her waist and marvelling at its narrowness. Encouraged by his worshipfulness, Sheba took to wearing more cosmetics. Richard had never cared for make-up, but Connolly responded in the most gratifying way to the artifice. The first time that Sheba arrived for one of their assignations sporting red glossy lips and kohl around her eyes, she recalls Connolly's mouth sagging in wonderment.

'What is it?' she asked. 'The war paint?'

'You look just like a model,' Connolly whispered.

The affair did not have any immediate, adverse effect on her marriage, she claims. On the contrary, she says, her relationship with her husband was actually enhanced during those first few months. The nights on which she came home late from being with Connolly, she was struck by how warmly affectionate she felt towards Richard. Picking up the underpants that he had abandoned on the bathroom floor, or gently retrieving a container of dental floss from his sleeping hand, she felt neither resentful nor guilty: just grateful for the cosy fact of her husband's existence. It was comforting, after her strange, chilly assignations on the Heath, to climb into the warmed marriage bed—to feel Richard's body shift sleepily to clasp hers. On the nights when he wanted to make love, she submitted without protest. It didn't seem so awful at the time, she says, to go from her lover to her husband in the same evening. It seemed quite natural. She always showered before she got into bed. And she still liked Richard that way. These things don't just switch off, she says. □

GRANTA

THE ROLLERCOASTER CHAMPION OF THE WORLD
Andrew Martin

Richard Rodriguez (centre left) with Andrew Martin

The Rollercoaster Champion

I should have gone to Coney Island. I can imagine Americans reading this and saying: 'The guy's writing about coasters, and he's never been to Coney. He's never ridden the Cyclone!' Then again, everyone I spoke to advised me *not* to go, at least not alone, not on the subway.

I had always somehow known that Coney was once the rollercoaster capital of America, and I knew it was in decline. When I thought of it, I imagined a David Lynch world of gnarled hucksters, exploding coloured light bulbs and sweetness gone rotten. Such images came to mind the very moment my wife burst into my study to tell me about a question that had just been asked on the quiz show, *University Challenge*: 'Who holds the world record for spending the longest time on a rollercoaster?' I had no idea, but it came as no surprise to learn that the record-holder—Richard Rodriguez—was from Brooklyn, where Coney is located. His debut record was set on the Coney Island Cyclone in August 1977: 103 hours and fifty-five minutes.

Everything Richard said when I first spoke to him on the phone confirmed the importance of this particular coaster. 'It stands alone across the street from Astroland Amusement Park... It is a landmark ride of New York City. They can never tear it down.' They've torn down most of the other coasters built at Coney in the Twenties, most recently—just last year—the Thunderbolt, a coaster Richard told me I would have seen in some flashback sequences in *Annie Hall*: Alvy Singer (Woody Allen) grows up in a noisy house directly underneath it. But the Cyclone remains, and is Richard's favourite coaster. 'It has a steep angle, camelback, you know, lots of tight horseshoe turns. If you and I were to get on a plane tomorrow and go on the Cyclone, you would say, "Rich, this is a damn thrilling ride." And that's *today*, but think about 1927...'

I first shook hands with Richard in February this year in a bar in downtown Chicago; he's doing a doctorate in educational psychology at the city's Loyola University. The bar was pretty noisy, and I didn't get down all he said in that short, preliminary meeting. I remember his opening remark though, made after he had, with characteristic politeness, apologized about twenty times for being five minutes late: 'There is a serious side to the riding of rollercoasters.'

He told me of his interests in boxing, in ballooning—hot air and helium—and in Charles Lindbergh, who had ridden the Cyclone and reputedly declared it more thrilling than being in the cockpit of the *Spirit of St Louis*. As he spoke, I thought how much Richard himself looked like a flyer: at forty-three he is symmetrical and compact, like Scott Tracy, the handsomest of those idealized pilots in *Thunderbirds*. Unlike Scott Tracy, he talks fast, and is obviously very bright.

We stepped out of the bar, but the cacophony continued because we were now standing under the L—the railway on stilts that circles Chicago—which is itself quite coaster-like. Richard said something about 'romantic adventure in the modern world', and told me he had 'a thing' coming up in Holiday Park, an amusement park near Frankfurt, Germany: he intended to spend the entire summer, day after day, week after week, on one of the new breed of metal megacoasters that have done so much to revive the fortunes of amusement parks after the bad post-war years. We agreed to keep in touch by phone in the meantime.

Coney Island had come up a lot in our conversation, but another place had also been mentioned frequently: the Pleasure Beach at Blackpool. It was strange to hear those words spoken in a Chicago bar. Why, I knew the Pleasure Beach. Visits there had been the centrepiece of several holidays in my childhood in the north of England. I had been on plenty of the rides, although I'd never braved the coasters. My limit was the Log Flume, an enjoyable but fairly sedate matter of riding a plastic log along some water chutes. Part of the deal on the Log Flume circa 1975 was that a man took your picture as you came down the last drop. I had accepted my photograph politely enough, but soon arranged for it to be lost, because it had shown me screaming with delight, and I was ashamed of looking anything other than blasé on the Log Flume.

Today, if you include the kiddie coaster and the Wild Mouse, there are ten rollercoasters at Blackpool Pleasure Beach. I was most interested in the oldest, the Big Dipper, on which Richard had established five coaster marathon records, and the newest, the Pepsi Max Big One, one of the new megacoasters of the kind he would be riding in Germany during his forthcoming record-breaking marathon. I decided I would go and see him in Germany halfway through his record-breaking attempt, but first I would acclimatize myself to his world with a visit to Blackpool.

The Rollercoaster Champion

In 1978, a Dr Russell Nye told an American coaster conference that coasters are 'mirrors and parodies of transportation'. Certainly, they developed in parallel with trains, and a preposterously good example of this is the Mauch Chunk railway, which was arguably both America's first railway, and its first rollercoaster.

The Mauch Chunk gravitational railway was built in 1827 to transport coal from coal mines atop Mount Pisgah down to the Lehigh River at Mauch Chunk in Pennsylvania. It was being ridden for thrills almost immediately: coal in the mornings, day trippers in the afternoon. In 1884 LaMarcus A. Thompson, an engineering prodigy who had made a butter churn for his mother when he was twelve and ridden the Mauch Chunk as a tourist, erected the first true rollercoaster in America; at Coney Island, of course. Early coasters manifested a fascination with tunnels, and out of this developed what are known in the amusement park business as 'dark rides'—ghost trains and variants. In 1906 a kind of rollercoaster was constructed at Coney Island that might have been an early satire on motoring. People were put in small circular cars, and pushed down a slope cluttered with padded obstacles with which they would, if they were unlucky (or lucky), collide.

But if rollercoasters and conventional transport were once neck and neck, coasters have long since streaked ahead. There is, for example, one through train a day from London to Blackpool, and it takes three and a half hours to cover a distance of less than 250 miles, operating difficulties permitting. Meanwhile the Pepsi Max Big One is subjecting its victims to 3.5 Gs and speeds of nearly ninety miles per hour.

My first view of the Big One was from a taxi driving along Blackpool seafront. It was early June 2002, and Richard's marathon in Germany had been under way for a week, so I approached the megacoaster knowing he was on a similar ride at that very minute. The Pepsi Max Big One dominates the front at Blackpool, which is the least it can do with a name like that. Its first hill is 235 feet high, and for a few months after its opening in 1990 it was the tallest coaster in the world, until it was outdone by one in Japan. That's the way things go in the megacoaster world, which Richard dates from the construction of the Magnum XL-200 at a park called Cedar Point in Sandusky, Ohio in 1988.

Andrew Martin

The American comedian Steven Wright tells a funny story where he's given a lift by a deranged motorist, who says, 'Do you mind if I try something? I saw it in a cartoon, but I think it can work,' and that's what the first, sixty-five degree drop of the Big One looks like: something for Roadrunner to contend with. Yet every five minutes real people come over the brow of that hill, with a dull roar of metal on metal, intermingled with screaming. I knew I was doomed to experience the drop myself, and as a natural Log Flumer (i.e. easily scared) I felt the urge to get it over with straight away, but my first appointment was with the Big Dipper.

The older, wooden coasters at the Pleasure Beach are all sort of tangled up together beneath the Pepsi Max. To board the Big Dipper you walk beneath a wooden onion dome, past a fountain with dyed blue water. Next to the fountain is a plaque announcing that the Dipper was built in 1921, and is historically significant; next to this are plaques commemorating Richard's Dipper marathons. The first took place in early June 1979. At this point, apart from his debut on the Cyclone, Richard had ridden the Swamp Fox at Grand Strand Amusement Park, Myrtle Beach, South Carolina for 110 hours in June 1978 and, the following month, the Rebel Yell at Paramount's King's Dominion Park, Richmond, Virginia for 124 hours.

In 1979 he rode the Big Dipper for 140 hours and twenty-nine minutes, and to get some idea of the achievement, I climbed aboard.

The Dipper looks like the standard idea of the Loch Ness monster: a series of humps. Like the Cyclone it is a classic wooden coaster, a 'woodie', the sort that coaster clubs love. It gives you a lot of what coaster club members call 'air time', time spent in the air, bounced up from your seat—although not, ideally, out of it— by the negative G forces that come as you begin the descents. (Positive G forces, which come as you begin ascents, compress you into the seat). After one two-minute circuit of the Dipper, I felt thrilled to have graduated from Log Flume kindergarten but I knew I hadn't acquitted myself with much style. I was terrified of being pitched out of my seat and so didn't dare let go of the metal bar holding me firmly in, and I wasn't able to smile back when a fellow passenger smiled at me at the end of the ride. By my reckoning, Richard did the same trip almost 4,000 times during his first Big Dipper marathon.

The Rollercoaster Champion

It should be explained that most of Richard's records have been done under what he and the *Guinness Book Of Records* call the '60/5 rule'. He's allowed one five-minute break every hour—if he wants twenty minutes he must put in four straight hours first. The coasters are kept going all night, and Richard sleeps on them, cocooned in a nest of foam. Sometimes he wears a crash helmet. Richard has never had any problem sleeping on rollercoasters. He finds the steep drops 'quite lulling'. The Big Dipper is certainly no kiddie coaster, but the top speed is only thirty-five mph and a crash helmet is not required; Richard told me he could even read on it: 'Well, you couldn't get into any real literature, but you could look at the pictures.' Every day the crew brought him a copy of *USA Today*. He was allocated a lavatory and rest quarters in an anonymous building next to a nearby kiddie ride called the Grand Prix, where he took his meals.

When he was preparing for his debut marathon on the Cyclone, Richard went to a dietitian to ask him how he might survive without eating solids, an idea that lasted 'about two minutes'. He found he liked to feel full on a coaster, so now he eats frankfurters, hamburgers, milkshakes and so on—'park food'.

During the marathons, any member of the public is allowed to sit beside him, pretty girls especially. At night, when he's not sleeping, he talks to the operating crews, who'll ride with him for a while. Richard is proud of his relationship with the Blackpool Dipper crews—he feels he's bridged a big cultural gap—but looking around the clamorous Pleasure Beach after my Big Dipper ride I wasn't so sure. Even though at any given moment it is full of spindly Northerners eating chips, there's an American energy about the place. All the staff seem to be snappy and smart; the men have short hair and wear ties. You might walk past a candy floss stall and although there's nobody waiting to be served the man behind the counter will be frenziedly whirling the floss on to the sticks, accumulating a stockpile in anticipation of a rush. Most of the Pleasure Beach coasters were designed by Americans. The Pleasure Beach's founder, William George Bean, the dynamic son of a Thames lighterman, was inspired by a visit he made to Coney Island, and opened its British equivalent in 1896—the present managing director, Geoffrey Thompson, is Bean's grandson. I imagine the Pleasure Beach is to Coney Island what Tommy Steele is to Jerry Lee Lewis, but Richard Rodriguez loves it, and after setting three more records in America in 1979, he returned to the Big Dipper in 1980. He did 209 hours on it in June.

The big question with Richard Rodriguez is obvious, really: why? As a child he was afraid of coasters. He would ride the fairly mild Tornado at Coney (he didn't brave the Cyclone until he was sixteen) but only with his mom on one side and his dad on the other. When he was nine, though, his parents divorced, and thereafter he went to Coney with his uncle Tommy or either parent, but never again both, the result being that Coney means to him, in microcosm, what it seems to mean to the whole of America: lost innocence. This is his root connection to rollercoasters.

At high school Richard was an excellent student—long before he began the coaster marathons he was known as 'Bookathon'. He started a degree in medicine at the University of Pennsylvania, but gave it up after the first semester. It was like the divorce again. 'I felt I had left my friends behind, I felt alienated, shocked.' In 1977 he was working as a runner on Wall Street when the fiftieth anniversary of Lindbergh's flight across the Atlantic prompted a series of newspaper articles. Reading about Lindbergh, Richard thought he would like to have a go at flying, so he looked up aviation in the Yellow Pages, but before he got to AV he found AM—AM for amusement parks, which means, if you happen to live in Brooklyn, Coney Island. He recalled reading of a man who in 1968 had set a record by riding a rollercoaster for about eight hours, the first ever coaster marathon; he thought about Lindbergh, thought about the Cyclone, and stopped leafing through the phone book there and then because this would do; in fact it was a very happy elision. It was a romantic adventure in the modern age.

When he did his first marathon people he knew from high school showed up at the Cyclone to say hello, and he liked that. 'When you're from a divorced family you feel an outsider, an outcast, and this was a way of my getting attention and setting myself apart.'

By 1983, Richard's record stood at 384 hours, but later that year he encountered his first, and so far only rival in a French Canadian fireman called Norman St Pierre who spent 502 hours on a coaster at Belmont Park, Montreal. Shortly after hearing of this feat Richard retired from coaster marathons for ten years, not out of despair at being bested but because he was finally getting round to his bachelor's degree, this time at Columbia University. It wasn't until 1994—by which time he was teaching history at schools in Chicago—that the St Pierre record began to bug him.

After arranging a relatively brief residency on the Cyclone in order to reacquaint himself with the motion of a coaster, Richard got in touch with the managing director of Blackpool Pleasure Beach again. 'Mr Thompson was very gung-ho. I went 549 hours on the Big Dipper.'

In 1998 he decided to try for 600 hours. He cleared his diary, the his room near the kiddie ride was prepared, *USA Today* ordered, and then it emerged that Norman St Pierre was going for another record at the same time, on a coaster called La Monstre at La Ronde Park, Montreal. It became an international coaster competition. 'They did it on all the shows,' Richard told me, '*MSNBC*, *The Jay Leno Tonight Show*. We had these satellite hook-ups. Norman would call up from the park in Montreal, and I would be on the platform of the Big Dipper, and it was like Frasier and Ali, when Ali says, "You're going down."' Except that, this being Richard, it was more like 'You're going down, if that's all right with you.'

St Pierre stopped at 670 hours. 'He got off, I kept going,' Richard told me. 'I said I'd like to shoot for a thousand hours.' It should come as no surprise that Richard achieved his thousand hours. In the immediate afterglow, he talked to Geoffrey Thompson, who casually enquired, 'What about 2,000 hours in the year 2000?'

In 2000, Richard duly did 2,000 hours on the Big Dipper. 'That was a long time—three months on a coaster. I mean, you're *living* on a rollercoaster. Your body gets tired.'

I asked him how he coped, and he replied laconically: 'You pad the car out with the help of the crew, you know. You talk about football with the crew, you talk about America, talk about England.'

After my ride on the Big Dipper, but before my ride on the Pepsi Max Big One—the prospect of which was beginning to get me down—I went to meet Geoffrey Thompson. He was ebullient and disarming: half circus ringmaster, half Cambridge-educated economist. He works at a desk the size of a banqueting table in the beautiful art deco Pleasure Beach offices, untroubled by the round-the-clock cackling just outside his window of 'The King of Fun', an animated and loudly amplified mannequin dressed in regal clothes.

Knowing I was going to see Richard on the megacoaster in Germany, Mr Thompson wanted to pass on his best. 'In a place like this we live for publicity,' he explained, and Richard's marathons had attracted a lot of it, especially his last one, during which he had raised £25,000 for a charity called Give Kids The World. While the marathon was in progress, Mr Thompson's publicity people had pumped out press releases about Richard being the rollercoaster king, explaining that he was engaging in the equivalent of a coaster ride to Australia and back. (Richard himself, however, had been a bit vague about some aspects of the hype: at one point he'd been joined on the Dipper by a professional football team—he couldn't say which one.) I told Mr Thompson I'd been reading about coasters, and mentioned the idea that they were parodies of transportation. 'I'd say that was crap really,' he said, after a pause for consideration. 'A coaster symbolizes spring. It's the excitement and fun, with the spring wind in your hair... A chance to cuddle your girlfriend all in the fullness of spring.'

I was then introduced to a young Pleasure Beach employee called Laura, who would be my chaperone on the megacoaster. She had ridden the Big One hundreds of times, implying a tremendous confidence in it that was surely, I fretted, ripe for puncturing. I went through the turnstiles in a daze, only half aware of the recorded announcements: 'Welcome to the Pleasure Beach. You are about to ride the highest and fastest rollercoaster in the world', or something like that, something almost-but-not-quite strictly accurate.

Laura led me to the front seat of the coaster, explaining that this was the most frightening position and therefore the most fun. A klaxon sounded and we started our ascent of the first hill. The safety ratchets that prevent roll-back clattered behind us. These create the clanking chain noise that coaster fans love, but to me the sound had all the balefulness of Marley's chains in *A Christmas Carol*. The ascent was slow—first hill ascents generally are, to allow you think about what you've let yourself in for. 'You don't need a degree in engineering to design rollercoasters,' said the American coaster engineer John Allen, 'you need a degree in psychology.'

At the summit I was eyeball to eyeball with a Civil Aviation Authority Approved aircraft warning beacon. 'You can see Southport from here,' said Laura happily. Then we went over the top, and I was inhabiting one of those falling nightmares. I think I shut my eyes halfway down, and they stayed that way for the rest of the eighty-mph ride.

I still felt shaken—though also elated—an hour later, as I sat on the slow train back to London with half a bottle of wine. Basically I was celebrating not being on a rollercoaster.

Why had I ridden the Pepsi Max? In the interests of research. Why do regular coaster users ride coasters? There are many answers. Coaster histories tend to start with the sporting events of Ancient Greece, or the gladiators in the Coliseum, some token acknowledgement that humans have always sought excitement, but they rapidly home in on sledging, the original gravity ride.

The first rollercoasters were sledging plus technology plus leisure time. In the late eighteenth century the public around St Petersburg could go on ice slides known as Russian Mountains. Fir trees enclosed the slides; some had Chinese pagodas on top. According to *The Incredible Scream Machine* by Robert Cartmell, there was a wheeled coaster in St Petersburg by 1784, but it was the French who were the pioneers in this field. A highly dangerous wheeled coaster, Les Montagnes Russes, was built in the Ternes quarter of Paris in 1804. Some riders were injured, which only increased its popularity. About ten years later the Niagara Falls, an ancestor of the Log Flume, was constructed in Ruggiery Gardens, Paris. It involved a boat car being pushed at tremendous speed into an artificial river, and was preceded by a very elemental notice: THE POLICE WOULD NOT HAVE PERMITTED THIS AMUSEMENT IF IT COULD JEOPARDIZE THE LIVES OF ITS CITIZENS.

Do people ride coasters because they know they're dangerous or because they know they're safe? The popularity of the lethal Les Montagnes Russes suggests the former, the sign at the Niagara Falls the latter. I would say it has to be the latter, that coasters are a celebration of our trust in technology. It takes a churlish sort like me to actually peer under the cars to verify the presence of the 'under-friction wheels', which clamp the cars to the tracks.

In any event the French did not seriously pursue rollercoasting. Who knows why not? I associate coasters firstly with a reasonable degree of prosperity (they are surplus to requirements if your daily life is a struggle to survive), and secondly with a culture that sanctions the expression of emotions. France has the first, but possibly not the second; the United States has both. Coasters boomed in the States until the Great Depression, suggesting that— unlike alcohol—they complement good times but do not distract from bad ones. Between 1930 and 1972, 2,000 amusement parks disappeared across the States and almost as many coasters. They were pulled down, burned or left to become lonely, dark skeletons. The amusement parks that survived were thought of as tawdry and dangerous, a notion Walt Disney sought to counteract with his wholesome Disney World.

Disney World was a big factor in the revival of amusement parks, along with the megacoasters which were enabled by greater understanding—through computer modelling—of what the human frame can stand. Mention of which reminds me that I ought to modify an earlier remark: strictly speaking, only the first half of my half bottle of wine on the train back from Blackpool was drunk to celebrate no longer being on the Big One; the second half was drunk to ward off my terror about the one coming up, the one Richard was riding at that very moment, the megacoaster in Holiday Park near Frankfurt: the Ge Force.

As it turned out my worries were fully justified, although my thoughts on entering Holiday Park—a much more countrified affair than the Pleasure Beach—were not initially on the megacoaster, but on dwarfs. Geoffrey Thompson had asked me to pass on his regards to the Schneider family, Holiday Park's owners, and had mentioned in passing that they had once run an all-dwarf circus, some of the performers from which had been retained. Within seconds of my arrival in Holiday Park, however, all such whimsy was banished. My host, Mr Beitz, looked up and waved; at once I heard the thunder of the megacoaster, saw the coaster cars flying on their orange metal tracks above the tree tops, caught sight of Richard sitting in the middle of the coaster train. He was the only one not waving his arms in the air and screaming with delight. Instead, he looked *wryly amused*. I glanced back and saw the first drop of the Ge Force, the one Richard had just come down: eighty-two degrees, and twisted.

When the coaster had passed, a man wearing clown's make-up sauntered by on stilts. I looked at the ride we were standing alongside. It was called the Tour des Fleurs (don't ask me why it's in French): a small train on a five foot high monorail nosing past some pretty floral displays at about three mph. I wanted to stay looking at this peaceful scene but Mr Beitz was urging me on towards the Ge Force for my rendezvous with Richard.

As we approached the ride we passed the motor home where Richard took his breaks, and many medical warning signs. You were not to board the Ge Force if you had back problems, heart or nervous difficulties, or if you were too fat. Why couldn't Richard be doing his record on the Tour des Fleurs? Physical defects were no problem on that—the more the better.

The coaster cars were in the station as we arrived. A member of the crew was placing a paper cup of black coffee on the running board of Richard's car as he signed bags, flesh, T-shirts, and autograph books for the crowd of coaster riders around him. His seat was not at this point padded, and the only things to mark him out were his windburned face, and a shirt with badges on the epaulettes announcing his GE FORCE MARATHON. I had rehearsed meeting Richard on the Ge Force many times. 'Hi, Richard,' I would say, 'Obviously there's no need for me to come on with you. I can get a much more objective impression of the ride if I stay on the ground and watch.' But in the end I just capitulated, and stepped into the seat of honour, the one next to Richard. We fastened our seat belts, the klaxon sounded and the coaster began to climb the hill. His fans behind him, Richard turned his attention to me, shaking my hand, asking how my journey had been. As we climbed, I said something—something not very coherent. Between Richard's knees, I noticed, was a rolled up copy of the New York Herald Tribune.

Mr Beitz contends that the Ge Force—opened in 2001—is the most ferocious coaster in Europe, and the second most frightening in the world, behind only the Superman Ride of Steel at a park called Six Flags New England in Agawam, Massachusetts. A feature of the Ge Force that the purists do not like is the lack of the clanking chain noise. A feature they do like is the seven occasions during the ride on which you experience negative Gs. That's a lot of air time. You're whisked quite rapidly to the top of the first hill. As we went over the top (from where, incidentally, you can see a range of presumably quite famous German hills) I realized that, compared to the Ge Force, the Pepsi Max Big One presents only an approximation of the falling nightmare. The Ge Force is its precise equivalent, and you appreciate that its defining characteristic is the sensation of going down and also, thanks to the negative Gs, forwards. This is the true meaning of 'headlong'.

Richard had told me that the Ge Force was a 'lively ride', which, paradoxically, meant that after the first drop there were about six further points when I was absolutely sure I was about to die. I stayed on the coaster with Richard for three circuits, sitting patiently as he signed autographs every time we came into the station, and while the subsequent torments of the Ge Force—the sudden sideways tilts through ninety degrees for example—became more manageable by the third time, the horror of that first drop did not yield.

As I climbed off the Ge Force, I arranged to meet Richard that evening for dinner in a pizza restaurant in Hassloch, the nearest town to Holiday Park, which ought to prompt the wide-awake reader to ask: 'How, if he's supposed to be spending all his time on the coaster?'

'See,' Richard had explained a few weeks earlier, 'this one in Germany is a different category of record—it's about the number of *days* spent on a coaster.' A day is defined as from nine a.m. to seven p.m., again with a five-minute break per hour. The record was inaugurated in 1998 when two men rode the Scream Machine at Six Flags Over Georgia for sixty days. Last year, Richard broke that with one hundred days spent on the Boss at Six Flags St Louis. 'I went May 3 to August 10. I had done more hours but fewer *days* in Blackpool in 2000.' At Holiday Park he is aiming—and the present tense is strictly right because the marathon is ongoing at the time of writing—to do 'something over a hundred days'.

I spent most of the rest of the day in Holiday Park, which is dominated by the Ge Force just as the Pleasure Beach is dominated by the Pepsi Max. As I stared at some flamingos on a pretty ornamental lake, trying to work out if they were real, Richard flew overhead. As I sampled Wiener schnitzel in a mock Bavarian village while idly looking out for dwarfs, Richard rocketed above the nearby tree tops.

In the pizza restaurant that evening, Richard looked a little tired. He explained that while riding the Boss the previous year he had fractured the middle finger of his lateral brace hand, the left, and was still feeling twinges from this, his first injury sustained during a marathon. 'The Boss is a megacoaster but it's wooden, and a wooden coaster really throws you around.' I said never mind the finger, what might the coasters be doing to his brain? Richard grinned: 'I have thought about that, but I've been doing these marathons for twenty-five years... And my doctoral programme is going fine.' Every few days in Holiday Park he is examined by a doctor. 'My blood pressure's 120/8, my pulse is sixty. My heart's better than the doctor's.' He added that he was also being periodically examined by a Dr Pongratz, a colonel in the German air force curious about the effects of prolonged exposure to substantial G forces.

I was tired myself, and our conversation tended to go in circles. I asked how he felt every morning, waking in his rented flat to face that first drop. 'I'm not going to bullcrap you. When I first went on the ride I felt it. But now? I don't feel it. I get my enjoyment out of meeting the people, them saying, "Rich, we saw you last week, you're still going."'

We were back to the social idea of coasters—'a mom and dad family thing', although you'd be hard pushed to find a family all of whose members would agree to ride the Ge Force. I asked Richard whether he liked the fame his marathons had brought him—which is sufficient for him to be asked about on *University Challenge*, but insufficient—if my wife remembers correctly—for the question to be answered correctly or in fact at all. 'I am the only one who does what I do and that has meaning for me. The parks recognize it, some people write about it. But while you get some people saying that's neat, that's kind of cool, others say, "God, that's really *strange*, are you all right?"'

I suggested that the satisfaction he derived seemed to have little to do with the physical act of riding the coasters, but he disagreed. 'See, my kick is the endurance, seeing if I can take it. For me to ride a coaster for one day wouldn't mean anything. The Wright Brothers flew for ten seconds in Kittyhawk in 1903. Lindbergh flew the Atlantic in thirty-three and a half hours. It was the endurance, the phantoms that visited him. I'm not Lindbergh but he certainly inspired me.'

I asked Richard about the phantoms that had visited him on coasters at night, and he mentioned something about dreaming of being with his uncle Tommy at Coney Island. I then suggested that in his marathons he was actually subverting the whole point of a coaster, which is meant to give a single, sudden flash of excitement; I argued that the marathons were akin to the sort of witty conceit dreamed up by conceptual artists wishing to provoke; that they might be taken as meaning that in modern consumer society, we aspire to make intense pleasure the norm. He said, 'That's a good insight...I suppose,' which I suspect is the nearest he would ever get to saying, 'That's rubbish.' I had not meant that he was being disloyal to coaster history, to the legacy of Coney Island, but perhaps he thought that's what I was saying.

When the bill came I apologized for keeping Richard up late, but he was so polite and charming that it was impossible to know whether I really had. It was left open whether I would come and see him again on the Ge Force the next morning, and in the event I decided not to. In his hospitable way, he would only invite me aboard, and I would once again have to master my fear of that first drop—a fear he has entirely transcended. I thought of his uncle Tommy whom I had never met, the Cyclone, which I had never seen, and realized I did not understand Richard Rodriguez. He existed on an entirely different plane to me. But that, I suppose, is the whole point about romantic adventurers, in the modern age or any other.

□

GRANTA

DEAR TYRANT
Riccardo Orizio

TRANSLATED FROM THE ITALIAN BY AVRIL BARDONI

Dear Tyrant

I was writing a book about fallen tyrants. Since my early days as a reporter for Italian newspapers, they have always interested me. What goes through the mind of someone who has had everything and lost it? How does a man grow old with his infamy? What does he tell his grandchildren about himself? What does he tell himself? But the first question, of course, is: how do I persuade them to see me? Ingratiation, unfortunately, is usually the key, but sometimes the courteous letter works and more often it doesn't. My most remarkable reply came from the former Panamanian dictator General Noriega.

General Manuel Antonio Noriega
August 2, 2000

Distinguido Senor Orizio

Thank you for sending me your book about 'Lost White Tribes'. With the help of my dictionaries I am reading this interesting book and today I started the chapter about German slaves in Jamaica.

With reference to your request for an interview in connection with a projected book about certain 'forgotten individuals', once-powerful people who have been blamed for the problems encountered by their respective countries, etc., my response is that I do not consider myself to be a 'forgotten individual', because God, the great Creator of the universe, He who writes straight albeit with occasionally crooked lines, has not yet written the last word on MANUEL A. NORIEGA!

Thank you also for your elegant and generous letter/s of June and also for your telephone call to Don Arturo Blanco.

Respetuosamente,
Manuel Antonio Noriega

But I succeeded, on a different occasion, with Jean-Bédel Bokassa. It was Bokassa, the former self-proclaimed emperor of the Central African Republic, who had set off my interest in the subject of fallen tyrants many years before when I read a report about him in the British *Guardian*. I still have the cutting in my wallet: FORMER EMPEROR GOES HOME AND PROCLAIMS HIS SAINTHOOD. On June 8,

1995 I sat in a large house on the outskirts of Bangui, the capital of the Central African Republic. After some effort I had managed to secure an interview. The house we were in, the Villa Nasser—named for the Egyptian leader—had once been the residence of the Empress Catherine, Bokassa's estranged wife. Now its courtyards were filled with weeds, its walls crumbling, but the small old man in front of me seemed oblivious to the ruin. Bokassa sat on a large white sofa. Behind him a white curtain was pulled across the window, shielding him from the blazing equatorial sun.

Leaning against a white wall at the far end of the room were the last relics of his empire: a gilded throne upholstered in red velvet, and a suit of armour. 'See that?' Bokassa asked me, pointing at the armour with his ivory-tipped cane, the same cane that he had used to beat Michael Goldsmith in 1977, after the English reporter had somehow upset him. With his so-called 'canne de justice' he had beaten Goldsmith until he bled, and then forced him to sign a document in which Goldsmith confessed, quite falsely, to being a South African spy.

'See that?' Bokassa asked again. I took my eyes from the cane to the armour. 'It's medieval. It comes from Spain. General Franco's gift for my coronation. That day all the powerful people had to come to Bangui. For the first time they bowed to an African emperor. Oh yes,' he added with a rapt expression on his face, 'right here in Bangui. And each one had to bring me a magnificent present.' He stopped and looked at me, his eyes shining like a boy's on his birthday. I concentrated on taking notes. He seemed disappointed by my failure to share his delight, but he carried on anyway. 'That day I ceased to be the one who always had to give presents— diamonds, ivory, women... The international leaders respected me because I was an emperor.' He gestured at the suit of armour again, as if the ancient relic contained—besides a handful of African insects baked to a frazzle by the heat—proof of his imperial dignity.

In 1965, Jean-Bédel Bokassa led a military coup against David Dacko, the president of the Central African Republic. He seized control of the government; Dacko was thrown into prison. Having annulled the constitution, Bokassa made himself President, then President for Life in 1972, then Marshal of the Republic in 1974. In 1977 he decided to crown himself Emperor. His coronation was held on December 4, 1977, in the Palais des Sports Jean-Bédel Bokassa, next to Jean-Bédel Bokassa University, on Bokassa Avenue. (The Vatican had refused permission to use the cathedral.) But it had not gone quite as the former emperor remembered it. The absentees had been more notable than the attendees. Despite Bokassa's claim, the coronation had not been the first where the 'civilized world' had bowed to an African emperor. At Haile Selassie's coronation in 1930 the celebrations in Addis Ababa had lasted for three days. All the great powers had sent delegations or members of their royal families, despite the difficult journey. George V's son, the Duke of Gloucester, travelled from London. Prince Eugenio di Savoia came from Rome. Moscow and Washington supplied senior diplomats.

The coronation of Bokassa the First was, by contrast, snubbed even by his fellow autocrats. General Franco stayed away. The Spanish suit of armour travelled alone, by ship. Emperor Hirohito of Japan and Shah Reza Pahlavi of Iran, the first to be invited, made their excuses. Of the 500 foreign dignitaries who did make the journey, the most prominent were a relative of the Prince of Liechtenstein, Count Emmanuel, and the Prime Minister of Mauritius, Sir Seewoosagur Ramgoolam. Even Bokassa's old friends—Idi Amin of Uganda, Mobutu Sese Seko of Zaire and Omar Bongo of Gabon—declined the invitation.

Many of the 'magnificent presents' later turned out to be worthless; only France's gifts were truly substantial. I reminded Bokassa of the French government's generosity to the country they had regarded in colonial days as their 'poor relation'. They had supplied twenty-two million dollars for the coronation. The money had gone towards ceremonial dress for thousands of guests, a throne in the form of a Napoleonic eagle, a gilded imperial carriage with eight white Belgian-trained horses and a crown by the Parisian jeweller, Arthus Bertrand, studded with eighty-carat diamonds. A troop of mounted soldiers in brocade uniforms made especially for the occasion escorted the imperial carriage.

Bokassa also bought 24,000 bottles of Moët & Chandon and 4,000 bottles of Château Mouton-Rothschild and Château Lafite Rothschild. He had sixty Mercedes cars shipped from Germany to Cameroon and then flown 740 miles over the forest of Central Africa to Bangui. He commissioned a French composer to write music for the ceremony. He paid a German artist, Hans Linus, to paint two official portraits of himself.

Bokassa's eyes lit up as he listened to me run through this catalogue of European luxuries that he had had flown into the heart of Africa, luxuries never before seen in Bangui, a town still permeated with the smoky smell of an African village, on the banks of a muddy river filled with hippos.

'All true,' he said, 'but is there anything wrong with that?' It was the least the French could do, he said, to repay him for his services as a soldier who had once fought for France and for all the personal favours he had done for French politicians. 'I am the son of a king. My coronation was organized to give dignity to my country in the eyes of the world. The Central African government did not incur the debt of a single franc for the coronation. I did what any other African king would have done. And if Mobutu and Idi Amin chose not to come, it was because they were jealous of my becoming emperor. Jealous of my idea.'

His eyelids drooped and for a moment I thought he had fallen asleep. A man in a tailcoat tiptoed across the big room towards us, treading warily on the rotten ceramic tiles and flinching whenever one wobbled and grated against its neighbour.

Bokassa opened his eyes at the sound. 'My cabinet secretary,' he explained, jabbing his cane in the man's direction with less enthusiasm than he had jabbed it at the suit of armour. The courtier bowed his head.

Bokassa launched into a tirade against the French. Having spent a few hours in his company I knew this to be a favourite theme. He listed his grievances in a monotonous voice, like a lawyer reading a will whose contents are already known to the family of the deceased.

There was the volte-face of the once-loved adoptive country. He had fought for France in three continents, and what had France done for him in return? Robbed him of his castles, crown and reputation. His 'dear cousin' Valéry Giscard d'Estaing, the former French president, a keen hunter of elephants and women, had betrayed him by backing the coup that in 1979 had ended his reign. Then there was the infidelity of the Empress Catherine, who Bokassa claimed had slept with d'Estaing and—worse—shared some of the imperial treasure with him.

'I fought for France in Indochina—oh yes, Indochina. I fought against the Nazis with the forces of the Free French. I sacrificed my youth to France, even though the French killed my father before my very eyes, right in front of M'Baiki's police headquarters. My father was a chief who opposed the colonial occupation. My mother killed herself shortly afterwards, in desperation. I was six years old. And yet I fought for France for twenty-two years.' He listed his honours: one Croix de Guerre, two Croix de la Résistance, the Légion d'Honneur, an officer's pension. But now he hated the French. 'If I still had those decorations I'd throw them in a dustbin.'

The cabinet secretary began to laugh in an official, practised kind of way. While Bokassa had been berating France, the cabinet secretary had positioned a china tray laden with medicines—small boxes and bottles, all labelled in French—in front of the former emperor, who pretended not to notice. But the cabinet secretary stood resolutely in front of us. Bokassa looked at the tray with disgust. 'I'm very ill, it's difficult for me to move now. I can stand up for two minutes, two seconds, that's all. The French have tried to poison me on several occasions. They did poison me. They have poisoned me.'

The cabinet secretary nodded, and nudged the tray nearer to Bokassa. 'But I survived. Not thanks to the medicines, but thanks to this.' He suddenly picked up a heavy silver cross from the coffee table in front of him and waved it at me. It was about half a metre tall, a solid cross with an emaciated Christ in the centre. 'Paul VI gave this to me when he secretly nominated me thirteenth apostle of Holy Mother Church.'

I looked up from my notebook. Perhaps I hadn't understood properly. Now for the first time I began to appreciate the former emperor's outfit. He was dressed in a white priestly robe that reached down to his flip-flops, with a crucifix hanging on a chain around his neck, not at all the Bokassa I remembered from photographs posing in his glorious 'Marshal of the Republic' uniform. (In one of these pictures, he was standing in his presidential office holding two enormous rough diamonds. He held them delicately between his thumb and forefinger as if they had just appeared from a drawer in the imperial desk.)

At first Bokassa didn't respond to my glance. Another distraction had arrived. A small girl wearing a blue school uniform had run into the room and curled up beside him on the sofa. I assumed she was one of his many daughters—he addressed her as 'Petite'; he had told me earlier that he found it difficult to remember all of their names.

Then, registering my scepticism on the apostolic question, he asked rather angrily if I didn't believe him. The large cross, he said, had been given to him by the Pope during his visit to the Vatican on July 30, 1970. 'Shortly beforehand, he baptized me with a special ceremony in his private chapel. He asked if I was prepared to receive a great honour. I said I was and he celebrated the rite. My role in the Catholic Church has been a special, secret one ever since. When I was in power I acted as a mediator for the Vatican in various conflicts, such as that between Libya and Egypt. After my overthrow, the Vatican offered me political asylum. I refused. When I was in prison here in Central Africa, awaiting execution, and then when I was expecting to serve a life sentence, an Italian missionary, Brother Angelino, visited me. We became friends. He gave me a Bible. For seven years it was the only book I read and it made me realize that my being sent to prison was an act of divine grace. Now that the life sentence has been quashed and I'm free, I'm also poor. I don't possess anything, not a square metre of land nor a single diamond. I don't want anything any more. My only possession is the title of apostle, like Peter and Paul.'

Another lapse into silence. Outside the curtained room the afternoon sun seemed to grow stronger. The cabinet secretary repeated the date of the Vatican visit, presumably to give the revelation greater credibility: July 30, 1970. The former emperor struggled to his feet, and his daughter leaped up to help him. In the silence of the crumbling villa, he repeated, 'The Pope himself gave me this crucifix. Together with my thirteen Bibles, it is the only thing I have left. Everything else—land, decorations, power, women—belongs to the past. This house, Villa Nasser, I have given to my ex-wife, Madame Catherine, even though she doesn't deserve it after her adultery with Valéry Giscard d'Estaing. The man stole my diamonds and my wife. A pirate. He treated me like that because I am an African. But no matter. Today, thanks to divine intervention, I am a man of peace and faith. Inside, I am still His Majesty Bokassa the First, Apostle of Peace and Servant of Jesus Christ, Emperor and Marshal of Central Africa.'

The next day I went with him to court. He wore his white robe and his crucifix, and his hands clasped the larger cross he'd waved at me during our interview. Tucked under his arm was a framed print of Christ. We walked in a small procession—myself, the former emperor and his Christian symbols, several of his children, and, still in tails, the cabinet secretary. A few youths in jeans and sunglasses followed us, sniggering. Passers-by greeted him respectfully. Not far away were the muddy banks of the Obangui river where we could see women washing clothes and fishermen in dugout canoes.

Bokassa was in court to apply for the return of his property, nearly all of which had been confiscated after the bloodless coup of 1979, when d'Estaing's government sent a team of paratroopers to restore David Dacko to power in a mission called 'Operation Barracuda'. Bokassa, who had been visiting Libya at the time, was forced into exile. Now the current government of the Central African Republic were asserting their ownership of his castles in France. The Bokassa clan, led by 'Petite', seated themselves on the public benches. The session was adjourned after only a few minutes.

We trooped back to the Villa Nasser, where Bokassa asked me if I would like to take a photograph of him in uniform. He disappeared into one of his rooms, and then re-emerged into the courtyard in full military rig with the Napoleonic cross of a Marshal on his left breast and seven rows of insignia below it. He once again carried his *canne de justice*, the weapon that had descended upon his ministers, his opponents, and his own children.

Gazing into space, Bokassa recited his autobiography.

'My name is Jean Bédel-Bokassa. I was baptized in 1950 at Fréjus, where my old French regiment was based. I received my baptism as thirteenth apostle on July 30, 1970 from Pope Paul VI. I was president from 1966 to 1976. I was, indeed still am, emperor of Central Africa, being crowned on December 4, 1977. On September 20, 1979 the French removed me from power with a coup d'état. On November 20, 1980 I was condemned to death in absentia. In the same year I was extradited to a prison in the Ivory Coast, then extradited to France, where I remained under supervision for two years before being finally repatriated to Central Africa on November 23, 1986. My trial lasted from November 23, 1986 until June 2,

1987, when I was again sentenced to death. The sentence was subsequently commuted, first to life imprisonment and twenty years' forced labour, then to ten years' forced labour. I was finally freed on September 1, 1993. That is the story of my life, that's who I am. I am Jean-Bédel Bokassa. And I no longer have any political ambitions. The present Central African leader is President Patasse.'

The recitation over, Bokassa hurried indoors and changed back into his priestly robe. 'They gave me this robe in prison. It comes from Jerusalem,' he whispered softly, and then repeated, as if in a reverie, 'From Jerusalem. From Jerusalem.'

The real story of his life was rather different.

After the success of Operation Barracuda, and following the confiscation of his properties in Switzerland and Central Africa, Bokassa applied to his friend Colonel Gadaffi for asylum, but Gadaffi had his hands full with Idi Amin who had just escaped from Uganda and was now a temporary guest in Tripoli. So the French government turned to Felix Houphouet-Boigny, the President of the Ivory Coast, and persuaded him to accommodate the deposed emperor. Bokassa stayed for several months at the elegant Villa Cocody in Abidjan (he was to remain in the Ivory Coast for four years altogether). The Empress Catherine, meanwhile—having anticipated the coup—was already safely installed in Geneva (some said under the personal protection of D'Estaing). She spent much of her time reading tarot cards.

The deposed emperor was in shock. He spent his days playing, at maximum volume, a patriotic record called *Brass Marches and Red Pompon* performed by the band of the French Navy. From Bangui came news of statues pulled down, relatives arrested, houses destroyed, former mistresses fled abroad or absorbed into the harems of the new leaders. Then one day a flamboyant French businessman, Bernard Tapie, telephoned him. A few days later Tapie arrived in Abidjan without an appointment. Having gained entry to the villa by bribing the guards, he informed Bokassa that France was about to confiscate all of his French properties. These included four or five chateaux, a villa in Nice and a hotel in the Loire Valley. These properties were the last remnants of Bokassa's fortune. Apart from them he had nothing. Claiming to have the discreet consent of the

French government and Houphouet-Boigny, Tapie offered to buy the lot for 12.5 million francs. This sum amounted to less than half their actual value, but by seven o'clock that evening Bokassa had signed the contract.

Interviewed by the French press a few days later, Tapie admitted that the story of the imminent confiscation was a bluff and declared that he had 'swindled the brutal Bokassa for the good of France'. The emperor sued and, two years later, won the case: the contract of sale was declared invalid. His French properties were returned to him, though they were later to be confiscated again by the government of the Central African Republic (hence our trip to court during my visit).

This story was not the only one Bokassa omitted from his autobiography. He also left out a discovery that had been made at one of his former residences, the Villa Kolongo. The house stood on the banks of the river in a district called Kilometre 12 outside Bangui. It had been occupied by his Romanian concubine. It was one of Bokassa's favourite residences, with pools, fountains, tropical gardens, an enormous circular rotating bed, ceilings of rare woods and chandeliers of French crystal. When the French paratroopers searched the house they found diamonds in the safe and a museum which Bokassa had devoted to himself, spread across several rooms. And in the gigantic freezer adjacent to the kitchens they claimed to have discovered human cadavers, including those of the leaders of the student organizations that had opposed Bokassa's reign. The paratroops cited this find as 'evidence that [Bokassa] is a cannibal and deserved to be overthrown'.

Bokassa also left out his business dealings, though that would have been an exhausting recitation. He used to describe himself as 'first peasant and first businessman of Central Africa'. In his presidential residences, in Villa Kolongo and Villa Berengo, Bokassa installed workshops producing textiles and copra. He had a butcher's shop and a restaurant, both open to the public. He owned two airlines, two condominiums (Pacifique 1 and Pacifique 2) and a boutique which sold clothes made in a factory belonging to the Empress Catherine. He granted exclusive rights to trade in ivory to a Spanish company, La Couronne, in exchange for a third of the profits. La Couronne slaughtered at least 5,000 elephants every year. Then there was the Central African Republic's diamond trade, at one point run by Bokassa's Lebanese friend, Adrien Geddai, and his Arab associates, Adnan Khashoggi and René Tamraz.

He had also forgotten, to mention the student massacre. Impressed by the orderly cadres of Chinese students he had seen during a visit to Beijing, and angry at his nation's disappointing results in the 1977 French baccalaureate examinations, Bokassa decided to bring a degree of military discipline to the classrooms of the Empire. On February 2, 1978, the Education Ministry announced that from October 1 all schoolchildren would be required to wear uniforms designed by the emperor himself. The girls were to wear dark blue dresses with light blue collars and belts, the boys dark blue trousers and light blue jackets. The uniforms were to be manufactured by the 'Compagnie Industrielle Oubanguienne des Textiles' or CIOT, a company owned by Bokassa, and they could be bought only in certain shops—shops also owned by Bokassa.

The order was largely ignored. Four months later, the Lycée Bokassa and the Lycée Boganda began to turn away children not wearing uniform. On January 15, 1979, 3,000 students took to the streets shouting, 'Bokassa, pay our student grants!' and 'After the Shah, Bokassa!' Reza Pahlavi had just been driven out of Teheran by the ayatollahs. In Kampala Idi Amin was about to go. The students smashed the windows of Pacifique 2 and took over Bangui.

At six in the evening the imperial guard intervened, led by Bokassa in army fatigues. Over the next twenty-four hours 150 students were killed by machine-gun fire. There were protests from Amnesty International and other bodies. Bokassa broadcast a speech rescinding the school uniform law. A few weeks later Giscard d'Estaing offered the Empire of Central Africa a loan of one billion French African francs—from 'cousin' to 'cousin'.

The horror of Bokassa's reign was accompanied by the absurd—two qualities which so often go together. In 1970, he solemnly announced to the nation that he had awarded himself the title of 'Grand Master of the International Brotherhood of Knights Collectors of Postage Stamps'. On November 12, 1970, the day of

General de Gaulle's funeral, he appeared at the Elysée dressed in the uniform of the French parachute regiment. He proceeded to weep noisily in front of de Gaulle's perplexed widow, crying '*Mon père, mon Papa*. I lost my natural father when I was a child. Now I have lost my adoptive father as well. I am an orphan again.' (De Gaulle had always ridiculed him as 'Papa Bock'—*bock* being a beer glass.)

Now he stood in front of me and said: 'God has absolved me. The people of Central Africa have absolved me, too. Now I don't owe anything to anybody. Neither to God nor to the people. We're quits. My people saved me. If the accusations spread by the French about me had been true, I would not be alive today. In Africa one pays with one's life for evil deeds like cannibalism. I obeyed my people. I disobeyed France. They wanted it all their own way, they wanted to sell us their products at hugely inflated prices and buy our raw materials for a pittance. For years the French vetoed the construction of a cement plant in Central Africa in order to export their own cement. The English were different: they colonized in a more honest way. The only Africans in power today are the puppets of France. But you can't build a nation like that. I built up this nation in thirteen years. And that did not please France. And for that they stripped me of power.'

I went back to Villa Nasser the next day, this time with Raphael Kopessoua, a journalist with Central African Radio and the local stringer for the Associated Press. It was thanks to him that Bokassa had agreed to talk to me. 'Come to Bangui,' he had said eventually when I called him from London, 'and I will do what I can to help you.'

Raphael was a quiet and unexpressive man, who only grew animated when describing the many scandals and corruptions he felt characterized the workings of the current Central African administration. Despite the humid heat he invariably wore a jacket and tie and he always carried a leather briefcase. After my first couple of visits to the old emperor, I always took Raphael with me. In the morning I would go and pick him up from the radio station, which had neither windows nor chairs and where the only equipment, so far as I could see, consisted of old-fashioned manual typewriters. Many of his colleagues were related to politicians, he said, and rarely turned up for work. He himself was not so well connected. He was a fervent campaigner for honest government and good leadership—so fervent that he has since spent time in prison for agitating against perceived abuses of power.

Yet Raphael seemed oddly well disposed towards Bokassa. He appeared to regard even his most outlandish statements as tolerable eccentricities. I watched in amazement as he nodded at the former emperor's boast: 'Of all the African leaders I was the greatest. Why? Because I was the emperor. One step below me was the King of Morocco. A king and a great head of state. Then came all the others: simple presidents. I was the emperor...'

In 1978, at the annual summit of Francophone African nations, Bokassa had asked the French government to ensure that he was addressed as 'Your Imperial Majesty' and put first in order of precedence. The French diplomats had refused the request. Only the president of Gabon, Omar Bongo, was in favour, because he too had imperial ambitions.

I tried to press him on the subject of Giscard's diamonds. Why had he given them to him? The emperor looked at me as if I was mad. 'He asked for them. Besides, I was his friend, almost like a relative. He came to Central Africa twice a year. I supplied him with virgin women and virgin territory where he shot dozens of elephants without paying a single franc. Sometimes he came with his mistresses, some famous, some not. And I gave him diamonds. He wanted lots. To give to his mistresses. There you have your answer.'

I returned to the apostle question. He came out with a new revelation. 'At twelve years old, yes, at twelve years old, at twelve... I had three visions of Christ. When I went to Rome I informed the Pope. And he, forty years after the visions, baptized me as an apostle.'

Raphael remained inscrutable. I asked Bokassa about the medals and the jewels, two subjects close to his heart. The emperor replied simply, 'All stolen by the French. Now all I have is this cross.' Then he began to list the names of the French officers who had taken part in Operation Barracuda, accusing them of having appropriated his imperial kepi, his pearls, his clothes. When he got to the end of the list, he said, 'I am prepared to go and live in poverty with my children on the street. This house is Catherine's. Beautiful woman, but with a cold heart.'

He sighed like a boy in love. 'I've had the most beautiful women in the world. So I forgive Catherine, because her beauty was a ray of sunshine in my life. If she comes back I will hand over Villa Nasser and go and live in the market at Kilometre 5.'

The following day Raphael and I hired a car. He was going to show me the former imperial residences. A friend of Raphael's came with us, to act as a driver.

The red earth road out of Bangui took us past the Palais des Sports, where the emperor's coronation had taken place. This was where the presidential guard had held its march pasts. And where, in 1986, Bokassa was tried for the second time by the new government of the Central African Republic. (He was originally tried in absentia in 1980. That trial concluded in the death sentence—later commuted.) The charges against him included cannibalism, misappropriation of public funds and concealment of children's bodies.

I asked Raphael if we could pull over. Tossed to one side of the stadium, under an arch of crumbling concrete, was Bokassa's famous throne. It was rusty but instantly recognizable, three and a half metres high, shaped like a Napoleonic eagle with two huge golden wings. Papa Bock had had it constructed in France and placed in the middle of the stadium for the coronation ceremony, surrounded by ermine pelts and swathes of red velvet. The chair of the throne was carved out of the belly of the eagle. At the coronation, Bokassa sat in his eagle, picked up the crown and put it on his own head, in a conscious imitation of Napoleon's famous gesture at his coronation.

Leaving Bangui we passed Bokassa Stadium. The oval of cracked concrete was deserted. No one in Bangui appeared to play football any more.

Just beyond a roadblock two kilometres outside the capital, we ran over a large porcupine. Raphael got out and dumped it into the boot of the car. 'Delicious roasted,' he said.

The eighty-kilometre road between Bangui and Berengo was built by Bokassa in the 1970s. It was the country's first and only motorway, now reduced to a potholed single lane. In the course of a two-hour drive we saw just two cars and three lorries.

Our destination was the Villa Berengo. During Bokassa's imperial reign Berengo had been a self-sufficient compound. It had had its own farms, cattle, staff quarters, offices and private houses. There were flats for foreign visitors, carefully furnished with reproduction antique furniture and gilt mirrors. This African Versailles was the home of the Imperial Council, a second government with protocols copied from the court of the Shah of Iran. The Imperial Council's power and influence was far greater than that of the official government of Prime Minister Patasse.

Before me now lay a wreck surrounded by empty fields. We went inside the main building. Kalashnikov bullets littered the floors and vegetation had invaded the bare rooms. The initials JBK were still visible on the walls, also laurel wreaths in the style of Caesar Augustus and the motto of the empire: DIGNITE, UNITE, TRAVAIL. I wondered in which of the rooms the heir to the throne, Prince Saint-Jean de Bokassa de Berengo de Boubangui de Centrafrique, had played.

Raphael suggested we visit one of the bungalows near the entrance to the estate, where the custodian of the grounds lived. The custodian asked where I was from, and when he discovered I was Italian, he invited us to dinner, which consisted of one of the chickens that roamed around the ex-imperial courtyards. His wife served us silently, not sitting down to the table herself. Then, at the end of the meal, her duty done, she spoke at last, in perfect Italian. She had just returned from Rome, where she had worked as a housemaid for many years. A city, she remarked—with no hint of irony—that reminded her of Berengo because it had once been the seat of another imperial court and also had some interesting archaeological ruins.

On the drive back from Berengo a small antelope ran out from the bushes next to the motorway. Instead of swerving to avoid it, Raphael's friend deliberately ran it over. Raphael got out and put it in the boot of the car with the porcupine. 'Delicious roasted,' he remarked.

Our next stop was at Villa Kolongo, at Kilometre 12. A group of baby-faced soldiers took us to see the villa where the Romanian concubine Gabriela Drimba and the imperial babysitter Martine N'Douta had been caught in bed with soldiers of the garrison. N'Douta was killed immediately. Drimba, Bokassa's favourite among his women, defended herself by accusing Bokassa of ignoring her in favour of his Vietnamese and Gabonese concubines. Bokassa threatened to throw the men to the crocodiles, then relented and had them killed in prison instead.

Kilongo with its courtyards and fountains was like a Mexican hacienda. The ceiling of the banqueting hall had been dismantled. There was no longer any sign of the long table at which, according to statements made by David Dacko, twice president and a cousin of Bokassa, fillet of opposition leader was once served. Delicious roasted, perhaps.

The soldiers marched us round the perimeter of the estate to where Bokassa and Drimba, seated on a kind of altar, had improvised summary trials of their enemies, real or presumed. The emperor and the dancer decided the method of execution, deliberating between the firing squad, the prison, or the crocodiles.

Apart from cadavers in the kitchens, the French soldiers claimed to have found human bones at the bottom of Villa Kilongo's swimming pools.

The swimming pools were still visible, although they had long since been drained and their blue tiles were now buried beneath layers of soil. The youngest of the soldiers scrambled down into the smallest of the pools. He scrabbled about beneath the weeds and pulled out a smooth white bone, declaring, 'Human. Eaten by Bokassa. One hundred francs.' Raphael seized the bone and studied it for a couple of seconds before pronouncing, 'Goat.' Faced with such certainty, the soldier conceded. 'OK. Goat. But eaten by Bokassa.'

On July 29, 1972 the following order, Decree No. 29.058, was issued by the Republic of Central Africa:

Any person discovered in the act of theft shall be subject to the following punishments:
1. The first time such an offence is committed one ear shall be amputated.
2. The second time such an offence is committed the other ear shall be amputated.
3. The third time such an offence is committed one hand shall be amputated.
Amputations will be performed by suitably qualified surgeons within twenty-four hours of sentence being passed.

The decree was put into practice on several occasions. The amputations were carried out in the middle of the market square at Kilometre 5. Bokassa—who was at the time President for Life, Minister of Defence, Minister of Justice, Minister of Home Affairs, Minister of Agriculture, Minister of Health and Minister of Aviation—presided over the operations. The Secretary General of the United Nations, Kurt Waldheim, made a strong protest. Bokassa responded by describing him as 'a ruffian', 'a colonialist,' and also, strangely, as 'an imperialist'.

New Year's Eve 1985 was the twentieth anniversary of the coup that brought Bokassa to power. He spent it in one of the properties he'd won back from Tapie, the Chateau Haudricourt, near Paris. The vast rooms with their portraits of the Empress Catherine, busts of Napoleon and photographs of the battle of Dien Bien Phu (with the legend: 'They gave their lives for Liberty') were cold. There was no money for heating. 'I haven't got the money to feed the fifteen children who live here with me,' he told journalists. 'Every day more bills arrive and I don't know how to pay them.'

Bokassa was a penniless prisoner. He couldn't sell his chateaux because Dacko's government had now laid legal claim to them. He had been forbidden to leave Haudricourt by the French secret services. A book he had written, *Ma Verité*, was pulped on the orders of Giscard d'Estaing before it reached the shops.

Six months later, however, the situation changed. The tribunal in Paris gave him back the 'Corvette', a plane worth six million francs that had been seized by the Central African Republic after Operation Barracuda. The gendarmes guarding the entrance to the chateau were recalled. Papa Bock found himself some new French friends, a lawyer and two former army officers with links to the extreme right. They helped him to sell the plane. The proceeds were invested in a new plan: escape.

On October 21, 1986 Bokassa told his new wife Augustine (whom he had met during his stay in the Ivory Coast) that they would be returning to Bangui next day on a scheduled Air Afrique flight, using forged papers. During their escape someone informed the captain of the plane about his famous passenger. But the captain assumed that if Bokassa was indeed on board he could only be there with the permission of the French government. He saw no reason to divert the flight.

At first, when Bokassa arrived in Bangui airport, no one recognized him. Then someone in the baggage hall shouted, 'It's Bokassa!' The crowd began to buzz. 'The boss is back... Get to the presidential palace! Get to the presidential palace!' The airport police fled in terror. The crowd applauded. Bokassa began to make a speech.

Twenty minutes later, Colonel Jean-Claude Mantion, on secondment from Paris to command the new presidential guard, arrived in the baggage hall at a run, followed by dozens of soldiers. He arrested Bokassa, suspecting that the former emperor's return to Bangui signalled his intention to seize power once again.

'I'm here just to clear my name,' Bokassa protested. Eight months later his first trial took place. He was sentenced to be executed. No one could explain why he had left Haudricourt.

'It was the French secret service. They kidnapped me, my then-concubine and my children and put us on the first plane to Bangui,' Bokassa told me. 'I still have the names of all the officers in charge of the operation.' He appeared to have forgotten about the letter he wrote to President François Mitterrand on the eve of his departure, which began: 'I return a free man to a free nation. And if I am invited to be of service to it, I shall accept immediately, because my dearest wish is to serve the people. Indeed, to serve all men: a philosophical concept natural to those of us imbued with French culture.'

The crippled children encamped in front of Bangui's only hotel now recognized me. Morning and evening they greeted me with cries of 'Bonjour!'

The hotel, which belonged to the French chain Novotel, stood on the banks of the river. Every evening the bar was full of French soldiers in army fatigues. They talked about Rwanda, but only among themselves. Occasionally a girl dressed in yellow came to visit them. She walked barefoot up to the hotel door, with her very high-heeled shoes—also yellow—tucked under her arm. The leader of the crippled children watched the little ceremony. He addressed her as 'sister' and earned a tip from the soldiers.

At his home Bokassa often referred to 'the fruit of my blood'. At first I assumed he meant the child he called Petite, of whom he seemed especially fond. Eventually I realized that he was referring to his French army pension, earned partly through spending 'six months in a military hospital in Indochina'. The pension allowed him to survive. It also allowed over a hundred of his legitimate and illegitimate children, spread over Africa and France, to survive.

One day, tired of talking about his military experiences, Bokassa returned to the subject of the Bible. He recited the Lord's Prayer. He compared Christ to Nelson Mandela, saying, 'He suffered a lot in prison, like me. Mandela is a gift of God to the African people, to compensate them for centuries of suffering.' Then he told me that he had seen the Italian prime minister Silvio Berlusconi on the television just after he was elected. 'I liked him immediately.'

There was The Romanian, The Tunisian, The Gabonese, The French, The Vietnamese, The Belgian, The Libyan, The Cameroonian, The German, The Swede, The Zairean and The Chinese (a 'present' from Chiang Kai-shek). And then there was Catherine, the Empress.

Bokassa's mistresses were the only visible outcome of his frequent official visits abroad. He claimed that they were mostly 'given' to him by foreign heads of state as tokens of friendship. Sometimes he would catch sight of a woman while he was on an official engagement, and ask to be introduced to them. If he liked them he took them back to Bangui. He installed each woman in a separate villa.

He met 'The Gabonese', Joelle, at the airport in Libreville at the end of an official tour in 1979. She was among the throng of notables who had come to see him off. She was very beautiful. According to the magazine *Jeune Afrique*, Bokassa whispered to her not to move. 'I'll be right back.' Then he embraced President Omar Bongo and boarded his plane.

Fifteen minutes later he commanded the captain of the presidential jet to turn the plane around. Bongo, who was already being driven away from the airport, was informed that Bokassa had changed his mind. He returned to the airport in a hurry, to find the smiling emperor. 'Earlier I was here as a head of state. Now I'm here in a private capacity. And I'm about to marry one of your fellow citizens,' Bokassa announced. A few hours later 'The Gabonese' was in Bangui.

Most famous of all his concubines was 'The Romanian', Gabriela Drimba. Bokassa had spotted the blonde dancer in a Bucharest night-club during a visit to his ally Nicolai Ceaucescu. She initially refused to marry him, but turned up a few weeks later in Bangui.

Most mysterious were the three Vietnamese women. One was Bokassa's wife. Two were his daughters. One daughter was real, the other false. Both bore the name Martine Nguyen. They came to Bangui from Vietnam after Bokassa had searched (with the help of the French government) for his daughter by the wife he married in Saigon in 1953 and then abandoned. The first to arrive in Bangui was the False Martine. But she was exposed as a fraud. The French press fell on the story, ridiculing 'the monster of Central Africa'. Bokassa responded to his critics by adopting the girl, to show the world how generous he was. Then he found the Real Martine working in a Vietnamese cement factory. She too was persuaded to leave Vietnam for Africa.

Once in Bangui, Bokassa offered both of them in marriage via a kind of public auction. Hundreds of young Central African men bid for them. The eventual winners of the competition were a doctor and an army officer. The sumptuous wedding in the cathedral was even attended by a few heads of state, the most prominent being the ever-faithful Bongo.

The False Martine's husband, the army officer, eventually attempted a coup and was shot. The Real Martine's husband, the doctor, remained loyal to Bokassa. He too was shot, but by Bokassa's enemies after Operation Barracuda.

On my last visit to Villa Nasser I found the emperor alone, holding a Bible. I still had to ask him about the most serious charge, the one that worried him most. 'The story about cannibalism was invented in order to destroy me. It's a lie. Do you really believe that a much-decorated French officer could be a cannibal? It's a lie,' he repeated. And indeed the famous trial cleared him on this charge. But what about the other crimes? The murders? Bokassa did not deny them. 'But I was not the only one. What about that Israeli politician, what is he called? Yes, Ariel Sharon. Why has he been forgiven for the massacres at Sabra and Shatila, while I have been forgiven for nothing? Just because I'm African?'

Riccardo Orizio

Jean-Bédel Bokassa died a year after we met, on November 3, 1996. He was seventy-five years old. He is buried at Berengo. In its obituary, the Central African state radio described him as 'illustrious'. Ten years previously, the same radio station described him as 'the Ogre of Berengo'.

The Empress Catherine lives in Lausanne and refuses to speak about Bokassa.

Giscard d'Estaing remains an influential politician. Few still remember the scandal over the diamonds.

Bernard Tapie has been a government minister, a convict and the owner of the Olympique Marseilles football team, which he had to sell but to which he has subsequently returned. He now works as an actor.

Patasse is president of the Republic of Central Africa. He is an ally of Colonel Gadaffi.

'The Romanian', Gabriela Drimba, returned to Bucharest, leaving her daughter, Anne de Berengo, behind in Bangui. Nothing more has been heard of her.

The Real Martine escaped from Bangui after the coup. She now runs a Vietnamese restaurant in Paris.

The False Martine was killed by Bokassa's bodyguards a year after her husband's failed coup.

Augustine, the last concubine, returned to Haudricourt where she now lives with several of Bokassa's children.

Omar Bongo has been president of Gabon since 1969. A wealthy man (unlike surviving members of Bokassa's family), he has been one of the main private clients of Citibank since 1970.

Ariel Sharon is prime minister of Israel.

Raphael Kopessoua is not, for the moment, in prison. ☐

GRANTA

THE MIRACLE BOY

Tom Stoddart

In the time it takes to look at the photographs on the following nineteen pages, another twenty people will become HIV-positive. The rate can be calculated at five people every minute. An estimated forty million people throughout the world have now contracted HIV and 21.8 million have died since the disease was first recognized just over twenty years ago. In Africa attempts to slow the pandemic are failing. In Kenya alone, 700 people die every day. In the capital, Nairobi, where two million people live crammed together in shacks made of mud and tin, one person in every six is HIV-positive. Most can barely afford to feed themselves, let alone pay the $200 a month or more for drugs that might help them.

For those who are believers, God is the answer. But even God costs money. Every week Kenya's poorest people give what little they have to the hundreds of religious sects and healers who claim to be able to cure Aids.

At the God's Power Church and World Centre of Healing, the Reverend John Nduati is the hottest act in town. Nduati calls himself the 'Miracle Boy' and attracts thousands of HIV/Aids sufferers to his eight-hour long sermons held in the shed which serves as a church. Dressed in his smart suits, gold watch and cufflinks, Nduati summons the sick to stand and confess the reason they have contracted Aids. 'If the sinner repents,' Nduati shouts, 'I tell you, "You are healed, go home!"' The crowd then explodes into wild cheering and tears of joy. Later the preacher and his associates gather up discarded crutches and burn them, dramatically, outside the church.

'The more you give, the more you are healed. Somebody say Amen,' he will chant during the 'Giving Hour' while his followers queue to deposit money in baskets, or offer their crops or chickens for collection. 'Nobody has to pay, but if those sick with Aids give a donation, then it goes towards my work,' Nduati told the photographer, Tom Stoddart, who has witnessed several of his services. Stoddart has spent eighteen months travelling extensively throughout sub-Saharan Africa to document the catastrophic effects of the disease, which has orphaned fourteen million children. He found it hard to understand the stoicism of a proverb hanging on a wall in an Aids sufferer's home: I WAS BORN WITH NOTHING SO EVEN IF I DIE WITH NOTHING I HAVE LOST NOTHING. BUT I HAVE ENJOYED THE JOURNEY. □

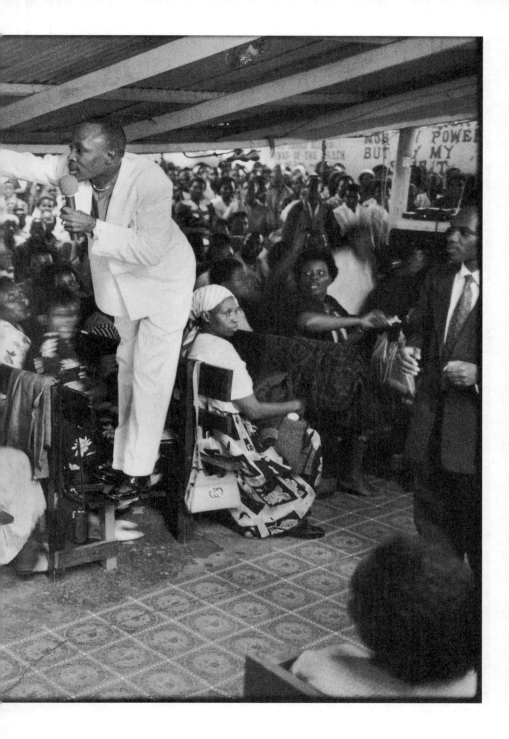

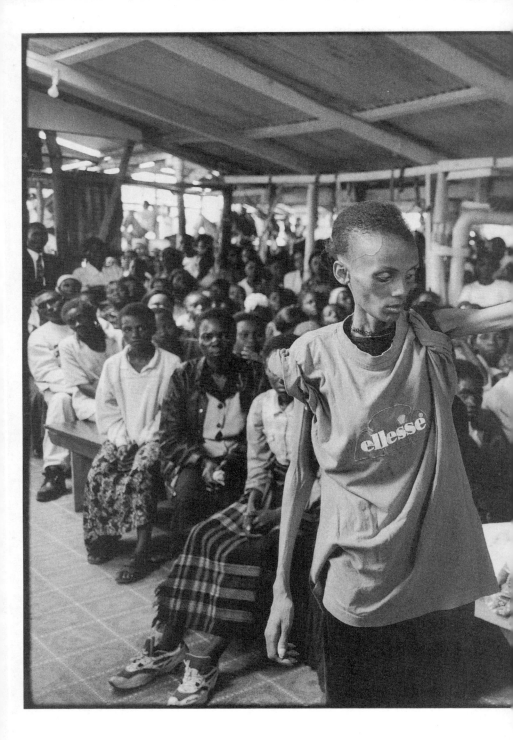

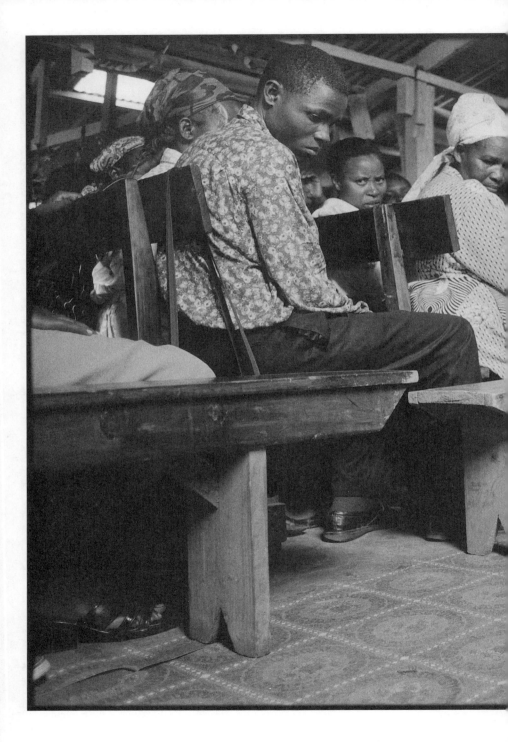

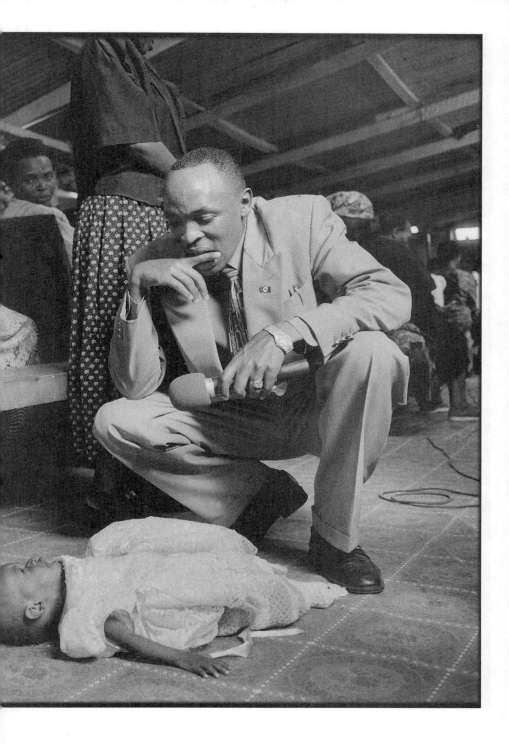

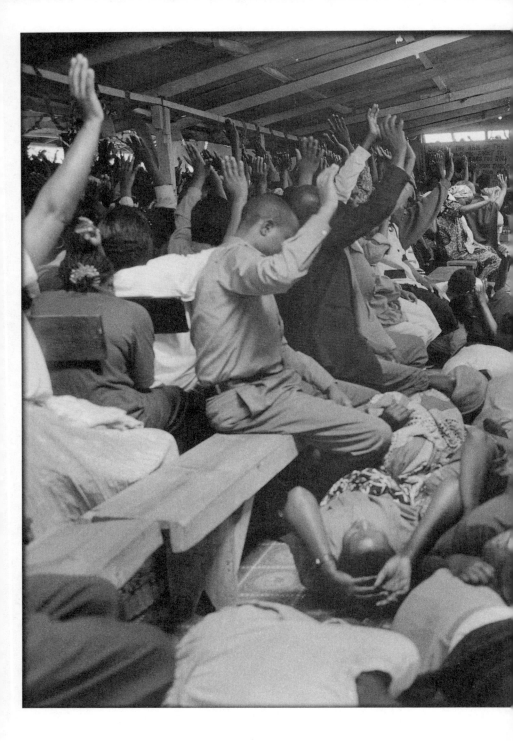

AP/WIDE WORLD PHOTOS

to be the poet

MAXINE HONG KINGSTON

"I have almost finished my longbook," Maxine Hong Kingston declares. "Let my
life as Poet begin…I won't be a workhorse anymore; I'll be a skylark." *To Be the
Poet* is Kingston's manifesto, the avowal and declaration of a writer who has
devoted a good part of her sixty years to writing prose, and who, over the
course of this spirited and inspiring book, works out what the rest of her life
will be, in poetry. Taking readers along with her, this celebrated writer gathers
advice from her gifted contemporaries and from sages, critics, and writers
whom she takes as ancestors. She consults her past, her conscience, her time—
and puts together a volume at once irreverent and deeply serious, playful and
practical, partaking of poetry throughout as it pursues the meaning,
the possibility, and the power of the life of the poet.

The William E. Massey Sr. Lectures in the History of American Civilization
$22.00 / £14.95 cloth

harvard university press
US: 800 405 1619 • UK: 020 7306 0603
www.hup.harvard.edu

GRANTA

THE SEARCH
FOR DR BLOCH

Jason Cowley

My Patient, Hitler

By Dr. Eduard Bloch as told to
J. D. Ratcliff

The physician of the Hitler family tells about the dictator, who was his patient as a boy in old Austria

PHOTOGRAPHED FOR COLLIER'S BY LAWRENCE A. MONAHAN

Early in 1943, an operative of the Office of Strategic Services or OSS, the wartime precursor of the CIA, made his way to an unkempt attic apartment on the fifth floor of a building in Creston Avenue, the Bronx. The operative, Walter C. Langer, was compiling what would become the world's first psychological profile of Adolf Hitler, and that day he took with him Gertrude Kurth, a psychotherapist who was also acting as his translator. Together they climbed the stairs to see a seventy-one-year-old doctor who two years earlier had fled from Austria to New York: a Jew, Dr Eduard Bloch. Dr Bloch had an interesting story to tell. He had known Hitler at first hand; nearly forty years before he had been the Hitler family's doctor. He had treated Hitler's mother, Klara, during her final illness, as well as the young Hitler himself for various routine ailments. Obviously, in any study of Hitler's personality the evidence of such an intimate witness to illness and trauma—his mother's death had grieved Hitler deeply—could be important. No less interesting—though its relevance to Langer's research might be debatable—was Dr Bloch's account of how he had escaped the usual fate of Austrian Jews in 1940. Hitler personally, he told Langer and Kurth, had intervened to allow his departure.

In other words, he was a Jew who had been saved by Hitler— from Hitler. This became the conundrum of his life.

What Bloch told Langer in his two interviews with him—a second conversation occurred a few weeks later—can be found in the OSS's Hitler profile, a 300-page document which was declassified only in 2001, and which, with its disquisitions on Hitler's voice, eye-colour, childhood and uneasy sexuality, prefigured an entire industry of lurid psycho-historical speculation. Titled *A Psychological Analysis of Adolf Hitler: His Life and Legend*, the document is organized into five parts: 1) Hitler—as he believes himself to be; 2) Hitler—as the German people know him; 3) Hitler—as his associates know him; 4) Hitler—as he knows himself; 5) Psychological analysis and reconstruction (with a long concluding subsection on his 'probable behaviour in the future'). There is an extensive bibliography and a complementary sourcebook, in which Langer discusses the reliability of much of the evidence on which he has been working.

From his comments in the sourcebook, it is clear that Langer was as sceptical as he was intrigued by the doctor's remarkable story. It wasn't the first time Bloch had told it. Soon after he reached New

Jason Cowley

York in January 1941, Bloch had given a long, detailed interview about his experiences with the Hitler family to *Collier's*, the weekly magazine. The interview was published over two weeks in March that year in the form of a piece in the first person ('as told to J. D. Ratcliff'). America was then neutral in the European war; Pearl Harbor was still nine months away. By the time Langer met Bloch, however, Hitler was no longer a merely disquieting transatlantic phenomenon. The world had come to know him, as Langer wrote in his introduction to the profile, for his 'insatiable greed for power, his ruthlessness, cruelty and utter lack-of-feeling, his contempt for established institutions and his lack of moral restraints'.

Langer didn't doubt that Hitler would one day be defeated, and moral order restored. But how to prevent 'similar eruptions' in the future? There was only one clear answer: 'We must discover the psychological streams which nourish this destructive state of mind in order that we may divert them into channels which will permit a further evolution of our form of civilization.'

A meeting with Bloch offered Langer an opportunity to paddle in these psychological streams, to return to the primal scene of Hitler's childhood and adolescence and to what the British historian Hugh Trevor-Roper later called 'the darkest, the most formative, and therefore in some sense, the most interesting period' of Hitler's life. Langer believed that Bloch was particularly well placed to provide insight into the years, sometimes since mythologized as the missing years, when, from 1908 to 1913, Hitler was a striving but unsuccessful young painter in Vienna. And what did Bloch tell him? That Hitler had been 'a nice pleasant youth'.

'Favours were granted me which I feel sure were accorded no other Jew in all Germany and Austria,' he told Langer. Hitler had honoured an earlier promise of gratitude for the doctor's care of his mother; he had helped him escape persecution in Austria and smoothed his passage to America. There is no other reported instance of Hitler intervening to save the life of, or of extending compassion to, a Jew, certainly not once he took power in Germany. In this, Bloch was uniquely chosen.

Dr Bloch was to remain forever a stranger to America. It wasn't his natural home, nor did he wish it to be—it was where his life narrowed and reduced. To the end, he was a cosmopolitan servant of the old Habsburg empire, who is revealed in photographs to have an old world dandyish charm—a wide-brimmed hat, stiff collars, elaborate double cuffs, a cigarette in hand, a moustache that twisted at the edges like a bow tie. This is what we know about his early life. He was born in 1872 into an assimilated bourgeois Jewish family in Frauenburg, a small German-speaking village in southern Bohemia—which, he said, had been 'under three flags' in his lifetime: Austrian, Czechoslovakian and German. He studied medicine in Prague and then, once qualified as a general practitioner, he joined the Austrian army as a military doctor. In 1899, he was 'ordered to Linz', the provincial capital of Upper Austria and the home town of Adolf Hitler, where, on completing his army service, he decided to stay on; in 1903, he married a local Jewish girl, Emilie Kafka, a distant relative of Franz Kafka, and opened his own public practice.

In the course of this story I went to Linz, and there the town archivist, Dr Joseph Mayrhofer, showed me a photograph taken on a March day in 1938 when Hitler returned to his home town after an absence of thirty years. As a young man, he had dreamed of rebuilding the town on a monumental scale, so that Linz would become one day not just an architectural rival to Budapest and Vienna, but *the* city on the Danube, a place of colossal dimensions. In the photograph Hitler stands in his open-topped, six-wheeled Mercedes-Benz at the head of a motorcade which is moving along the main street, the Landstrasse. A crowd in the street salutes the Führer; even people in the windows above have raised their arms. A closer inspection of the picture shows that it was taken as the motorcade reached 25 Landstrasse, which means that Hitler was about to pass directly beneath the upstairs window of a fine baroque house, 12 Landstrasse, where Eduard Bloch happened to be watching. The two men had last seen each other after the funeral of Klara Hitler, at the end of 1907.

In the photograph, Hitler's face seems to be fixed in that very direction, upwards, to his right, and ahead. Who is it he sees up there? What absorbs him? Dr Bloch thought he knew. 'It was a moment of tense excitement,' he told *Collier's*. 'For years Hitler had been denied the right to visit the country of his birth. Now that country belonged to him. The elation that he felt was written on his features. He smiled, waved, gave the Nazi salute to the people that crowded the street.

Then, for a moment, he glanced at my window. I doubt that he saw me but he must have had a moment of reflection. Here was the home of the *Edeljude* who had diagnosed his mother's fatal cancer; here was the consultation room of the man who had treated his sisters; here was the place he had gone as a boy to have his minor ailments attended to. It was a brief moment. Then the procession was gone. It moved slowly into the town square—once Franz Joseph Platz, soon to be renamed Adolf Hitler Platz. He spoke from the balcony of the town hall. Historic words: Germany and Austria were now one.'

Edeljude: a noble Jew. Bloch told Langer of how in 1937 a group of local Nazi supporters from Linz had visited Hitler at his mountain villa at Berchtesgaden in the Bavarian Alps. 'The Führer asked for news of Linz,' Bloch said. 'How was the town? Were people there supporting him? He asked for news of me. Was I still alive, still practising? Then he made a statement irritating to the local Nazis: "Dr Bloch," said Hitler, "is an *Edeljude*—a noble Jew. If all Jews were like him, there would be no Jewish question."'

D r Bloch and his wife Emilie reached New York from Lisbon on January 8, 1941, aboard a small Spanish liner, the *Marqués de Comillas*. Their daughter and only child, Gertrude (Trude), had reached New York with her husband eighteen months before. She earned money as a cleaner while her husband, Frank Kren, who like Bloch had practised as a doctor in Linz, studied for the qualifications that would enable him to work as a doctor in America. The Krens lived with their two young children, George and Joanne, in a five-room flat at 2755 Creston Avenue in the north Bronx, which also became home to Bloch and his wife. Bloch, unlike his son-in-law, was too old to continue as a doctor, and he spoke only rudimentary English. He spent many of his afternoons at the cinema, watching westerns. And then somehow he came to the attention, or brought himself to the attention, of *Collier's* magazine. Perhaps, as an obscure old man in a strange country—in Linz, he had been a known and respected individual in the middle class community—he wanted to claim some importance, some celebrity. In the *Collier's* pieces, he speaks as though he were already famous. During his passage across the Atlantic, for example, he describes an episode when his ship was stopped by 'British control officers' aboard a trawler. The passengers were assembled in the main lounge and their papers examined by the British officers. 'There was a feeling of tenseness,' Bloch said, as the officers made their way down the line. Finally they reached Bloch. 'The officer in charge took my passport, glanced at it and looked up smiling. "You were Hitler's physician, weren't you?" he asked. This was correct. It would also have been correct for him to add that I am a Jew.'

This is an unlikely incident. Hitler had not seen his former doctor since Christmas 1907; even in Linz, Bloch was no more than a local hero, best known for being what the town archivist, when I met him, called a 'poor person's doctor', a compassionate friend to the hard up. Beyond Linz, how many people could have heard of him? The officers aboard a British trawler heaving up and down in mid-Atlantic, three days' sail from the coast of Portugal? Perhaps the *Collier's* rewrite man is to blame—or perhaps not: Walter Langer, in the OSS sourcebook, often expresses scepticism about Bloch's reliability as a witness. He notes at one point: 'Dr Bloch's impressions of the family's life—"quiet, the only bone of contention being Adolf, who refused to become an official and wanted to become an artist; his mother backing him against his father"—seem to be based on his reading of [Konrad] Heiden's biography [1936] rather than on actual knowledge'. Elsewhere, as Bloch talks about Hitler's time in Vienna, Langer notes that his memories are here 'obviously very much mixed up with his reading'. Yet, for all his scepticism, Langer quotes extensively from *Collier's* and was intrigued enough by Bloch to visit him a second time 'to get more facts from him which seem of importance'. These included information on Hitler's sisters, on his performance at school and on whether he had had 'some trouble' as a teenager, an incident that 'was hushed up' involving young girls or boys. Bloch had heard about the incident, confirmed that it involved girls, but suggested that it was 'nothing too serious'. He also confirmed that Hitler had 'no physical deformity, and definitely no tuberculosis, though tuberculosis was hereditary in the family from the father's side'.

How reliable was Dr Bloch? Perhaps reliable in one important way: he does not seem to have been a revisionist witness, adjusting his experience of Hitler and his family to suit Hitler's later beliefs and behaviour and his then current position as the civilized world's greatest enemy. Largely, he spoke as he had found. He never once condemned his former patient: if anything, he exhibited an understandable touch of wonder at what the mature Hitler had achieved, the improbability of it all. Nor did he ever disparage Klara Hitler, whom he consistently portrayed as a gentle, modest woman, attentive to her children and religiously devout: 'Outwardly, his love for his mother was his most striking feature,' he told Collier's. 'While he was not a "mother's boy" in the usual sense, I have never witnessed a closer attachment. Some insist that this love verged on the pathological. As a former intimate of the family, I do not believe this is true.' To the OSS, he described the 'reciprocal adoration' of mother and son as most 'unusual'.

After the first OSS interview, according to the psychotherapist Gertrude Kurth, Bloch followed her and Langer down five flights of stairs to stress once again, and by now in the street, what 'a nice pleasant youth' Hitler had been. More than fifty years later, when Kurth was interviewed by Ron Rosenbaum for his book Explaining Hitler: The Search for the Origins of his Evil, she could not forgive Bloch for the awful innocence of his remark. 'Outside in the street,' she said, 'Langer and I laughed and laughed at that—bitter laughter.'

Bloch died in 1945. According to his grandson, George Kren, he was to the end of his life ignorant of the full horror of what had taken place in central and eastern Europe between 1939 and 1945. That may be true. Less easy to explain, however, is his reluctance to condemn the man who had forced his family's displacement and that of many other thousands of Jewish families—all this he had experienced and witnessed for himself. And yet, as he told Collier's, 'Even today I cannot help thinking of him in terms of his grief and not in terms of what he has done to the world.'

We will come later to the details of what Hitler did for Dr Bloch. The first question is: what did Dr Bloch do for Hitler? What effect did Bloch's treatment of Klara Hitler, as she succumbed to breast cancer, have on her son?

Klara Hitler had been a widow for four years when she visited Bloch at his surgery in January 1907. Her husband, Alois, had been twenty-three years older, her second cousin, and married twice before (both wives died). Her first three children had died in infancy. Another son, Edmund, Adolf's younger brother, died of measles at the age of six. As a child, Adolf was weak and sickly; his mother feared that he would not live to maturity, and, after Edmund's death, she became extraordinarily devoted to her only living son, the soft, maternal buffer into which he was propelled by the rage and aggression of his father. Perhaps Adolf was strengthened by her attachment. After all, as Freud said, 'A man who's been the indisputable favourite of his mother goes through life with the feeling of a conqueror'.

During his examination, Bloch found a tumour the size of a hen's egg in Klara's right breast. 'I thought immediately of cancer,' he told *Collier's*. He did not, however, tell Klara of his immediate fears; instead he called her 'children'—presumably Adolf, who had recently returned from Vienna, his sister, Paula and their elder half-sister, Angela—to his consultation room, where he 'stated the case frankly'. Their mother, he told them, was very sick. 'Without surgery, there was absolutely no hope of recovery. Even with surgery there was but the slightest chance that she would live. In family council they must decide what was to be done.' Bloch described how Hitler reacted to what he heard. 'His long, sallow face was contorted. Tears flowed from his eyes. Did his mother, he asked, have no chance? Only then did I realize the magnitude of the attachment that existed between mother and son.'

Klara Hitler's mastectomy was performed four days later by Dr Karl Urban, the chief of the surgical staff at the Hospital of the Sisters of Mercy in Linz, who was recognized as one of the most experienced surgeons in Upper Austria. After examining Klara, he agreed that she required immediate surgery if her life was to be prolonged. (The Nazis later persecuted Urban: together with his son, a brain surgeon, he was forbidden from practising medicine.)

Bloch was present during surgery at the family's request. Klara was discharged from hospital on February 5, 1907 and enjoyed a brief recovery; Bloch would meet her out walking by the river or see her shopping at the market. But by midsummer the cancer had metastasized; she was once more in severe pain and there was little he could do for her, beyond reducing her pain with regular morphine injections.

'I shall never forget Klara during those days,' Bloch told *Collier's*. 'She was forty-eight at the time; tall, slender and rather handsome, yet wasted by disease. She was soft-spoken, patient; more concerned about what would happen to her family than she was about her approaching death. She made no secret of these worries, or about the fact that most of her thoughts were for her son. "Adolf is still so young," she said repeatedly [he was eighteen]. On the day of December 20, I made two calls. The end was approaching...so the word that Angela Hitler brought me the following morning came as no surprise. Her mother had died quietly in the night. The children had decided not to disturb me, knowing that their mother was beyond all medical aid. But, she asked, could I come now? Someone in an official position would have to sign the death certificate... Adolf, his face showing the weariness of a sleepless night, sat beside his mother. In order to preserve a last impression, he had sketched her as she lay on her deathbed... I sat with the family for a while, trying to ease their grief. I explained that in this case death had been a saviour. They understood. In the practice of my profession it is natural that I should have witnessed many scenes such as this one, yet none of them left me with quite the same impression. In all my career I have never seen anyone so prostrate with grief as Adolf Hitler.'

The most complex explanation of the effect of Bloch on Hitler during this time comes from Professor Rudolph Binion in his book *Hitler against the Germans*. Binion is half psychologist and half historian—a psycho-historian—and he identifies Bloch as the latent trigger for Hitler's anti-Semitism. Bloch, after all, replaced Hitler's dead father, Alois, in Klara's bedroom; Bloch saw his mother naked; Bloch, in Binion's view, increased her suffering through the excessive application of iodoform, a strong-smelling antiseptic which is toxic when absorbed into the bloodstream in high doses.

Bloch makes no mention of iodoform in his interviews. Binion discovered it in Bloch's patient records, which he found in a National Socialist party archive—Bloch's papers had been seized by the Gestapo before he left Linz. The records for 1907 showed Binion that Bloch had used iodoform gauze to cover the open wound left by her mastectomy. The treatment, Binion argued, was poisonous, with side effects which would have included insomnia, muscle spasticity, extreme thirst, severe migraines, fever and visual disturbance—all consistent with Klara's symptoms as described by Bloch, by Hitler, and by Hitler's closest friend from adolescence August Kubizek.

Ergo, according to Binion, a dedicated Freudian, Hitler nurtured an unconscious hatred of Bloch. He unconsciously blamed the suffering of his mother on the doctor's incompetence. To Hitler, he became not just a Jewish poisoner, he was poison itself. Hitler would speak later of the need to remove the 'Jewish poison from the breast' of the German nation. Professor Binion is unequivocal: Hitler relocated his mother in Germany.

Throughout his life, Bloch, Freud's fellow countryman, took a simpler view. He told *Collier's* of how, a few days after Klara's funeral, Hitler and his two sisters had visited him at home on the Landstrasse. 'They wished to thank me for the help I had given them. There was Paula, fair and stocky; Angela, slender, pretty but rather anemic; and Adolf. The girls spoke what was in their hearts while Adolf remained silent... Adolf wore a dark suit and a loosely knotted cravat. Then, as now, a shock of hair tumbled over his forehead. His eyes were on the floor while his sisters were talking. Then came his turn. He stepped forward and took my hand. Looking into my eyes, he said: "I shall be grateful to you forever." That was all. Then he bowed.' Later, Bloch claimed that Hitler sent him several postcards and sketches from Vienna, including a postcard on which Hitler had painted a hooded Capuchin monk raising a glass of champagne. The picture was captioned: PROSIT NEUJAHR ('A toast to the New Year'). On the reverse, he had written: 'The Hitler family sends you the best wishes for a Happy New Year. In everlasting thankfulness, Adolf Hitler.' When I spoke to Bloch's grandchildren, George and Joanne, they said that their grandfather had indeed kept these souvenirs, but that they had been taken by the Gestapo when they confiscated his medical records.

Gratitude: that was what Bloch felt certain Hitler had felt. Otherwise, why the postcards? Otherwise, why in 1940 would Bloch and his wife have been granted passports and permitted to emigrate unhindered to America?

Klara Hitler is buried in a small churchyard in the market town of Leonding, which was once a small, isolated agricultural village but today is part of the south-western suburbs of Linz, which lies surrounded by wooded hills in the Danube valley. The Hitlers themselves had once lived in Leonding, in a cottage that backed on to the cemetery. It was in Leonding that the family patriarch, Alois Hitler, a retired minor customs official in the Austro-Hungarian bureaucracy, died suddenly from pulmonary bleeding as he sat drinking in a tavern on January 3, 1903. The Hitler family plot lies under a big tree by the graveyard wall. On the morning I went there I saw that flowers had been laid at the foot of the headstone—white lilies and red roses. There was no sign of greater pilgrimage; in the 1930s Nazi flags had been laid over the grave, and visits became popular again, I was told, just before the reunification of Germany. But neither was there any sign of desecration. On the headstone, the photographs of Klara and her husband, Alois, were undamaged. A brief inscription recorded the dates of their deaths.

I'd gone to Linz to find out more about Bloch. My hotel, on the square in the old quarter of the city, was only a short walk away from his old house at 12 Landstrasse. From the window of my room, I could see the Rathaus, the town hall, from where on March 12, 1938 Hitler had addressed an estimated 60,000 people on his homecoming to Linz. Later that night, encouraged by the mood of celebration in the town, he declared the Anschluss of Austria, which he saw as predetermined, the fulfilment of his long-standing ambition to unite the German Volk. On April 10, the Anschluss was ratified in a mass vote.

Hitler had great plans for Linz. During the war, he commissioned the architect Hermann Giesler to lead its redesign and rebuilding: new bridges, avenues and public squares, a new city hall, sports stadium, theatre and opera house, its own monument to Bismarck and, most spectacularly of all, a 160-metre high Gothic 'Tower on the Danube', in which the Führer's parents were to be reburied in a vaulted crypt. There was also to be a new art gallery in which to display the great works that had been looted from public and private collections during the Nazi conquest of Europe.

During his final weeks in the Reichskanzlei, when the war was lost and the Soviets were rampaging towards Berlin, the sleepless Hitler would return repeatedly to the underground room where Giesler's model of the new Linz was still taking shape; pictures of Hitler at this time—some, uncharacteristically, of him wearing spectacles—show the fierce concentration with which he studied Giesler's plans and models, though he must have known long before that Linz would never be rebuilt, that his home town would remain forever provincial.

Today the Nibelungen Bridge across the Danube, linking the old main square of Linz with the northern suburb of Urfahr and completed before Germany's reversals on the Eastern Front, remains the chief monument to Hitler's mission to rebuild Linz. It replaced the old iron bridge across which Dr Bloch used to travel in his carriage on his daily visits to the dying Klara Hitler at the family's three-room apartment at 9 Bluetenstrasse. Bloch later spoke of how the apartment afforded fine views of the surrounding hills; but these views have since been altered by a sprawl of office blocks, shopping malls and high-rise concrete car parks. This was the result of the Allied bombing and postwar redevelopment of Linz, a city which, until the signing of the State Treaty in 1955 gave independence to the newly neutral Austrian state, was occupied north of the river by the Soviets and by the Americans in the south.

A hundred years ago, when Bloch began to practise there, the dominant political culture of Linz was a kind of provincial patriotism: conservative, folkish, agrarian, clerical, anti-Slavic and Judaeophobic. It was part of the Austro-Hungarian Empire, the Dual Monarchy, but, close to the Bavarian border, it leaned away from the cosmopolitanism of Vienna and towards Germany. Many Upper Austrians felt uneasy about the absorption of their German identity in the polyglot amorphousness of Dual Monarchy; they increasingly looked west to the new unified German state for leadership and security. Newspapers such as the *Linzer Fliegenden* and the *Linzer Post* supported the pan-Germans and published caricatures of the Yiddish-speaking 'Eastern' Jews—the so-called kaftan Jews—who were moving west to escape Tsarist pogroms and the insularity of shtetl life. The city council was intermittently under the control of the pan-Germans, as were many of the local guilds, student groups and institutions of wider civil society. In a population of 60,000, only one per cent were Jews.

After the Anschluss, the Nazi elite was determined to modernize and industrialize Linz—the industrial base of the old Dual Monarchy had been in Czech Bohemia. In 1938, work began on a huge iron, steel and coking works—the 'Hermann Goering Works'—which once completed became an important engine of the war effort. Within six months of the Anschluss, unemployment in Linz had been eliminated. In the years that followed, and partly by exploiting the resource of slave labour at the nearby Mauthausen concentration camp, Linz became one of the leading industrial centres of Europe. Today heavy industry is still responsible for much of its affluence—and for thickening its skies with smoke. Its economic transformation remains one of the great successes of National Socialism, as the right-wing Austrian populist Jorg Haider likes to remind his supporters, omitting to mention that a large part of this prosperity has its foundations in slave labour. The present popularity of Haider's Freedom Party is often cited as an example of how Austria, unlike Germany, has failed to engage properly with its wartime history. Every autumn in Linz, for example, war veterans still meet to celebrate what some Austrians consider to be their national sacrifice. It was during one such meeting of veterans—this time in Klagenfurt, in the southern province of Corinthia—that Haider made a notorious speech urging his audience not to feel ashamed of themselves or of their country. They had, he said, only fulfilled their patriotic duty.

Talking to people in Linz, it seemed to me that Austria remained a humiliated and troubled state. Austrian schoolchildren have been taught to believe that their country was the first victim of Nazism. Perhaps, given Austria's immediate postwar history, it is a necessary untruth. As one young academic told me: 'It's very hard for people of my generation to tell our parents that they were wrong, particularly after the way so many of them suffered in the war in the East and under the Soviet occupation. [The 45th Linz Infantry Division sustained desperate losses on the Eastern Front.] It's hard to tell old people that their lives were a mistake.'

In this city, Bloch was nowhere. He'd slipped away when men were putting the finishing touches to the Hermann Goering Works. There was only his signature on Klara Hitler's death certificate, and the picture in the city archive; Hitler in the Landstrasse, looking—maybe—towards the dear doctor's house.

But Bloch had a child, Trude, and she had a husband, Frank Kren, and they had children, George and Joanne. Before I went to Linz, I had traced Bloch's two grandchildren. George Kren was a historian, retired from Kansas State University and living in a small town outside Kansas; Joanne, now Joanne Harrison, was a retired nurse who lived in Ewing, New Jersey. George and I had talked on the phone and exchanged emails. He said he was working hard to complete what would be his final book, a Holocaust study, and that he was translating a short memoir that had been left by his grandfather. I told him how interested I would be to read that memoir. He said nothing. I sensed a reticence about his grandfather, and in retrospect more than that: what now seems to me a reluctance to corroborate Bloch's story and even a suspicion of his motives for telling it. 'It was not so hard to get out of Linz for Jews,' George said once. 'Certainly not when I left for England in 1938.' Another time, he described his grandfather as 'a bit of a showman. He was a real character all right.'

George and Joanne had left Austria on the Kindertransport, on one of the trains that saved the lives of thousands of Jewish children. They travelled at night through Switzerland and France and then sailed across the Channel to Harwich, where they arrived in April, 1939. They stayed at first with a family in the East End of London and then moved south to Brighton, where they were separated from each other. In 1940, they were reunited with their parents in New York, shortly before their grandparents came to stay.

'How did you find living in England?' I asked George.

'I'll tell you about it when we meet.'

Kren had returned several times as an adult to Linz. He liked the tranquillity of the place, and recommended a restaurant that I should visit—high up on the Postlingberg heights, where there is also a baroque pilgrims' church, built in the late 1730s. You reach the summit of the Postlingberg on what is one of the world's steepest railways, completed in 1898. The air is thin and bracing up there. As dusk settles you watch the burnished blue of the distant Alps disappearing slowly into the surrounding darkness and follow the lamp-lit river below on its journey through the Danube valley.

In *Collier's* and with the OSS, Dr Bloch never talked about what Linz was like before the Anschluss—perhaps because he wasn't asked. The impression he gave of his life there was one of happy fulfilment. All that changed when, in the spring and summer of 1938, official anti-Semitism began to affect his friends and patients. Jews were, progressively, banned from hotels, restaurants, parks and certain clubs and associations; Jewish lawyers and doctors were forbidden to practise; Jewish shops, homes and offices were marked with what Bloch called 'the yellow-paper banners now visible throughout Germany—JUDE'.

On November 10, 1938—'Kristallnacht'—a ruling was issued that those Jews who had not yet emigrated, or declared (like Bloch's daughter and her husband) their intention to do so, were to leave Linz

Jason Cowley

within sixty-two hours. But Bloch, who was reluctant to leave, discovered that an 'exception' was to be made in his case. The Gestapo had visited previously to ask him to remove the yellow signs from his home and office—'the first suggestion that I was to receive special favours'. Then his landlord 'went to Gestapo headquarters to ask if I were to be allowed to remain in my apartment. "We wouldn't dare touch that matter," he was told. "It will be handled by Berlin."' Bloch told *Collier's* that he took that as a sign that Hitler had remembered. He had remembered his promise of gratitude to the Noble Jew.

During one of my phone conversations with George, I mentioned this episode. His tone hardened. 'My grandfather documented all that fairly accurately,' he said, briefly.

'Can you recall yourself what it was like to live in Linz as a child?'

'When you think of Linz at that time,' he said, 'you must remember that not just Hitler, but also Adolf Eichmann and Franz Stangel came from the town. That might give you some idea of its atmosphere.'

I was never to meet George Kren. Shortly before I was due to set off from England for Kansas to see him, I'd emailed him. The message bounced back. Perhaps he'd changed his address? I called Kansas University where I knew he still kept an office. A secretary said that 'Professor Kren had sadly passed away'. It turned out that he had been suffering from emphysema, something which he had never mentioned to me. He died without completing his final book, which I was told his wife was preparing for publication together with a collection of his academic essays. There was no mention of Bloch's memoir. When I called his wife at home in Kansas, she didn't want to talk about Bloch at all. 'That was all before my time,' she said. 'There's not a lot I can say about that anyway. You should speak to his sister.'

I called Joanne. 'My brother really hated our grandfather,' she said. 'I don't know why. To me, Dr Bloch was the nearest thing I ever met to a saint. But my brother, well, sometimes I wonder if in some strange way he blamed our grandfather for the Holocaust. He was obsessed with the Holocaust, he couldn't let it go.'

'Why was he obsessed?'

'He was a very bitter man. Life soured him. He hated his experiences in England—but I had a good time—and blamed that, I think, for his later unhappiness in America. He always felt out of place in the States, especially during his school years. He was very restless, very angry. He looked at the dark side of life all the time. He kept on looking into the darkness until he could no longer look away.'

'What about his Jewishness—wasn't that a source of consolation?'

'No. I don't think so,' she said. 'He was nothing. He believed in nothing. His funeral was held in a nondescript room with a few friends. He wasn't a believer.'

'What about you?' I said. 'Are you a believer?'

'Oh yes,' she said. 'I believe.'

Joanne said we could meet if I came to America, and the day after I got to New York I called her at her home in Ewing. She had disappointing news. 'I'm afraid I'm gonna have to cancel out on that,' she said. I explained that I had come all the way from London to meet her. 'No, I don't want to speak about any of that.'

I couldn't understand. Before on the phone she had been animated and candid about her memories of her grandfather and brother. The next day, I tried again; her refusal was adamant again. I decided to hire a car and drive out to Ewing the next day and do the simple, reportorial thing: knock on her door. Her husband opened it and invited me inside. Then Joanne came in from the kitchen, a small, slim woman with wavy grey hair and the unmistakable eyes of her grandfather. We had tea. It was a long time before I left.

Joanne Harrison was proud of her grandfather: she had never doubted the truth of his story. She was familiar with Binion's thesis about Hitler's unconscious hatred of Dr Bloch; her mother, she said, had considered legal action against 'that man' (Binion) until she realized that you could not libel the dead. (I later discovered that Trude Kren had written a letter to *Der Spiegel* in July 1978 which praised Bloch's compassion and loyalty to the Hitler family and mentioned Adolf's postcards from Vienna.) But something else also became clear: Joanne was no longer a Jew. There was a small ornamental cross on her mantelpiece. Her piety ('Oh yes, I believe') was Christian. She and her husband were evangelicals. How had this happened? Because, she said, she had never felt Jewish: 'Even at home in Linz, we used to celebrate Christmas. My mother was a disciple of Rudolf Steiner. She discovered his teachings when she was sixteen.' Then, during her brief stay as a child refugee in England, she had been told that she must attend church every Sunday, with the words 'because this is what we do in this country. You're not in Austria now.' Her mother, too, had converted. After her husband, the doctor Frank Kren, died, she had gone to live in an evangelical Christian community in upstate New York. Joanne remembered a conversation between her mother and her grandmother, Emilie Bloch, just before Emile died. 'She turned to my mother and said now we shall see who's right: you or me. By which I think she meant that she would at last be able to discover whether Christ was the Messiah, as my mother believed, or not.'

Joanne hinted that her own absolute faith was the source of much of the conflict between her and her brother, who, as she repeatedly stressed, 'believed in nothing'. She hadn't attended his funeral. 'His high intelligence isolated him from other people,' Joanne said. 'He was very hostile to our parents, hostile to Dr Bloch. I think he thought Bloch was too close to our mother, or something like that. Maybe he thought there was something sexual between them. Who knows what it was...'

She started again. 'It was the Holocaust, I think. He couldn't put it away. Deep down, I know he was really a good person—'

Joanne knew nothing of a memoir or a diary kept by Dr Bloch. Nor could she understand why, if her brother owned such a document, he would have waited for more than forty-five years before beginning to translate it. 'He never mentioned a memoir to me,' she said. 'And I wasn't aware that my grandfather was ever working on anything like that, not when we all lived together in the Bronx.' Might it be that there was something in the memoir—more generosity towards young Hitler, perhaps—that George Kren didn't want to confront? The thought hadn't occurred to her.

Joanne's husband, John Harrison, brought out the intricate family tree which he'd been working on for many years. The one important date missing from his research was that of Dr Bloch's death; all they knew was that he had died from cancer in 1945 and was buried 'somewhere on Long Island'.

So much about Eduard Bloch—as with his most famous patient—resists explanation. We can now know so very little of him; in the memory of his granddaughter, work was what had mattered most—'He loved being a doctor, loved his work'—and that had vanished once he left Linz, was vanishing even when he still lived there. After the

Anschluss, once the persecution of the Jews began, Bloch was permitted to treat only Jewish patients; as their numbers reduced, so his routine of more than thirty-seven years was destroyed. He was being prevented from doing what he knew best—from working. He seems to have found little or no consolation in religious belief. His fear grew. Joanne recalled how one day late in 1938 her father, Frank Kren, was arrested and imprisoned. He was, she said, guilty of no crime other than his Jewishness. In desperation, Bloch told his daughter, Trude, to show the local Gestapo the postcards that Hitler had sent from Vienna thirty or so years before. The move worked. 'My father was soon released,' she told me. 'After that, we had no more trouble.'

In the *Collier's* interview, Bloch described how a Gestapo agent later visited his wife at home, when he was out, and confiscated the postcards, his 'souvenirs of the Führer'. The next day, Bloch went to the Gesellenhausstrasse hotel, a Gestapo base, and requested their return. An officer asked him whether he were under suspicion for any anti-Nazi activities. 'I replied that I was not; that I was a professional man with no political connections. As an afterthought he asked if I was a non-Aryan. I answered without compromise: "I am 100 per cent Jew." The change that came over him was instantaneous. The cards, he said, would be retained for safekeeping.' Bloch never saw them again.

Still, he did escape. This is his story, as he told it and as his granddaughter believes it. At some point after the Anschluss, Bloch attempted to find out if, unlike other Jews in the town, he and his family would be able to take their savings with them if they got out. 'Getting any local ruling on such a matter was out of the question. I knew that I couldn't see Adolf Hitler. Yet I felt that if I could get a message to him he would perhaps give us some help.' So Bloch sent his daughter to find Hitler's now widowed half-sister Angela, who was living in Vienna. Because Angela was out, Trude left her father's written request for help with one of her neighbours; later that evening, the neighbour contacted Trude to say that Angela had received her message, that she 'sent her greetings and would see what she could do'.

By good fortune, Bloch told *Collier's*, 'Hitler was in Vienna that night for one of his frequent but unheralded trips to the opera.' He was 'sure' that Angela had met up with her half-brother and passed him the message. Bloch, it seems, never doubted Hitler's good intentions towards him. Soon after, he sold his property, and eventually left for America with 'sixteen marks' and a letter of recommendation from what he called the 'Nazi organization of physicians'. The letter said that because of his 'character, medical knowledge and readiness to help the sick' he had won 'the appreciation of his fellow men'. His final act in Lisbon, just before he left Europe forever, was to post a letter to the Führer which he had written in Linz. *Collier's* published it a few months later—perhaps Bloch retained a copy, or could reproduce it from memory; it seems an elaborate thing to have invented.

Your Excellency:
Before passing the border I want to express my thanks for the protection which I have received. In material poverty I am now leaving the town where I have lived for forty-one years; but I leave conscious of having lived in the most exact fulfilment of my duty. At sixty-nine I will start my life anew in a strange country where my daughter is working hard to support her family.
Yours faithfully, Eduard Bloch

Before I drove back to New York, Joanne Harrison showed me some photographs of Dr Bloch—of him on his wedding day in 1903, white gloves, white tie, dark morning suit; of him alone in his surgery on the Landstrasse, hunched in white-coated abstraction. She also showed me a facsimile copy of his application for American citizenship. His eyes, according to the form, were blue, his 'race' was 'German', his complexion was light, he weighed 165 pounds and he was five feet six inches tall. As ever, in the accompanying passport-sized photograph, he was wearing a stiff collar and thickly knotted tie, his wavy grey hair brushed back from the accordion creases of his forehead. But this time his expression was more melancholy—a certain downturn of the mouth and a sad shine in his eyes. The best was behind him then.

I asked Joan a last question, as difficult to ask as, I thought, to answer. How did it feel to have a Jewish grandfather who owed his life to the friendship, or gratitude, or mercy, of Adolf Hitler? In a voice just above a whisper, she said: 'Hitler kept his promise to us, didn't he?'

She paused, perhaps aware that she was echoing the words of Dr Bloch himself. 'Which means...'

'Which means, what?' I said.

'That there must be some good in everybody, in Hitler, in those people who flew the planes into the World Trade towers. You have to believe in the possibility of goodness, don't you? Who knows what Hitler went through as a child to make him the person he became.'

Ron Rosenbaum, while researching his book *Explaining Hitler*, met and interviewed the world's leading authorities on Nazism, only to conclude after more than 400 pages that in fact there was nothing to conclude: Hitler remained resolutely inexplicable, unknowable, what Joachim Fest had previously called an 'unperson'. The mystery of Adolf Hitler, then, is that there is no real mystery: he was no more than the sum of his atrocious actions. He was what he said and did what he thought. To search for what is hidden in his life—his sexuality, his secret hurts and slights—is to ignore what was manifest about him. The error of the pioneering OSS profile, of Ron Rosenbaum's book and so many others like it, is to assume, as Joanne Harrison did, that the 'real' truth about Hitler must lie buried somewhere, probably deep in childhood trauma. If it is, we shall never know.

On my final day in New York, I took the subway up through Harlem and deep into the Bronx, where I found the apartment building on Creston Avenue where Walter Langer had visited Bloch: red brick, dishevelled, Z-shaped fire escape, air-conditioning units scarring the outside of the building. Recent arrivals from Latin America and the Spanish Caribbean had made this once-Jewish neighbourhood their own.

How did Bloch feel as he reflected on his life and tried to find meaning there? What did he know of the fate of the Jews left behind in Europe, including members of the extended Kren family who, his granddaughter thought, had gone to the camps some time in the 1940s? Today Bloch lives on in the margins and footnotes of the Hitler industry—a victim of the cruelty of posterity, and the last of his own particular line of Jews.

☐

GRANTA

MILOSEVIC IN PRISON

Dragisa Blanusa

TRANSLATED FROM THE SERBIAN BY VANESSA
VASIC-JANEKOVIC WITH PETER MORGAN

Milosevic arriving at The Hague, June 28, 2001

Milosevic in Prison

Iwas born on March 31, 1945 in Bajina Basta. My star sign is Taurus with Sagittarius in the ascendant. I am married to Radmila, a nurse, and have two daughters and four grandchildren.

The fact that I was ever born at all can be blamed on Bilja, the most popular midwife in Bajina Basta. She was a short but determined woman and very talkative. My mother had already given birth to three boys, and our family had fallen on hard times. Our house had been destroyed in the war and my mother was going to pay for an abortion by selling the valuables left in the rubble. But Bilja the midwife scolded her. The baby will be a boy, she said, and he will be the most obedient of all your children. And so it was.

Later I qualified as a teacher and got a job at the Interior Ministry. I worked as a police inspector in the drugs squad and then became chief of the Department of Public Order in Belgrade. I received several decorations—including one from Scotland Yard for organizing security for an England–Yugoslavia football match. In 1994 I resigned and went to work for private security companies. Until 1999 I was a member of the Socialist Party of Serbia, the SPS. I then became a member of the Serbian Christian Democratic Party, and worked as a nightwatchman at their headquarters. On February 9, 2001 I was appointed warden of the district prison in Belgrade.

The next month, on March 30, I received instructions from the district attorney's office to be on a state of alert: Slobodan Milosevic was coming to my prison. The next day was my fifty-sixth birthday but that was a small event, overshadowed by the news that I was about to have in my charge the world's most famous prisoner. For two nights I didn't sleep.

April 1 At four-thirty a.m., the Interior Ministry warned me that Milosevic was on his way. I immediately opened the prison gates, and saw a swarm of journalists and photographers waiting outside. Within minutes, a Chrysler jeep and two BMWs with darkened windows swept through the gates and screeched to a halt in the jail yard. Out stepped Milosevic's lawyer, Toma Fila, the investigating judge, Goran Cavlina, a young politician called Cedomir Jovanovic, the district attorney, Rade Terzic, and several plain-clothes policemen with machine guns. They were all chattering into their mobile phones, pacing around nervously trying to get the best signal.

Slobodan Milosevic stepped out of one of the BMWs. He was not handcuffed. He too was talking into his mobile phone, pleading with his wife to calm down. 'Mira...Mira...' he said.

For a while, the men stood around awkwardly, as if postponing the moment of separation. Cedomir Jovanovic asked me what sort of cell Milosevic would be given. I had been planning to put him in with all the other prisoners but Jovanovic asked me to give him the best possible treatment. 'After all,' he said, 'he was president of Serbia and Yugoslavia, and over a million people voted for him.'

Milosevic was taken to our reception department, where a guard confiscated his belt, shoelaces and tie.

'Don't worry,' Milosevic smirked. 'I'm not going to hang myself.'

He had no personal ID on him. He asked if he could keep his watch. I agreed, even though it's against our rules.

The ex-president was taken to Cell 1121 in a rarely used part of the jail. Other prisoners call this wing 'The Hyatt'. Each room has a shower and a toilet, a sink, and hot water all day long. There are two iron bunk beds, and a metal cupboard. A twenty-four-hour suicide watch was set up outside Milosevic's door, and for a while I studied him through the spyhole. He took off his raincoat and washed his face and hands. Then he clambered on to the bottom bunk bed, covered himself with two old military blankets and fell fast asleep.

Milosevic woke up at eleven a.m. He ate his breakfast: two hard-boiled eggs, some jam, bread and tea. Soon afterwards, his lunch came too: a potato stew and a hot loaf. Each prisoner receives one loaf a day.

After that, the duty physician examined him. Milosevic had moderately raised blood pressure and a slight tachycardia. I asked the doctor to take his blood sugar level, but Milosevic refused. He was not diabetic, he insisted. That was old gossip from his time as a banker.

At noon, Judge Cavlina arrived in my office with prosecutor Terzic; Milosevic's lawyer, Toma Fila; and a minute-taker. Cavlina asked to see the former president. Two guards brought him to my office.

Milosevic wore a blue suit, sky blue shirt, black shoes without shoelaces and a thin blue mohair coat draped over his shoulders. He walked quite steadily. We greeted each other. He was very pale, and held my hand for a long while, repeating my name.

'I'm glad we have met,' he said. 'Although it would have been better under different circumstances.'

'What can you do?' I said. 'That's fate. Do you need anything?'

'Nothing,' he replied. 'I've eaten an excellent stew. I know this is not a hotel, by the way.'

The first interrogation took place in my office without me. Milosevic was charged with abusing his position and conspiring to obtain financial gain and to preserve his power. He chain-smoked as the charges were read out. He had to borrow the cigarettes, a cheap brand called Drina, from a prison guard.

Milosevic wrote an appeal against his arrest. He has been detained on the grounds that he could flee and/or try to influence witnesses. Milosevic denied this and addressed some of the charges. He admitted money was paid through the Belgrade Bank, but insisted it was always for 'legitimate purposes' including weapons and ammunition for the Bosnian Serb and Croatian Serb armies.

After the interrogation, I gave him two copies of the prison rules and told him to read them. I suggested he gave one copy to his wife.

Milosevic's wife Mirjana Markovic—'Mira'—arrived at three p.m. Milosevic angrily threw the prison rule book on the table.

'Here. Take this,' he said. 'Your minister wrote this!'

Mira ignored him. Their home had been searched, she said. The police were very professional and issued receipts for all the weapons they confiscated.

Later that night, the ex-president complained his cell had 'surplus inventory' and was badly lit. We removed some furniture and brought him a reading light. He was very pleased—but had one other request. 'Could my wife please come over and make my bed for me?' I couldn't allow this.

April 2 At nine a.m., I found Milosevic talking to his lawyer, Toma Fila. I gave them the morning papers. One of them had the headline DICTATOR ARRESTED.

'Look what they're writing about me!' Milosevic said angrily. 'A dictator!' Toma Fila tried to calm him down. 'Mr President, don't take it to heart. It's nonsense.'

Later Mira said that their son Marko had called wanting to hear about the arrest.

The ex-president has already established a very orderly routine. He washes his hands frequently and brushes his teeth several times a day. Sometimes he lies on his bed for two or more hours, facing the same spot on the wall, without moving at all. He sleeps several times a day. He hasn't yet bothered to unpack the clothes from his check canvas suitcase.

There was polenta for supper tonight. Milosevic didn't like it. 'For the first time in my life,' he said bitterly, 'I'm eating without a knife and fork. I'm eating with my fingers.'

April 4 Mira comes every day at noon. The Milosevices usually talk for about an hour. Mira constantly checks her Sixties hairstyle in a make-up compact.

April 6 Milosevic had a visit from Boro Drakulovic, a Socialist Party MP. He brought messages of support from party members, and told Milosevic that women are coming to the jail with flowers. He also advised the ex-president to get rid of some disloyal people in the party. 'Of course, there aren't many,' he added.

Milosevic then spoke bitterly about his arrest. 'If only I had been imprisoned by Albanians or Germans,' he spat. 'I wouldn't have minded that. But by my own Serbs!'

Toma Fila said The Hague indictment was due to arrive on the Justice Minister's desk any day now. Milosevic said, 'I don't recognize The Hague Tribunal.'

They agreed Fila should go and see the new President of Yugoslavia, Vojislav Kostunica. Milosevic claimed Kostunica was a stickler for the rule of law, and knew that he was in jail for 'no reason'.

April 7 Milosevic got up at seven-thirty a.m. and asked for the morning papers. The guards told him that no papers are delivered on Saturdays. Milosevic said, 'There's nothing to read in them anyway.'

Saturday is also cleaning day. Prisoners take their bed sheets out into the yard and shake them. Milosevic joined in.

April 8 Milosevic's daughter, Marija, came to visit with Mira. A guard named Savic, known as 'Tomcat', took them to Milosevic's cell.

'How do you like my daughter?' Mira asked Tomcat. 'Do you think she's pretty?'

'She's pretty,' said Tomcat.

Marija was furious. 'Why are you asking him that? Even if I were as ugly as a wart, he'd say I was pretty.'

Milosevic was delighted to see his daughter. 'Where have you been?' he bellowed. 'My little terrorist!'

Marija was upset to see her father in such reduced circumstances: 'When you leave prison I will never allow you to go into politics again. This country doesn't deserve you. You are too clever.'

During his walk, Milosevic asked for some stale bread to feed the pigeons.

In the evening, Milosevic confided that he 'really loved' the bean soup today. 'Good enough for any restaurant. I could eat it all the time.'

April 10 Milosevic's wife and daughter were late and he was very upset. When they arrived, he said that his blood pressure had gone up. Mira burst into tears.

The family have asked if they can bring him a TV and radio. They claim the Justice Ministry has approved their request. I told them that no one had bothered to ask me, and that I couldn't allow it; the families of other prisoners are already complaining about Milosevic's special treatment.

April 11 Milosevic was examined by his physician, Colonel Zdravko Mijailovic, and by several prison doctors. Although the first results seemed fine, the second batch indicated a possible heart attack. Milosevic reacted angrily: 'You are all paranoid. I feel excellent and my health is very good. My blood pressure is usually a little high.'

Colonel Mijailovic has already told the press that his patient's health has seriously deteriorated.

I agreed with the prison doctors that it would be best to transfer Milosevic to the military hospital where his doctor also practises. Milosevic refused. We summoned a team from Dedinje hospital, but he refused to let them examine him either; according to Milosevic they were all members of the opposition and incompetent. Finally we called Mira. She knelt next to Sloba's bed and said: 'If you die, we will all disappear with you.' She then turned to me, put her head on my shoulder and started to cry. 'Thank you,' she said.

At last Milosevic agreed to be transferred to the military hospital. He asked anxiously which floor his suite would be on. He was worried about being kidnapped from the hospital because there is a helipad on the roof.

April 12 During one of my conversations with Colonel Mijailovic, I mentioned that Milosevic was a very intelligent man.

'Hitler was very intelligent, too,' he replied. 'Milosevic has always been a difficult man. If he finds something that suits him he sticks to it, if it brings him profit. But only then.'

April 13 The doctors decided that Milosevic's treatment can continue in prison, so we took him back in today.

April 16 Toma Fila informed Milosevic that The Hague indictment has arrived at the Justice Ministry. The ex-president said he would not receive it, as he doesn't recognize the court. He also complained about his health.

I wondered whether it might be better for him to see his wife and daughter less often. Whenever they visited, they took his blood pressure and talked all the time about doctors and drug treatments. This irritated Milosevic immensely. Yet his blood pressure would jump with worry if Mira was even five minutes late. On one occasion, he told the prison doctor: 'Doctor, I don't know what to do. Marija screams, Mira cries, and I have to put up with it all.'

April 17 I'm struck by the conspicuous absence of Milosevic's closest associates. Very few of them have come to visit him.

April 19 Another visit from Boro Drakulovic. They discussed a rally planned for next Saturday. Milosevic insisted that several 'ordinary citizens' be allowed to speak. He also wanted to know when the party newspaper will be published again. Soon, Drakulovic promised.

April 23 During a walk with Tomcat, Milosevic said that the Montenegrin government would stay in power after the coming election because, unlike him, they'd steal all the votes they needed.

April 27 Statehood Day, to mark the establishment of the Third Federal Republic in 1992. Milosevic received forty-three telegrams from Socialist Party branches across the country. Mira and Marija remarked how sad it was that on the day Yugoslavia celebrated its creation, its creator was rotting in jail.

April 28 Milosevic was surprised to hear that Tomcat lives in the jail too. He advised him to get married as soon as possible. Tomcat got his nickname in childhood, when he used to wear a jumper with a cat on it. He has now acquired a new nickname—'Senta'—after Milosevic's former personal bodyguard.

April 29 The first quiet day since Milosevic arrived. The phones were silent. It wasn't until the evening that I realized this was merely the calm before the storm. Tomorrow is the last day of his thirty-day detention.

April 30 Toma Fila told Milosevic that his sentence has been extended by two months.

May 1 The Labour Day holiday has also been quiet. Milosevic spent a long time walking in the prison yard. He talked a lot about Serbia's natural beauty. Then he spoke about his relatives, regretting the fact that he'd not seen very much of them. In all these years, he has only attended one family function—a funeral. He said that he can barely remember any of his relatives.

May 3 Goran Cavlina delivered The Hague indictment. 'I won't even touch that pile of shit,' Milosevic declared.

The judge was not deterred. He put the envelope between the bars of Milosevic's cell. Milosevic asked the guards to take it away.

'We're very sorry, but we can't do that,' they said.

So the indictment sits between the bars, with Milosevic grumbling that it's been left there without his consent.

May 5 Milosevic reads a great deal both in English and in Serbian.

He reads thrillers mainly, as well as mysteries and spy novels. Among the books he has read are:

Wilbur Smith	*The Seventh Scroll*
Robert Ludlum	*The Corsican Story*
Ivo Andric	*The Bridge on the Drina*
Petar Petrovic Njegos	*The Mountain Wreath*
Joseph Murphy	*The Power of Your Subconscious Mind*
John Steinbeck	*The Grapes of Wrath*
C. S. Forester	*Captain Hornblower, RN* and *Lieutenant Hornblower* and *Admiral Hornblower*

May 7 Milosevic has been demanding a haircut for several days now. He wanted his personal barber who has cut his hair for over twenty years. But I told him we had a very experienced barber in the jail. When the prison barber finished, Milosevic said: 'Sorry, Boss, but I don't have a tip to offer you.'

May 8 Members of the student protest movement tried to visit Milosevic. They left him a few sarcastic presents: a packet of cheap cigarettes, a newspaper from his home town and a book called *Cry Mother Serbia*, dedicated to all the students who had been beaten on his orders. Milosevic turned up his nose when he heard who the gifts were from: 'I've said all I'm ever going to say about that lot.'

May 11 Mirko Marjanovic, the former Serbian prime minister, finally paid a visit. He complained about his health too, but boasted to Milosevic that his company 'Progress' is doing well. Milosevic wanted to hear about the Socialist Party newspaper.

May 19 'I haven't slept as well as last night in years,' said Milosevic. 'Ever since I came here, I have been sleeping like a righteous man.'
Mira and Marija told him that 500,000 Ukrainian peasants have signed a letter of support and sent it to President Kostunica.

May 20 Another visit from Mira and Marija. 'Five million people have signed a petition supporting you,' said Mira. Yet the newspapers reported that only 15,000 people bothered to sign—and that the petition was abandoned soon after that.

May 22 I told the ex-president that the Helsinki Committee for Human Rights wants to come and visit him.

'I'm not an animal to be displayed for everyone to stare at,' Milosevic snorted. 'Let them stick it up their mother's cunt. They are world-class shits. Scum.'

May 27 Mira and Marija came again. Whenever Sloba and Mira meet they indulge in long romantic kisses. They look like a young couple in love and they don't seem to care who's watching them. Mira will kiss his hands and he'll kiss hers. I once saw her kiss his knee. Mira calls Slobodan 'My little one,' and he says it back to her. She'll call him 'My puppy', and he'll call her 'My little kitten'.

Sometimes the kisses go on for so long that the guards have to pull them apart. Marija gets very upset at this and her father tells her: 'Marija dear, they are simply doing their job.'

Today Mira left her husband a home-baked pie. Milosevic was very touched by this gesture, and offered a slice to his guard. 'Come on,' he said. 'Mira cooked this.' (A few days later, we learned that the pie was cooked by Mira's private chef.)

June 2 Milosevic complained of a headache all day. He asked for his windows to be opened, read, took his blood pressure, read again, took his medicine and went to bed. He complained that the doctors and nurses do nothing but take his blood pressure and said he wants to get rid of them.

June 10 I was feeling unwell so I asked to borrow Milosevic's blood pressure monitor.

'Warden,' he said, 'this is your jail, you are the boss. Do as you please.'

My blood pressure is higher than his. Milosevic complained about his heart. He said that it was enlarged. I told him that sportsmen usually have enlarged hearts.

'What are you talking about?' he snorted. 'I've never run in my life.'

Mira once told me that her husband has experienced high blood pressure for several years. It would go up on Tuesdays, when he had to attend difficult meetings. They called it 'Sloba's Tuesday'.

June 11 Milosevic will certainly remember this day. For the first time, his daughter-in-law Milica brought his grandson to the jail. Grandpa Milosevic was overjoyed. He drew animal pictures for baby Marko, crocodiles mostly. But he thinks that it might be better for his grandson not to spend too much time in prison.

June 14 Toma Fila arrived with a team of five lawyers. They are going to see Lepa Karamarkovic, President of Serbia's Supreme Court. They decided to hold press conferences as often as possible to highlight Milosevic's 'illegal' detention.

June 15 As the number of visits keeps growing Tomcat needs help and I have assigned another guard called Vulovic to look after Milosevic.

The ex-president's lawyers talked about press conferences again. The pressure must be kept up. Serbs must be told that a 'sick and innocent man lies in jail'. They told Milosevic that ordinary people have been calling Mira, offering their houses as security for his bail.

A Canadian lawyer called Christopher Black came on behalf of the International Committee for the Defence of Slobodan Milosevic. He assured Milosevic that he, Black, was a free-thinking individual who believes that the Hague tribunal is an extension of NATO invented to justify the bombing of Yugoslavia. According to Black, the Hague tribunal is a kind of a theatre whose sole aim is to convict people without any regard for evidence.

Milosevic agreed with him wholeheartedly and said his only crime had been to oppose the world's most powerful nations.

June 16 Some 4,000 Milosevic supporters gathered outside the prison. They climbed the gates, threw stones and bottles and even large firecrackers. Milosevic paced up and down his cell listening to the noise and chain-smoking.

'Even more will come,' he told me. 'Soon there will be 30,000 of them and they will get me out of here.'

Milosevic was worried about Mira.

'My poppet. You are very tired,' he said. 'Sleep a little. Don't come and see me like this.'

'I love the rain,' she replied. 'This is my weather.'

Marija added: 'We love the night, not the sun. The night is our time, we sleep in daytime, and live at night-time.'

June 17 A visit from the lawyer Mihajlo Bakrac. They spoke about the Russian President Vladimir Putin's visit to Yugoslavia. Milosevic praised Putin for relying on his own resources. 'That was my Yugoslav policy,' he said.

But he also remarked wearily: 'I was convinced the Russians would give us military help in the spring of 1999 when Yugoslavia was bombed. But throughout history they have never helped us when it really mattered, and that's what happened this time. If only Vladimir Putin had been leader then, and not that Yeltsin.' He said Yeltsin was a sick and frightened man. All important statesmen, including himself, knew that Yeltsin could not speak for longer than twenty minutes. After that, he had to be 'refreshed' by his physicians.

Later on Mira and Marija arrived with his grandson. Mira told her husband that yesterday's rally was 'magnificent, divine, with lots of people from all over Yugoslavia'. Even parents of young men killed in Kosovo expressed their support. She was surprised by how many people kissed her face and her dress. She concluded triumphantly: 'Sloba, no one in Serbian history was more popular than you.'

June 18 Milosevic's legal team asked him to answer some of the questions journalists put to them most frequently:

'Do you know why you are in prison?'

'Because I stood up against NATO.'

'Who is keeping you in prison?'

'NATO, or rather NATO's exponents in Yugoslavia.'

'Do you think you've won?'

'Of course. That's why I'm here in prison.'

The lawyers suggested setting up an American-style TV duel, pitting one of the lawyers against a spokesman from the Justice Ministry. Milosevic was very enthusiastic. 'Good idea,' he said. 'They don't stand a chance. We are morally and intellectually superior, and sure to be the winners.'

Dragisa Blanusa

They talked about the past decade, agreeing that the Balkan crises were 'artificial' and 'created by the Great Powers'. Milosevic added that Putin has finally realized Western bank loans are worthless:
'We understood that much earlier... This is why we were bombed. Western intelligence agencies created the Kosovo Liberation Army...and when we defeated those terrorists in 1998, they threatened us with bombs. There was no humanitarian and civilian catastrophe. They invented the Racak massacre as an excuse to bomb us.

'I'll tell you a story about Ibrahim Rugova [the current President of Kosovo]: Rugova telephoned me once, asking me to help him move his family to a safe place. His own side were trying to kill him. So I called Italy's Foreign Minister Lamberto Dini and arranged for Rugova to go to Italy with his family... I told Dini to send a plane for Rugova straight away, and that's what happened.

'The fact that Rugova tells a different story is a matter for his soul and conscience.

'Our enemies wanted the impossible from us: our total surrender. That's why we were bombed. It's normal to defend oneself when attacked. And we inflicted significant casualties too, destroying more than 250 cruise missiles and shooting down over sixty planes. They know that very well, but hide it from their public.'

June 19 Milosevic's lawyers agreed that it was time to spread rumours to help his case: for example, that Milosevic is very ill and that prison health care is poor; that there's a risk he could be kidnapped during his daily walks.

They then promised to see President Kostunica. They will ask for their client's sentence to be overturned on the grounds that Slobodan Milosevic is 'the number one political prisoner in the world today'.

June 21 Bishop Amfilohije came to visit. Milosevic was very pleased, and kissed the Bishop three times.

'I am so glad to see you,' he said, 'and sincerely regret not having met you earlier.'

'I thank the court for allowing me to see you,' said Amfilohije.

They discussed Montenegro and the Serbian Orthodox Church's influence there. They were chatting away like old political buddies. At the end, Amfilohije wished the ex-president all the best, and said the Hague Tribunal was 'an inquisition against the Serbs'. Again, they kissed three times. Amfilohije left Milosevic a copy of the New Testament.

Later, Mira asked her husband if he wanted any books. He mentioned the New Testament and remarked on its beautiful binding.

'You're not going to read the New Testament, are you?' she asked.

'No!' Sloba said quickly. 'No way!'

June 22 Boro Drakulovic complained of apathy in the party. But he praised some of the rallies and mentioned that at one he'd attended, women had read poems about Milosevic. He said this brought tears to his eyes.

Toma Fila told Milosevic that many foreign journalists shake their heads in disbelief when he shows them the charges which keep his client in jail.

'Of course it's ridiculous,' said Milosevic. 'Who thought about theft at that time, when we selflessly helped the Republika Srpska— even though we were under sanctions. We are not ashamed of what we did. On the contrary, we're proud of our success!'

That afternoon, while Milosevic was feeding the pigeons, a group of hawks scared his flock away.

June 23 At eight a.m., around ten supporters, all women except for one young man, gathered outside the jail to protest. At the same time, a group of Albanian women in traditional dress came to visit their men. The protesters made the Albanians kiss pictures of Milosevic and say, in Serbian, 'Sloba, we love you!' My men took the Albanians inside the jail for their own protection. Then the protesters spotted a foreign journalist. 'Whore, go back where you came from!' they shouted. She fled.

Around noon, Mira, Marija and his daughter-in-law Milica arrived. Milosevic asked Marija to make some coffee. She exploded with anger. 'You think I came here to make you coffee? I hurt all over, my kidney, my stomach, everything is failing. I shan't live to be forty! You obviously love it in here, don't you? Mum likes it too. It's like the partisan days all over again, isn't it! Both of you should stop behaving like partisans in the woods. I don't belong here with you! I'm from another story. The end of the world has come to

Serbia! Everything is flooded, volcanoes are erupting, earthquakes shatter the earth! And you just laugh!'

Which they did. The conversation turned to family and other matters.

June 24 Toma Fila brought a copy of the law on cooperating with The Hague tribunal to Milosevic. At one point, Milosevic said: 'You ought to go and see our man and tell him to stick to the bargain.'

'I can't reach him at the moment,' said Fila.

They are all worried, and so is Milosevic's family.

In the evening I visited him to see how he was. 'I'm completely at peace,' he said. 'My conscience is clear. I have never done anything I ought to regret. I am the moral victor and I am being held here as a political prisoner.'

There was a great deal more in the same vein before Milosevic declared: 'The Germans are to blame for the disintegration of Yugoslavia. They did this because they wanted revenge on us for defeating them in two previous wars.'

He signed off with a few thoughts about the Kostunica government: 'They're all motherfuckers. They'll end up here instead of me.'

Milosevic and his party comrades are becoming more and more nervous. Milosevic got angry with Dragutin Milovanovic, a member of the Party Executive. 'Why the fuck have I been fighting for this party for ten years if you don't know what to do now? You can't start learning to walk now!'

His request for bail has been refused. At first, Milosevic left the judgement between the bars of his cell, together with The Hague indictment. Then he changed his mind. 'Well,' he said. 'This did come from our court. I'd better keep it here on the table...'

June 26 The extradition process has begun. Toma Fila advised Milosevic to appoint legal representatives within twenty-four hours.

Milosevic was visibly upset when his wife and daughter arrived. Marija burst into tears. 'If only you had resisted the arrest!'

Milosevic tried to comfort her. 'Life consists of ups and downs. Was I supposed to let all of you get killed that night? I am content when you are safe and well. Don't worry. I shall take it all with dignity. I shan't kill myself. I'm not ashamed for having defended my country.'

Milosevic invited me to join him for a drink in the evening. He has no alcohol in his cell. It's not allowed in the prison.

I found him reading. I'd heard that he liked bourbon, but couldn't find any. So I entered with a bottle of cheap imitation whisky called Grant Williams. He was worried about the glasses.

'Don't be alarmed,' I said. 'Both glasses have been washed and you can choose which one you want.'

'Have you come to bid me farewell?' asked Milosevic.

'You invited me.'

In a resigned tone of voice he added, 'Do you know what it's like in the Hague jail?'

'Everything is computerized, the prisoner is treated more like a robot than a man.'

He thought for a while and then said bitterly: 'Those motherfuckers. They really are about to send me to The Hague, aren't they?'

'Tell me,' I asked, 'why didn't you quit while you were ahead, while you were still popular? You could be lying on a beach somewhere now.'

After a half-hearted attempt to justify his clinging to power out of concern for the nation, Milosevic paused. 'Yes. You're right,' he said. 'I did make a mistake.'

I had the impression that he was tired of politics.

June 28 A family lunch. Everyone knew that Milosevic was about to go to The Hague but no one talked about it. Mira brought him a clean shirt. Their last meal consisted of a cake, some cheese, deep-fried courgettes, potato salad, watermelon, peaches, pears and one sardine. They drank mineral water and milk from plastic glasses.

Mira has hurt her right shin. The ex-president placed her leg in his lap and changed the dressing. They talked about their childhood. At one point, Milosevic put his hand in his pocket and took out seven little boats made out of cardboard. They were for his grandson, he said. Mira started to cry and a tear also rolled down Milosevic's cheek. 'Please don't bring my little grandson Marko here any more,' he said. By now they were all crying.

'You have to be very strong,' said Milosevic. 'I have everything I need. I feel best when I know you're all healthy and okay.'

Milosevic spent the afternoon feeding his pigeons.

Operation 'Dove', as we called the extradition, began at 18.00. I walked into the ex-president's cell and said tersely: 'Get up and get ready.'

Milosevic looked up in surprise. 'Where are you taking me?'

'To The Hague.'

He didn't seem unhappy or shocked. 'Warden, let me at least call my wife and my lawyers. Give me a bit of time to pack my stuff.'

He dressed slowly, packing things into his suitcase. He took four books at random from his bookcase, his sponge bag and raincoat. As we walked down the corridor, he turned to me and asked, 'Warden, what's this? It's not right. This is a kidnapping!'

We got into the back of a police van and drove slowly through the Belgrade streets. We reached the helipad at 18.50. Milosevic stepped very slowly out of the van. He dismissed us all with a wave of his hand. 'Well done, you lot. You can take your money now.'

Two men and a woman were standing by the helicopter. One of the men was an investigating officer from The Hague, the other was a Dutch police officer. The woman was an interpreter.

When the investigator read out his indictment, Milosevic simply said: 'I don't recognize The Hague Tribunal.'

'Which languages do you speak?' the official asked.

'Serbian,' replied Milosevic.

The interpreter then translated the indictment into Serbian, but Milosevic pretended not to listen. He looked around, staring intently at each of us in turn, and lit a cigarette. The investigator then turned to Milosevic and declared, 'I am arresting you. You are now under the jurisdiction of The Hague Tribunal.'

As we walked to the helicopter, Milosevic turned and said proudly: 'You know, Serbs—it's Vidovdan today!'

He took one last look at the Belgrade skyline and then entered the helicopter. As he stepped inside, Milosevic asked the pilots, 'How are you lads?'

One of the pilots mumbled back, 'All right, Mr President.'

We put him into a seat, with two security personnel.

'Warden, where is my raincoat?' he asked.

It was 18.57. Those were Slobodan Milosevic's last words on Serbian soil. □

NOTES ON CONTRIBUTORS

Dragisa Blanusa's memoir, *Cuvao sam Milosevica* (I Guarded Milosevic) was published last year by Glas Javnosti in Belgrade. He was removed from his post following the book's publication and now works as an adviser in the Ministry of Justice.

Michael Collins is a writer, photographer and curator. His photographs of the English Channel appeared in *Granta 76*.

Jason Cowley is the literary editor of the *New Statesman*. His novel, *Unknown Pleasures*, is published by Faber.

Geoff Dyer's books include *Paris Trance* and *Out of Sheer Rage* (Abacus/North Point Press). 'Hotel Oblivion' will be included in *Yoga For People Who Can't Be Bothered to Do It*, to be published by Abacus in the UK and Pantheon in the US in 2003.

Andrew O'Hagan was born in Glasgow in 1968. 'You, the Viewers at Home' is taken from his new novel, *Personality*, which will be published next year by Faber. His previous novel, *Our Fathers*, was shortlisted for the 1999 Booker Prize (Faber/Harcourt).

Zoë Heller is a columnist on the London *Daily Telegraph* and was named Columnist of the Year in the latest British Press Awards. 'What Sheba Did Wrong' comes from her second novel, *Notes on a Scandal*, which will be published in summer 2003 (Viking/Henry Holt). She lives in New York.

Andrew Martin is a freelance writer living in London. His third novel, *The Necropolis Railway*, is published by Faber.

Riccardo Orizio is the author of *Lost White Tribes* (Vintage). His forthcoming book, *Talk of the Devil—Encounters with Seven Dictators*, will be published by Secker & Warburg next year.

Fintan O'Toole is a columnist and chief drama critic with the *Irish Times*. His books include *A Traitor's Kiss: The Life of Richard Brinsley Sheridan* (Granta Books/Farrar Straus & Giroux) and *Shakespeare Is Hard But So Is Life* which will be published by Granta Books this autumn in the UK and next spring in the US.

Tom Stoddart is a founder member of the Independent Photographers' Group (IPG). He has worked as a photojournalist in many countries including Bosnia, Lebanon, Rwanda, Sudan, India and China. He has won many international awards for his pictures.

Kyle Stone is a journalist living in Toronto. She is producing and directing a film on Ethiopian music.

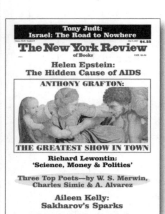